Young Children
and Their Families

Young Children and Their Families

Needs of the Nineties

Shirley Hill
B.J. Barnes
California State University,
Fullerton

LexingtonBooks
D.C. Heath and Company
Lexington, Massachusetts
Toronto

Library of Congress Cataloging in Publication Data

Main entry under title:

Young children and their families.

Includes index.
Contents: Needs of the nineties/Irving Lazar—Parent education: under-
standing parents so that they can understand themselves and their children/
Helen F. Durio and Robert Hughes, Jr.—The adaptations of mothers of tod-
dlers to multiple social roles/Elizabeth C. Ringsmuth—[etc.]
 1. Children—United States—Congresses. 2. Parenting—United
States—Congresses. 3. Family policy—United States—Congresses.
I. Hill, Shirley. II. Barnes, B.J. (Betty J.)
HQ792.U5Y68   305.2'3'0973   81–48463
ISBN 0-669-05372-4   AACR2

Copyright © 1982 by D.C. Heath and Company

Published simultaneously in Canada

Printed in the United States of America

International Standard Book Number: 0-669-05372-4

Library of Congress Catalog Card Number: 81–48463

Contents

Preface

This book grew out of a conference on research related to young children and their families and the implications of that research for both practice and public policy. The conference was held in Anaheim, California, in June 1981, under the leadership of Shirley Hill. It was sponsored by the Institute for Early Childhood Education at California State University, Fullerton and the university's Office of Extended Education, in cooperation with the Bush Foundation Training Program in Child Development and Social Policy at the University of California at Los Angeles; the California Association for Childhood Education; the California Association for the Education of Young Children; the California Community College Early Childhood Educators; the California Child Development Administrators Association; the California Children's Lobby; and the California Professors of Early Childhood Education. The twelve chapters in this book are representative of the issues discussed in the fifty-three conference presentations.

To improve the quality of life for young children and their families, we must examine research findings for their meaning, and for directions for further study. If life in the 1990s is to be better than in the 1980s, we must use the information available to us and seek further knowledge in relation to anticipated needs. The papers published as chapters of this book synthesize information from earlier studies with findings from current research and suggest directions in which we need to focus our attention and energy.

Irving Lazar's introductory comments raise issues and anxieties about the current national political climate which threatens the well-being of young children and their families. He implies that unless the needs of each member of society are adequately met, all members of the society will suffer.

Chapters 2 through 5 offer data and suggestions as to ways in which we might approach meeting society's needs—particularly the needs of young children and the family members on whom they depend for nurturance. Helen Durio and Robert Hughes declare that support systems for parents must include child-rearing information and must be strengthened by considering parental learning styles as well as their patterns of information seeking. Elizabeth Ringsmuth points out that parent education programs must take account of the developmental levels of parents and of the complexities of the interactions between mother and child, each of whom is progressing through personal developmental stages. Mildred Pagelow notes that children are frequently victimized by the abuse they observe at home as well as the abuse directed at them. Recommendations for treatment and prevention of family violence are suggested. Richard Valencia points out that the historical victimization of minority children is unjustly supported by school practices and prevents equal access to educational opportunity. He urges policymakers and researchers to provide increased support to quality research.

Chapters 6 through 11 address specific needs of particular persons and groups in society and suggest policy implications for leaders of our social agencies and institutions. Alan Ziajka's study furthers our understanding of the mutual communication between mother and infant, so critical to human development. Sylvia Ann White examines the quality of care giving and the interaction with infants in group care programs, and points out the need for training and evaluation of care givers. Rosemary Peterson and Barbara Tardif recognize that public policy directly affects the education of young children with exceptional needs. They describe the policy-making process that shapes California's response to federal legislation and to issues of equal access.

Looking forward to solutions of the problems of the 1990s, Jeanne Kohl reminds us that women and men will both need to work and to participate in family and child-rearing responsibilities. She suggests that the current sex-specific treatment of children will be counterproductive to society's goals as well as seriously limiting the fulfillment of individual potential. Stuart Reifel examines an often neglected element in human development: representational play, which he sees as critical to cognitive growth. He suggests that policymakers take a more holistic view of the instructional needs of young children. Doris Fromberg asserts that a transformational view of knowledge is vital for developing curriculum. She offers illustrative strategies for working with children to help them experience and define their own realities.

In chapter 12, Barbara Bowman and Elizabeth Brady declare that current reality—palatable or not—must be confronted, including many current anxiety-provoking issues which alienate individuals from each other and from social institutions. They maintain that a person-by-person solution to broad-based societal problems is inadequate and that public policy must emanate from a careful study of the issues, and of the values and needs of the people affected by policy decisions.

1 Needs of the Nineties

Irving Lazar

I gaze into my crystal ball and speculate on certain aspects of life in the nineties, but my speculations are not random. They are based on some knowledge about likely national choices, and the consequences which followed similar choices in the past, and of course, my own reading of the problems and opportunities which students of human development are going to face in the 1990s. Ten years is not a long time, and it makes sense for us to prepare now for the conditions of life we can reasonably expect to find in the next decade.

Certainly basic research will continue, but at a greatly reduced level. Our laboratories will explore the same issues in cognition and social behavior, in affect and bonding, that have occupied them for the last century. But their work, although undeniably important, will be only a small segment of our national investigative effort since most of the studies that people do are those that receive external support. Studies are supported to a considerable extent because they are relevant to practical problems or policy concerns. It is this kind of research question that I want to discuss; and this means making some guesses about what will hurt most in our society ten years from now. To me it makes no sense to predict the research questions we need to answer for the nineties outside of the political and social context in which we will then be working. So that you can better judge these guesses, let me describe the premises from which they derive.

First of all, I assume that we will be at peace during the remainder of this decade, although I would not give very good odds on it. The temptation to mask our economic ailments with a war is always attractive to certain kinds of American politicians. But I must assume peace if I am to assume that we will have a nineties in which research on children is a relevant activity.

Second, because of the demographics of our population, no matter what the government does, things will look better for middle- and upper-income youth in the nineties. There will be fewer of them; for the same reason, unemployment will have dropped, and the drudge-jobs will have been largely eliminated by technology. At the same time, things will look dismal to low-income youth. Technology will have eliminated the middle-level jobs they might aspire to; their numbers will have increased; and for reasons I will describe later, their opportunities to exit from poverty will have shrunk compared to 1980.

Third, I am assuming that our social and educational programs will be a shambles by the middle of the 1980s. Even if Congress saves some of the programs the present administration is seeking either to eliminate or eviscerate, they will be administered by cabinet officers who have clearly expressed their desire to demolish the programs. I have great faith in the ability of admininstrators to do by regulation those things Congress will not let them do by law. Few programs will be able to retain any vigor even if they do survive. The sequence of political blows to programs for children has been devastating. The Nixon years froze programs in their tracks; the Carter years set in place the deterioration inevitable with an intellectual vacuum at the level of program leadership. We now have appointees who actually believe that it is immoral for society to help its most troubled members. Radical Darwinism in the guise of anti-Darwinism has replaced fifty years of populism.

In concrete terms, what consequences can we expect from this wreckage of federal support for social programs? First, we may well slip back into last place among industrial nations in infant and perinatal mortality. The deterioration of our water and air, the removal of safety regulations on food and other essentials, the removal of prenatal care for the poor, the increased numbers of unwanted children, indicate clearly that the death rate, the handicap rate, and the rate of early mental illness will all shoot up, starting very soon.

The services that survive will do so under state auspices in those states that care. The variability will be great, of course, but in the states that care about people there will be more child care, more health care, and more services for the aging, I think, than we have now. Further, I expect that by the end of the 1980s, both state and federal governments will be reinvesting in the social services, including mental health, and that they will be rebuilding those systems. By 1990 I think that the failure to provide these services will have produced social unrest, deaths, and scandals on such a scale as to demonstrate to the whole country that the political mythology of the 1920s is too expensive to maintain in the 1990s.

The areas of reduced services from the state that I think will produce the most serious problems of the 1990s are ones we largely take for granted now. Their absence and change will educate us about their purposes. Parks, museums, libraries, and publicly supported recreation are America's system of afterschool care, and the groups that use these facilities—Scouts, and hobby clubs, and youth game teams—are America's system of character development and value transfer. The activities of such groups, of course, will remain available to the affluent, but they will be the first to vanish from local and state budgets. For the working classes, major child development services will disappear. The money saved from recreation will, of course, reappear with interest in the budgets of the juvenile justice systems a few years later.

The cuts in public health and public transportation will also affect us adversely. The energy situation cannot improve in the decade ahead because the lead time on all but one known partial solution to our energy shortage is at least twenty years. It is already clear that deregulation unleashed the profits of big oil—not for energy development, but for diversification into other industries. Oil wealth is going to real estate, computer companies, ball teams, and the closing down of potential competition in solar and sea power development. These are, of course, totally nonproductive investments as far as jobs are concerned. So energy will be tighter, public transportation less available and more expensive, and public health services in financial straits.

I predict that the administration and many states will try the voucher system in public education. This will accelerate middle-class flight to private and parochial schools, whose ability to grow is limited only by the scarcity of money. More significant, perhaps, is the fact that forty states now permit parents to educate their children at home, and the cost of home computers will in fact make education at home a feasible alternative for middle-class families. By the end of the 1980s, small computers will be common household appliances in middle-class families and software to teach reading and arithmetic will be readily available. When this happens, the gap in school readiness between the children of the poor and the rest of society's children will be greater than it has ever been. At that point, the public schools will be on their way to extinction, joining the poor farm and the foundling home as historical curiosities. Since the public schools take at least thirty years to incorporate research findings into practice, the self-instruction movement is another bus they will miss.

By 1990 institutions of higher education will reflect today's changes in student loans and federal grants. The small private school will be gasping for air. The older and larger private universities will revert to serving the rich and the very poor. The middle class will go to crowded and technologically underequipped state schools. We will have resegregated our society, reduced our human capital, and be on the way to being scientifically outclassed by our trading partners.

California is a good state in which to see the correlation between expenditures in higher education and economic productivity. Just as California had always led the country in showing us our future life-style, the rise and decline of the University of California portends what will happen to the rest of us in the next decade. Fewer doctoral candidates and faculty will do fewer and smaller studies, and a generation of potential scholars and professionals will be doing other things.

Additionally, our population and its distribution will, I think, change in noticeable ways. While Caucasians are marrying later and having fewer children, our Hispanic and black populations will continue to grow. With retail business continuing their efforts to keep downtown areas viable, and cornering the community development block grants as their special subsidy, poor and minority families will be increasingly driven into the older suburbs now decaying and being reestablished as ghettos isolated from central cities. The explosions of the inner cities which many people believe will occur in the near future will accelerate this process and rekindle the intergroup hostilities of the 1960s. Such hostilities will be made worse by the increased automation of low-skilled jobs which our new tax policies will reward.

Finally, one change for child development professionals is, I think, on its way. We are experiencing a very special baby boom right now. Educated women in their thirties are having babies; these women expect to continue their careers. As private child-care resources dry up, career women will begin to demand public support for high-quality day care. These women who came of age in the 1960s are not politically naive or passive. They will get a universal day-care system in at least half our states by the 1990s, and we are going to have to settle our differences and produce a system that will bring us on par, at least, with the systems of other industrial nations.

Now you have my picture of the 1990s and it is not entirely hopeless. There will be many opportunities to redesign our whole social service network. Also, we can begin to identify the kinds of issues that those of us concerned with applied research need to address. Among these are the following:

Premature babies. The prenatal services that used to be available under Aid to Families with Dependent Children (AFDC) have now been largely eliminated by regulation. We are going to have to deal with the consequences of prematurity, which are not very well understood, and we ought to get started now on some serious research on the long-term psychological consequences of prematurity.

Children whose parents do not want them to be born. We had better develop ways to compensate for parental rejection.

Early socialization and its relation to later pride, or the lack thereof. We can begin to study what that relation is, how it operates, and how it can be influenced.   ·

Day care. We must become realistic about standards and measures. Having a universal day-care system is going to mean a total restructuring of the way we train our teachers. My own belief is that they ought to be educated to be managers and trainers, and that at least two years of day-care experience should be required before they are accepted in a master's program.

Understanding modern learning theory. We are just about over being afraid of "behavior management." Computer-assisted instruction has helped us to recognize what reward and positive reinforcement can do. This is fortunate because we are going to need far more efficient and less expensive ways of dealing with behavior disturbance in children than we now have. One of the problems is that we do not know what mental health is. We can define mental illness, but we tend to forget that the concept of mental illness was originally a public relations device to increase the humanity with which afflicted people were treated. We have held on to that device as though it referred to something real, and we spend enormous amounts of time and money looking for the chemical imbalance or whatever it is that produces aberrant behavior. Instead of pursuing this, we need to develop more effective and more valid and more culturally sensitive diagnostic tools for assessing children's development. We have not made much progress on this for several decades.

Value acquisition and change. The current instruments and theories are, to put it kindly, antique. Psychology, and society itself have largely ignored this area. We are now paying quite heavily for that ignorance. We also need to restudy the role of religious belief in the development of personality.

These are not the only concerns we need to address.

We have a large public health problem: the need to find effective ways to change our bad habits, to change life-styles. Most deaths from the ages of about fourteen to fifty-five are caused by our life-style—not disease or broken bones, but how we choose to live.

We are going to face real changes in the life-style of the American family when energy becomes extraordinarily expensive; we will have to spend more time at home. I expect the divorce rate to plummet because people are marrying later, and therefore having a better idea of what they are getting into, and are marrying for reasons of personal choice rather than social pressure.

Of our precious human resources, gifted people are an extraordinarily important and very tiny part. Giftedness is distributed equally in all economic and ethnic groups; we have to find out how to identify giftedness of most kinds very early in life. The methodology is not unknown; we simply have been unable or unwilling to invest in the research. The total federal expenditures on gifted children of all ages and for all purposes in 1980 was under $30 million. Giftedness is really going to burgeon because of our new technology. The kind of computational power we can now put in the hands of a mathematically talented ten-year-old is extraordinary, and will, I think, lead to advances in every field of science.

In education I can see another set of problems we can begin to work on. We are going to have a lot more home-based instruction. Within five years good microprocessors will cost under a hundred dollars. The software companies, and probably the telephone company, will become the major

purveyors of educational material. There is an interesting book by Seymour
Papert (1980), of the Artificial Intelligence Lab at the Massachusetts Institute of Technology, *Mindstorms,* an account of what happened when he
taught young children a simple computer language which children call "tur-
tle talk." Papert suggests, almost too cautiously, that our current
understanding of how the learning process takes place really represents
what happens under conditions of ordinary stimulation, and that when intellectual stimulation and possibilities are increased in the way the computer
does, extraordinary things occur. When you give a child any kind of interesting electronic learning device, you cannot get it out of his hands.
Home-based instruction is on its way.

As educators we need to find ways of doing several things with home-
based instruction to make sure it is good. We need to find ways of devising
games that busy parents will be willing to play because the parents enjoy
them too; such games will promote interaction between parents and
children and will still have educational content. We are certainly going to
have to pay very close attention to better ways of providing home-based
special education.

The technology available to us is incredible—for example, the Kurzweil
machine. It looks like a videotape recorder with a glass top. It reads aloud
(with a slight Swedish accent) any printed material laid on top, no matter
what the type size or the column width. The machine's price has dropped
four times in one year. Incidentally, the Pentagon uses machines (which the
Japanese will soon market commercially) that will write down anything you
say to them.

I am concerned that the availability of these electronic learning aids to
middle-class children will increase the gap between them and the children of
the poor. One thing we can start doing now is finding ways of introducing
this technology into Head Start and low-income day-care programs, and
figure out how to use them. We need to learn what they are and are not
good for, and how to build them into the experiences of all children. They
are certainly going to be part of the essential equipment of whatever future
civilization we have.

In addition, we have very little information about what really happens
in our afterschool programs. We know that there is educational content,
but we do not know what it is or how to maximize it. We do not know how
to use afterschool programs appropriately, and yet they constitute a larger
segment of most children's educational experience than the public schools
provide. We have some research on informal education with adults, but not
much on children. Along with that research we should start seriously studying alternative models of afterschool care and its effects.

Our current methods of evaluating teacher effectiveness have a great
many problems. A movement, still around, called Competency Based In-

structional Certification, had merit, but it froze practice. We have to find some other way of measuring teacher competence along with adaptability in ways that permit invention.

The effect of the match between the personality of the child and the personality of the teacher is something else we have paid little attention to, partly because we have used an industrial mass-production model for schools. We look for the perfect curriculum and the perfect architectural design and the perfect lighting and the perfect materials and expect all children to fit. However they are very stubborn, and it is about time we began to show respect for their individual differences.

It is time for experiments in which we start assembling the children, not by their birthdate, but by the kind of people they are and the kinds of people they respond to. It has not been done, yet, to my knowledge, and I have looked.

Incidentally, we are going to have to define the goal of higher education. At this point there is at least one accredited university in the United States that is willing to offer a B.A. in nine months to anyone, anywhere, without their ever having to attend classes. Well, Robert Hutchins did say that he really wished he could issue a B.A. with a birth certificate to each child and get that over with, but we must think seriously about what we want a higher education system for.

We have done a terrible job of communicating what scientific thinking is and what findings mean. A number of studies show that educated people (Washington lawyers, for example) consider scientific findings to be just another form of advocacy—no more or no less valid than a logical argument. The extraordinary misuse of the IQ has plagued education for two generations. Endless examples show that the American people do not know anything about scientific thinking. For example, a group is now advocating "scientific-creationism," which has nothing scientific about it; it is a theological belief. A large part of the population reads the astrology columns—and a larger part is willing to be taken in by anything that is called scientific—and that is our fault as educators. We have not taught people what science is—what inquiry is—what evidence is.

Research money from governmental and private sources is going to be very limited, especially in the social sciences. Recently, I saw a list from the National Institute for Mental Health—almost anything with the word mental, social, behavioral, or psychological in it is not being supported. This might actually be a blessing in disguise, because, as the big computers have come along, it has been very easy to throw all kinds of garbage in and factor it out later. Before World War II, we did not have computers and we had little government support for research: what we did then was design something called a critical experiment, and it made us think. There is not much thinking in the current literature, partly thanks to computers, which make everything so easy. It may turn out that the budget cuts lead to the reinvention of critical studies, which may turn out to be a good thing.

Extraordinary problems in the area of program evaluation lie ahead, particularly in the field of epidemiology, which the privacy rules have virtually destroyed. For example, in many kinds of epidemiological studies one needs to review many hundreds of patients' records in order to find a small sample that meets certain experimental conditions. Hospitals are now requiring informed consent in advance from every person whose records are being examined. As a result, one needs to obtain five thousand informed consents to find ten cases in a search for correlation of events or conditions.

Similarly, it is now impossible to do longitudinal studies of the effects of preschool experiences, because we are now in a circle. The only way to find child subjects is through the school, and the school must have informed consents from parents. We need to find new ways of evaluating public programs. We have to find models that agencies themselves can use to do self-evaluation, and we need to teach our students how to use evaluation data to improve their own practices.

Evaluation should not be something that strangers come and do for you, but should be part of normal program management. We have a hard time teaching that, partly because we do not really have models to teach from. Tying practice to evaluation is part of instructional and methodological research that requires time and thinking, not money.

We also need to get ready to study the dynamics of social upheaval, which took us by surprise in the 1960s. Ways of using the family as a research unit is another thing we need. How to study the whole family as a single research unit is a methodological need that is ahead of us. When we know how to do that, then we will be able to understand what really happened in the Office of Economic Opportunity income maintenance experiment and not depend upon mere tabulations of divorce rates.

Finally, it is fairly certain that within ten years we are going to have to redesign our social and health service systems, and as part of that we have to reorganize the training of professionals. Now, we train professionals to be socialized to a single discipline and to be competitive with professionals in other disciplines. Until we change that, we are not going to be able to coordinate services into a meaningful package. Services are now fragmented along dimensions derived from academia and unrelated to each other—that is not how family problems are felt. Problems are related to one another within families and "solutions" are not being related to each other by agencies outside the family.

One of the things we need is to develop different administrative models. We keep trying new program designs, but use the same administrative procedures and hierarchical structures responsible for the organizational arteriosclerosis that characterizes many of our services. We do very little experimenting with new administrative forms. There are things that can be done. The U.S. Geological Survey has a practice of rotating its leadership.

The professionals take turns being national director, regional director, and laboratory director. They have a system in which everyone, after a while, understands the problems. Situations in which the regional offices fight the federal office and the federal office does not know the field problems do not exist.

When I was on the Appalachian Regional Commission we had an effective policy: no one could be an executive for more than five years. No one could have a career with the commission. That freed people to do things that they would not do if they thought it would affect their whole life. We did a lot of wild things. There is an organization in Southern California, an engineering firm, that is extraordinarily successful. It has a circular organization. Every engineer has his own problem; he is a consultant to someone else on *his* problem, and *he* has a consultant. There is one rule. In their consultant role they are not to prevent their consultee from making a mistake. It is a very high-quality staff and their mistakes are not likely to be random. There is one person who deals with clients—only one. He takes the flak but he has no projects and he has no authority over any project. The firm has enormous waiting lists of people who want to work there and there is no turnover except through death. The firm has more work than it can handle. There is a great deal of administrative research to be done in designing new and better programs for children and families.

Due to automation, many jobs will disappear in this society very soon. Every time we give new tax writeoffs for promoting the replacement of tools, we eliminate more jobs. We show no willingness to face up to the need for systematically creating new jobs. We seriously lack understanding of how to encourage youngsters to participate in the labor market and in citizenship. As a result, we have very low levels of participation in our democracy and the government we have is essentially what we deserve. The adult years are too late, I think, to build habits of citizenship. Waving the flag in kindergarten and first grade does not do it, either. I do not know what *does* do it, but it has terribly important consequences for the future of our country. How can we really make people feel some identity with the country as a whole and understand that participation is an important responsibility?

Finally, we need to start thinking about how we can avoid the externalization of frustration that will occur when we find out that the cost of saving a few bucks now is going to make us a second-class power—that our might lies not in guns, but in the universal recognition that we have more butter for everyone, and a better idea about how to live and share.

Reference

Papert, S. *Mindstorms*. New York: Basic Books, 1980.

2

Parent Education: Understanding Parents so that They Can Understand Themselves and Their Children

Helen F. Durio and
Robert Hughes, Jr.

The goal of providing effective parent education has been promoted frequently over the last fifty years (NSSE, 28th Yearbook 1929; Clarke-Stewart and Apfel 1979; McBrien 1980). Arguments for parent education have been based in part on research indicating that parents play a crucial role in the healthy development of their children (Bell 1976; White 1975). Strong evidence supports the role of parents as major contributors to children's psychological health and suggests that parents without capable parenting skills can contribute to psychological disturbances (Schwarz 1979). Staub (1979) presents evidence that parents are especially important in developing positive social behavior. These research findings emphasize the significant role parents play in the development of children's positive mental health.

In the last several years, specific social conditions make the need for providing education and support for parents an even more pressing social concern. Several recent studies have documented the confusing feelings of parents and their increasing need for support in the task of child rearing (Bronfenbrenner 1974; Goodson and Hess 1976; Keniston and the Carnegie Council 1977). The increasing number of teenage parents as well as the weakening of the extended or readily available family support systems through mobility signal the need for stepped-up efforts to channel support and information to parents (Orthner, Brown, and Ferguson 1976; Sparling, Lowman, Lewis, and Bartel 1978; Epstein 1980). Additionally, changing social structures and cultural traditions have contributed to a growing uncertainty among parents about their role and function (National Academy of Sciences 1976; Yankelovich, Skelly, and White, Inc. 1976–1977; Holtzman 1979). The particular conditions of our contemporary world make parent education an important topic of study.

Thanks to Mary-alayne Hughes and Melinda Longtain for comments on an earlier version of this chapter. This research was supported in part by a grant from the Hogg Foundation for Mental Health.

11

The methods for providing information and education to parents have taken a variety of forms. Parent education has been provided through workshops and seminars for parents (Dinkmeyer and McKay 1976) or in some cases, for parents and their children (Lehler et al. 1975). These types of parent programs generally focus on providing parents with a particular set of parenting skills. Other popular means of parent education are books, magazines, television, and other media sources. There are undoubtedly many other ways of educating parents. Throughout this chapter the term *parent education* will be used as a generic term encompassing all of these methods.

Despite the general support for parent education and the relatively long history of providing educational experiences for parents (Aries 1962), there is still little information about the most effective ways of providing parent education (Kazden 1979; Stevens 1978). The initial step is for parent educators to further understand parents as *information seekers* and as *learners*.

Recent research indicates that parents differ in the types of information they need and in the ways in which they seek information. Theories of adult cognitive processing and research on parents' conceptualization of parenting suggest ways in which parents' learning may need to be considered in the design of educational materials. The following sections review recent theory and research regarding parents as information seekers and as learners, and concludes with implications of this work for future of parent education.

Parents as Information Seekers

In general, parent education efforts have been developed with little regard for the ways in which parents seek information. Several recent studies indicate that there are several problems with current delivery mechanisms, including both parenting skills workshops and media sources such as books, magazines, and television (Clarke-Stewart 1978; Durio and Hughes 1980; James, Ethridge, and Coates 1980). These studies indicate that parent education has neither dealt adequately with the specific problems that confront parents, nor reached major segments of the population, especially minorities and nontraditional families.

Studies indicate that many parents are not satisfied with current information sources, and feel that the transmission of relevant information about child development is less than adequate (Clarke-Stewart 1978; Durio and Hughes 1980). In a recent study of the parenting information that can be obtained through the mass media, particularly books and magazine articles, Clarke-Stewart (1978) found that parents' use and reactions reflect some basic dissatisfactions; materials were seen as limited in application and influence to parents. While 94 percent of parents surveyed reported reading parenting publications, 81 percent felt that these materials were not directly applicable to their needs. Clarke-Stewart reported that over two hundred parenting books are currently in print and that the number of such publications has increased rapidly in the last ten years. Because of their wide circulation these materials must be very general and cannot be of help concerning very specific problems, nor do they address problems of parents from different family forms (for example, single parents, step-parents). Perhaps due in part to the general nature of the advice in these books, Clarke-Stewart reported that few parents found their parenting behavior had changed as a result of having read the books. Also, the books varied widely in the quality of the information provided, ranging from astrological guides to more carefully designed presentations of advice. Unfortunately, parents are rarely in a position to evaluate an author's suggestions critically, or to recognize that a suggestion may represent only one theoretical perspective.

Too often current parent education programs fail to address directly a parent's specific concerns. One of the conclusions voiced by James, Ethridge, and Coates (1980) is that in order to maintain parents' interest in the programs, the programmatic texts must be largely abandoned, to deal instead with the more specific concerns of the parents. In a survey of Texas parents conducted by Durio and Hughes (1980), 74 percent of the parents were not satisfied with available child-rearing information and 61 percent felt that their specific questions were not answered. Mass media education efforts can hardly be directed toward a specific parent concern. Alternative services must be developed that are sufficiently personalized to meet specific parental concerns.

Additionally, current resources fail to reach many of the parents most in need of education. Abram and Dowling (1979) found that the reading level of most of the parenting books required a high-school or better education. Certainly these materials are not going to have an impact on less well educated parents. While workshops and comprehensive parent training programs, such as Child Development Centers, have been shown to help parents, they have had only limited impact. These programs demand a great deal of time and motivation on the part of the parents. With today's greater number of working parents, fewer parents can take advantage of these programs. One recent report by a parent educator points to the problems of training low-income minority parents. James, Ethridge, and Coates (1980) report that only three out of twenty-five parents completed recent workshop programs and, amazingly, the authors suggest that this is a fairly good success rate! Clearly, programs of this sort are not reaching many parents. Alternative means must be found to reach parents who have less time for these high-commitment types of parent education programs.

Despite the existence of these dissemination problems, there has been very little study of alternative methods of delivering parenting information (Kazden 1979; Stevens 1978). In order to develop effective and efficient methods of educating parents, program designers will need to consider the patterns of child-care information seeking already used by parents. This work may provide clues as to where and when to intervene in the lives of parents to assist them in child rearing. Perhaps more effective methods than workshops and media sources can be developed. Some preliminary work regarding parents' information seeking will be considered.

Several recent studies have explored the sources to which parents turn when they need information (Clarke-Stewart 1978; Durio and Hughes 1980; Geboy 1981; Snow 1981). These studies have explored both the formal (doctors, teachers, psychologists) sources of advice to parents and the informal (friends, relatives). Additionally, these studies have considered the use of parent education workshops and reading materials.

The results of these studies indicate that parents consult a variety of sources. When asked in general who they would consult about problems, parents most frequently mentioned their own parents (37 percent, Snow 1981). Almost 60 percent of the parents stated that they would consult informal sources and only 35.5 percent mentioned formal sources (Snow 1981). When these results are examined more carefully in terms of specific problems, parents indicate that for school problems they generally turn to school personnel (92 percent, Snow 1981; 74.5 percent, Durio and Hughes 1980; 96 percent, Clarke-Stewart 1978). For health problems the most frequently mentioned source of assistance is the doctor (69 percent, Durio and Hughes 1980; 92 percent, Snow 1981). For other types of problems, parents' information sources are quite variable. Snow found that for social-emotional problems, parents most frequently turn to the schools, but this is only 36 percent of the parents. Somewhat similarly, Clarke-Stewart found that for problems such as stealing, 10 percent of the parents indicated they would consult a friend or relative, 27 percent a professional, and 19 percent a child-care book. In the case of a child fighting with parents, professionals were clearly more likely to be consulted (48 percent), with relatives and friends (17 percent) and books (19 percent) as less likely sources.

Durio and Hughes found that the spouse was the most frequently mentioned source of support and information for family problems (64.4 percent), personality development (54.6 percent), and antisocial behavior (43 percent). Snow reported that the clergy was consulted by 14 percent of the parents regarding parent information. Durio and Hughes found that parents frequently consulted the clergy for assistance with family problems (19.7 percent) and antisocial behavior problems (24.2 percent). Across all problem areas Durio and Hughes found that the spouse, parents or relatives, and friends were among the most frequently mentioned sources of information.

The study by Durio and Hughes also explored differences in information sources used by parents from various family types. While much of this information was similar for all families, there were some specific findings of interest. Except for health and school problems, single parents were more likely (19.9 percent) to indicate that they would consult no one when faced with family, personality, or antisocial behavior problems in their families (Hughes and Durio 1980). A much smaller proportion (7.5 percent) of adoptive, step, extended, and intact families indicated they would consult no one. As one might expect, one source of information and support, the spouse, is no longer easily accessible to many single parents. It appears that in many two-parent families one spouse would often consult the other. However, in the case of the single-parent family it appears that rather than consult someone, the single parent consults no one. This clearly illustrates the isolation of the single parent faced with a variety of child-care concerns.

The results of these studies seem to indicate that in the case of specific health and school problems parents turn directly to doctors and school personnel. However, even in these cases parents often mention several other less obvious informal sources. When the problems become more psychological in nature, and perhaps are less specific, parents frequently rely on friends and family or more familiar professional sources such as teachers or clergy. The findings regarding the high percentage of single parents that seek the aid of no one emphasizes the role of the spouse in the information and support system. Although these studies provide little about the patterns of help seeking that would indicate to whom parents turn first, second, and so on, they do provide strong support to the idea that parents generally rely on their own immediate community of family and friends for assistance in child rearing.

Parents as Learners

In addition to a further understanding of parents as they seek information, another issue for parent educators to consider is the way in which adults acquire knowledge. While understanding parents as learners is important to educators regardless of whether they present information via the media or workshops, it is especially important to those conducting parent training courses. Often parent education has been viewed as a simple matter of providing parents with the most current information regarding such child-rearing issues as health, social, emotional, and physical development. Matters regarding the process of education itself or the strengths and weaknesses of the parent as an adult learner have rarely been given much attention. In attempting to provide parents with information about child rearing, information regarding adult learning may provide help in assisting parents.

In the last several decades developmental psychologists and learning theorists have compiled a promising body of information that may be applied to educating parents. Developmental theorists can generally be considered to view adult learning from one or the other of two perspectives: age or stage. Age theorists are interested in determining if there are common concerns, interests, or tasks among adults at particular chronological times in their lives. The work of Berrin, Levinson, and Gould represents efforts to understand the ways in which age affects the thinking and behavior of adults. On the other hand, stage theorists have studied adults in terms of qualitative differences in modes of thinking. These theorists propose that adult thinking can be conceptualized as a series of hierarchical levels of information processing. Thus, rather than concerns and interests being organized in terms of age, these theorists suggest that adult thinking is organized by a set of rules, expectations, and understandings regarding the social world. Piaget, Kohlberg, Hunt, and Perry view adult thinking in terms of stages of cognitive development progressing from the concrete and undifferentiated to the more abstract and autonomous.

Theorists from both the age and stage perspective suggest that learning is affected by adults' particular mode of thinking. Generally, they suggest that different teaching strategies must be employed for different levels of functioning. For example, Hunt (1971) argues that individuals at more concrete levels of thinking learn better through highly structured teaching methods, whereas those at more abstract levels may gain understanding through less structured methods.

Neither age or stage theory assumes that the thinking of adults is permanently bound to a particular level or mode of processing. Rather the mode of thinking is viewed as a preferred method of functioning which may change through experience and/or education.

While both age and stage developmental theorists provide some insights into adult learning, the work of researchers in the stage theory tradition provides some of the most useful information regarding the teaching of parents. As yet there have been few attempts to use adult learning theory as a guide for parent education; however, the works of Hunt (1971), Newberger (1980), and Longtain (1981) provide useful ideas for considering parents as learners.

Hunt's Conceptual Levels

One theory of adult conceptual development that offers the possibility of application to parent education has been developed by Hunt and his colleagues (Harvey, Hunt, and Schroder 1961; Hunt 1971). Hunt outlines a sequence of stages called *conceptual levels* and a series of transition levels between these stages. According to this conceptual systems theory, a person's thinking about the social world is organized at one of the following levels:

Level 1. A person has a set of internalized norms and social conventions regarding the behavior of persons. These norms are applied to every individual in the same way and authority is viewed as the source of new ideas and the arbitrator of right and wrong.

Transition to Level 2. Persons begin to question the applicability of the norms to every situation and to all persons.

Level 2. With continued questioning the person begins to define a personal set of standards and norms for himself in relation to the cultural norms.

Transition to Level 3. The person begins to realize not only his or her own individuality in relation to norms but to others as well.

Level 3. There is increased understanding of the uniqueness of each individual.

Transition to Level 4. The primary conceptual task of this transitional stage is the attempt to reintegrate the individual standards into a coherent system recognizing individual differences within a framework of shared understandings and common goals.

Level 4. The attainment of an integrated framework involving an understanding of individual differences and common understanding and goals.

Based on work with this theory of conceptual development, Hunt (1971) has argued that the most effective means of education is through the matching of an appropriate teaching strategy to each conceptual level. Santmire (1979) has recently suggested a teaching scheme that can be applied to parent education.

The most effective role for parent educators working with Level 1 parents (those adults oriented to the practical, who tend to look to authority figures to define new ideas and right and wrong practices) would be to help them identify and define norms of parenting practices. With parents who are able to see that norms conflict and are not sufficiently specific for all situations (Level 2 Transitions), the parent educator could best foster parental acceptance of deviations from the norm. Level 2 Transition parents would need help in clarifying their own points of view. Level 2 parents could understand that their views were not completely different from parenting norms, despite some deviations. The parent educator's responsibility would be to help parents put together a coherent idea of their own parenting in relation to parenting norms. Parents at this level may prefer individualized parent education approaches rather than the group variety. Level 3 Transition parents would be able to view themselves as individuals capable· of deviating from parenting norms, but they might not be able to extend their conceptions of uniqueness to include their children's behavior. The parent educator would focus attention on how individuals differ from the parent (or the self) and from other children. Level 3 parents would be able to see the uniqueness of all individuals, including their children, and would emphasize this point to the degree that the parent educator needs to clarify the applicability of parenting as societal consensus. Collaborative exercises and sharing of experiences would be useful at this level. Level 4 Transition parents would understand that parents and children must relinquish some individual liberties for the sake of family harmony and in order to meet family responsibilities. The parent educator could thus focus on ways that parents and children could interact to solve mutual problems, rather than on singular parental practices or techniques of management acceptable to parents at lower conceptual levels. The Level 4 parents would operate in this interactive manner naturally and might only desire support and some justification from parent educators for their preferred mode of parenting. These parents would be more likely to desire further information on parenting and child rearing which they could utilize themselves. They would recognize that they would be adapting new information to their particular family situations.

In summary, lower conceptual-level parents would be likely to request and accept rules and specific explanations from parent educators. Those in transition between conceptual levels would be more likely to reject than accept or adapt the information not fitting their particular situations, and higher conceptual-level parents would be more likely to question specific practices, but adapt suggestions and parent education information to their own family styles. These examples demonstrate ways in which parent educators can apply Hunt's model of adult conceptual development to the task of educating parents. While there are still many issues that need to be considered, parent educators may find this framework useful in designing and conducting programs and workshops for parents.

Newberger's Parental Awareness

In a recent study Newberger (1980) has examined the thinking of parents regarding issues of parenting and has proposed a model of parent cognition. She defines the central construct of her work, parental awareness, as an organized knowledge system with which the parent makes sense out of the child's responses and behavior, and formulates policies to guide parental action (Newberger 1980). Newberger isolates two important dimensions in this process: the parental perspective-taking dimension and a parental moral dimension. The first dimension, role-taking, involves parental understanding of the child's level of understanding, or perspective. The second dimension, moral, involves rights and responsibilities, and requires parental resolution of competing claims for the distribution of his or her limited physical and emotional resources.

In a semistructured interview with parents, including some with a history of child abuse, Newberger discussed a series of issues and hypothetical dilemmas useful in examining parental reasoning. These issues were: identifying influences on development and behavior; understanding the subjective nature of experience, and how it is identified in children; defining personality qualities of children; establishing and maintaining communication and trust through closeness, sharing, and trust; identifying and resolving conflicts between child-child and parent-child relationships in the family; identifying the reasons for maintaining discipline in socializing children; defining needs; and identifying how parenting skills are acquired, and evaluating parental performance.

On the basis of this interview data Newberger identified four hierarchical levels of parental awareness:

1. *Egoistic,* in which the parent understands the child only as a projection of his or her own experience. Parental needs dominate reasoning.
2. *Conventional,* in which the child is understood in terms of external social forces of tradition, culture, and authority. Socially defined notions of correct parental practices dominate reasoning.
3. *Subjective-individualistic,* in which the child is viewed as a unique individual. Identifying the child's needs and meeting those needs dominate reasoning.
4. *Process or interactional,* in which the parent understands the child and him- or herself as growing and changing selves in an interactive relationship. Responsible harmonizing of the needs of both parent and child dominate reasoning at this highest level.

Newberger stressed that the levels of the parental awareness construct are hierarchical and reflect increasing cognitive flexibility and understanding and are not merely different parent value systems or positions. She found that parents' reasoning about a variety of child-rearing issues clustered around a particular level of understanding. Newberger also proposed that parental awareness is a developmental process and that parental reasoning may change from one level to another. Comparing the thinking of abusive and nonabusive parents, Newberger found that parents with a history of abuse reasoned at lower levels of parental awareness than parents without a history of abuse. Most of the nonabusing parents used conventional or subjective-individualistic modes of thinking. On the other hand, abusive parents were more likely to use egoistic reasoning in which the child is seen as little more than a projection of the parent's needs and desires.

The Newberger research on parental awareness also has implications for the education of parents. In particular the developmental nature of parental awareness suggests that the goal of parent education might be to encourage parental awareness at higher levels of reasoning. While further research is needed to link levels of awareness with parental behavior, Newberger's findings regarding abusive parents suggest that at least at the lowest level (egoistic), some possibility of problems in parenting may occur. Based on Newberger's work the parent educator may wish to pose hypothetical dilemmas regarding the issues of trust, authority, and conflict resolution in order to get parents not only to think about their position on these issues, but to stimulate thinking at higher levels of awareness. Activities to encourage critical thinking might include: role-playing (for example, the parent taking the child's perspective and having their own thinking reflected back to them) or reflective-questioning (for example, What does this issue mean for me? What does it mean for my child?). Parent educators may find several uses for the levels of parental awareness in their programs.

Longtain's Models of Socialization

In a study of parent models of child socialization, Longtain (1981) has collected several types of data from parents about their beliefs and values regarding child rearing that also has implications for parent education. She has identified nine different dimensions of parents' thinking about the issues of child rearing. There is no claim to a hierarchical pattern in these differing attitudes, although Longtain does suggest that cognition affects parenting behavior. The areas of parent attitudes are:

1. *Adult-centered.* The parent views child behaviors from the perspective of the adult (similar to Newberger's egoistic level);
2. *Child-centered.* The parent is aware of the child's perspective (similar to Newberger's subjective-individualistic level);
3. *Information-centered.* The parent is logical or rationally oriented in his or her child-caring role;
4. *Emotional reactiveness.* The extent to which the parent "thoughtfully responds" or "impulsively reacts";
5. *Intentionality.* The extent to which the parent positively or negatively evaluates a child's intentions;

6. *Role of the environment.* The parent structures the family environment to consider both the parent's and child's needs (similar to Newberger's interactional level);
7. *Child as a decision-maker.* The extent to which the parent encourages or allows the child to make decisions and live with the consequences;
8. *Fragility of child.* The extent to which the parent is influenced by child's delicate self-concept and feels responsibility for it;
9. *Confidence level.* The extent to which the parent feels confident in his or her role and will trust his or her own judgment.

Based on these nine attitudinal dimensions, Longtain proposed seven parenting models around which parents tend to organize their thinking and behavior: (1) Authoritarian, (2) Overprotective-Permissive, (3) Behaviorist, (4) Confused, (5) Romantic, (6) Consulting, and (7) Authoritative. She indicates that each of the nine dimensions must be considered in understanding the parent's model of socialization.

Applying this work to parent education, Longtain does not suggest that any one parent model is more effective than any other. She suggests that parent educators should direct their efforts toward assisting parents in understanding their own values and attitudes and helping them to be more comfortable with their particular model of socialization. Many of the previously mentioned activities, such as role-playing and discussions of child-rearing situations, would be useful for these tasks.

Adult Learning Applied to Parent Education

This section of the chapter has explored three models of adult thinking that have potentially useful applications for parent education. Each approach to adult thinking takes a slightly different perspective. The Hunt theory of conceptual development emphasizes the matching of teaching strategies to adult conceptual levels as a basis for education. The Newberger parental awareness model suggests that education should be targeted at stimulating the growth of parental awareness. Finally, the Longtain models of socialization emphasizes differences among parents and the need for each parent to come to understand his or her own attitudes and values regarding parenting. Despite these differences all of these researchers' work emphasizes the need to consider parents' thinking in designing parent education. Further research and application of these adult learning theories in parent education is needed to understand the strengths and weaknesses of each perspective.

The Future of Parent Education

This chapter has documented the many needs and problems of current parent education efforts. While several suggestions were offered regarding the further understanding of parents as information seekers and as learners, there are still numerous concerns, both research and programmatic, that need to be considered in the coming decades.

Research Needs

In regard to specific research needs, the work directed toward understanding parents has only just begun. From the recent research on information seeking by parents, a broad outline of this process can be identified. However, there are still numerous questions regarding differences in information seeking among different types of families, and differences due to such factors as education, socioeconomic status, and so forth. Likewise, there appear to be no data regarding the particular patterns of information seeking. While research indicates that parents often consult several sources, the pattern describing who they consult first, second, and so forth has not been examined. All of this information would be useful in designing intervention strategies to effectively target information to parents.

An additional area of applied research in parent education would be the examination of alternative information sources. While there have been some attempts to develop parent support groups (Powell 1980) and to provide information through audiotapes (General Telephone and Electric 1980), numerous other delivery methods are available to parent educators. Clarke-Stewart (1977) has suggested the creation of a family resource center offering a variety of information services and Stevens (1978) has suggested the use of food packaging (such as the backs of cereal boxes) as an outlet for parent information. Clearly there are many questions that can be asked about parent's information seeking.

While there has been considerable research on adult learning, there are many questions about how the thinking and reasoning of parents affects education efforts. There needs to be further research relating parental reasoning and actual parenting behavior. Also, researchers need to consider questions about what factors influence change in parental thinking. The further exploration of parents' ways of learning will undoubtedly be useful in providing guidance to parent education efforts.

Program Needs

In addition to the research needs of the future, there are also many program needs. On the basis of current problems with parent education and projected trends in family patterns throughout the coming decade, a variety of needs can be anticipated. As argued here, there are numerous problems in delivering adequate information to parents. On the basis of projected figures for the population in 1990 (from 1980 census figures), it appears that many of these issues will persist. Masnick and Bane (1980) project that over the next two decades there will be continued increases in families with two working parents. These authors also suggest that single parents will increase in number and that there may be a rise in single fathers as head of household. Considering these trends, it is clear that there will have to be continued parent education services to meet these parents' needs. On the basis of current studies (Clarke-Stewart 1977; Durio and Hughes 1980; Snow 1981) those parents who lack a familial support system or who have special family concerns are generally most interested in specific types of information about child rearing relevant to their needs. Parent education resources in the 1990s will have to be devoted to meeting the needs of these special groups of parents.

Another trend projected from the 1980 census relates to the increased number of children now enrolled in kindergarten and nursery school who will be teenagers in the 1990s. Anticipating this group of young people, parent educators should be prepared to handle an increase in the number of parents seeking assistance with adolescents' concerns. Many of these children will have been raised in homes with two working parents, which may pose additional challenges.

Perhaps the major issue that will confront educators will be assisting families that have broken apart through divorce, and the needs of reconstituted families handling problems with step and/or adoptive children, as well as the issue of coparenting with a previous spouse. Hetherington (1979) notes that currently 40 percent of marriages end in divorce and that 40 to 50 percent of children born in the 1970s will experience living in a single-parent family. An even greater number will be part of a step or blended family or will be reared through coparenting. Hetherington and others have thoroughly documented the numerous dangers and problems facing the families that experience divorce and remarriage. So far there are relatively few community support systems and educational opportunities to assist these families. The enormous challenge for parent educators is to develop a system of support for these parents and their children.

In considering parent education, professionals should think beyond the traditional methods of books, seminars, and workshops as delivery mechanisms. In the Carnegie Foundation report on families (Keniston and the Carnegie Council 1977), many of the major obstacles to effective parenting were found to be built into the social structure. Thus social change, rather than increased education, is needed.

Two types of changes in society should be considered by advocates of the family in anticipating the needs of the 1990s. These are: a more thorough integration of work and child care; and the development of community support systems. The first suggestion has largely been formulated as a plea for employers to offer on-site child-care services, but this is only one aspect of a larger problem. The central problem is providing opportunities for families to fulfill both work and family responsibilities. In part this may be child-care facilities at work, but it can also include such things as flexible work schedules and closer contact and coordination between schools and businesses. Effective adult functioning in either family or work role is largely dependent on success or failure in the other role. Parent education, whether through workshops or media sources, will not reach every family. Other means of providing parents with support must be considered.

Community support systems are one way in which development could occur. Research results clearly indicate that the primary support system for parents is still other family members and friends (Clarke-Stewart 1978; Durio and Hughes 1980; Snow 1981). Despite the increased availability of professional advice, parents continue to rely on their own personal resources. Parent educators may be able to exert the most influence by assisting in the creation of more and better community networks of support. This may take the form of both formal and informal networks. Current informal parent organizations for single, widowed, or separated parents should be encouraged and facilitated. Baby-sitting cooperatives and other types of informal parent assistance groups such as church organizations, parent-teacher groups, neighborhood organizations, and other organizations in the community should be strengthened to assist more parents. In addition to their roles as organizers of these types of groups or as advisors to the formal groups, parent educators can provide information through these networks via newsletters, workshops, and so forth. However, these activities would become secondary sources of support, the primary support coming from the community network.

These suggestions for a closer intergration of work and family within a community support system would seem to meet the emerging needs of the society as well as to fit within the political and economical climate of diminished resources. These ideas build upon the primary system of support for families and strengthen it with new direct ties to the secondary support system of professions. Not only is such a system more likely to be effective, but the costs of such an effort may be reduced when compared with efforts to provide more direct services to parents.

Perhaps such family support systems will be effective in diminishing other social problems that appear to be increasing in magnitude. They alone will certainly not be sufficient. At present there is little hope that such social problems as teenage pregnancy, violence, and the inability of schools to educate young people adequately will disappear in the 1990s. These issues are inextricably tied to the family, both through the family as part of the solution to these problems and the family as a victim of social situations.

Perhaps the development of community support networks can assist families in dealing with these problems as well as preventing their occurrence. Obviously, many other issues must be addressed in relation to these problems, but again the family stands firmly in the foreground as a factor whether one is talking about sex education, abortion, the role of television in promoting antisocial behavior, school reform, or home-school cooperation. While many of these issues and problems will not be solved by parent educators, those concerned with families will have to respond to changes in the family and in the social factors that affect family life. The role of the parent educator in these issues as they evolve throughout the remainder of this century may be multifaceted, but some role is absolutely necessary.

Summary

This chapter has reviewed current research related to two important issues for parent education: parents as information seekers and parents as learners. Recent studies of the sources through which parents seek information indicate that parents obtain information from a variety of both formal and informal sources. This research seems to indicate that despite changes in family life-styles during the last several decades, parents still rely on family and friends for much of their information.

With regard to theory and research on adult learning, much of the recent work with adults is potentially very useful to parent educators. Three different approaches to the study of parent cognition were examined. Hunt's theory of conceptual development proposes several levels of adult thinking and suggests that effective education can be facilitated by the careful matching of teaching strategies with parents' conceptual levels. The work of Newberger on parental awareness indicates that parents' reasoning can be viewed from a developmental perspective in which higher levels of parental awareness can be stimulated. Longtain proposes several parental models of socialization and suggests that parent education should focus on increasing parents' awareness of their own beliefs and attitudes regarding parenting. All of this work indicates that theory and research on adult learning can provide useful information to parent educators.

Despite the recent work on parents as information seekers and as learners, there are still numerous needs both in terms of research and programs. There must be continued research on ways in which parent education can be improved, and programs in the future must consider community support systems as well as the needs of working parents, single parents, and step and blended families. In the coming decades parent educators must continue to understand the lives of parents in order to assist them in understanding themselves and their children.

References

Abram, M.J., and Dowling, W.D. How readable are parent books? *The Family Coordinator* 28:365–369, 1979.

Aries, P. *Centuries of childhood: a social history of family life.* Translated by R. Baldick. New York: Knopf, 1962.

Bell, T.H. Formulating government policies on the basis of educational research. Address given at the University of Chicago, Chicago, Illinois, April 1976.

Bronfenbrenner, U. Is early intervention effective? *A report on longitudinal evaluations of preschool programs,* vol. 2. Washington, D.C.: Department of Health, Education, and Welfare, 1974.

Clarke-Stewart, K.A. *Child care in the family.* New York: Academic Press, 1977.

Clarke-Stewart, K.A. Popular primers for parents. *American Psychologist* 33:359–369, 1978.

Clarke-Stewart, K.A., and Apfel, N. Evaluating parental effects on child development. In *Review of research in education,* ed. L. S. Shulman. Itasca, Ill.: F.E. Peacock, 1979.

Dinkmeyer, D., and McKay, G.D. Systematic training for effective parenting. Circle Pines, Minn.: American Guidance Service, Inc., 1976.

Durio, H. F. and Hughes, R. Jr. *Assessment of parents' needs and attitudes in Texas.* Austin, Tex.: Measurement and Evaluation Center, The University of Texas at Austin, SR–80–7, 1980.

Epstein, A.S. *Assessing the child development information needed by adolescent parents with very young children.* Final report to the Department of Health, Education, and Welfare. Grant No. 90–C–1341. January 1980.

Geboy, M.J. Who is listening to the "experts"? The use of childcare materials by parents. *Family Relations* 30:205–210, 1981.

Goodson, D.B., and Hess, R.D. The effects of parent training programs on child performance and parent behavior. Stanford University, manuscript, 1976.

General Telephone and Electric. GTE infocenter. Austin, Tex.: *American statesman,* 1980.

Harvey, O.J.; Hunt, D.E.; and Schroder, H.M. *Conceptual systems and personality organization.* New York: Wiley, 1961.

Hetherington, E.M. Divorce: a child's perspective. *American Psychologist* 34:851–858, 1979.

Holtzman, W. *Delivery of mental health services: social, cultural, and family factors.* Austin, Tex.: Hogg Foundation for Mental Health, 1979.

Hughes, R. Jr., and Durio, H.F. The parent information needs of minority and nontraditional families. Paper presented at the annual meeting of the Texas Psychological Association, Austin, Texas, November 1980.

Hunt, D.E. *Matching models in education: the coordination of teaching methods with student characteristics.* Toronto: Ontario Institute for Studies in Education, 1971.

James, R.; Etheridge, G.; and Coates, B. Training inner city parents in child rearing: why fried chicken franchises for parenting won't work. Paper presented at the Urban South Conference, Norfolk, Virginia, 1980.

Kazden, A.E. Advances in child behavior theory: applications and interventions. *American Psychologist* 34:981-987, 1979.

Keniston, F., and the Carnegie Council on Children. *All our children: the American family under pressure.* New York: Harcourt Brace Jovanovich, 1977.

Leler, H.; Johnson, D.L.; Kahn, A.J. Hines, R.P.; and Torres, M. *Houston parent-child development center.* Progress report. Grant No. CG 60925, Office of Child Development, University of Houston, Texas, 1975.

Longtain, M. *Parent models of child socialization.* Executive summary. Austin, Tex.: Southwest Educational Development Laboratory, 1981.

Masnick, G., and Bane, M.J. *The nation's families: 1960-1990.* Cambridge: Joint Center for Urban Studies at MIT and Harvard University, 1980.

McBrien, R.J. Parent education research: a state of the art report. Paper presented at the annual meeting of the American Educational Research Association, Boston, Mass., April 1980.

National Academy of Sciences. *Toward a national policy for children and families.* Washington, D.C., 1976.

National Society for the Study of Education. *Twenty-eighth yearbook: preschool and parental education.* Bloomington, Ill.: Public School Publishing Co., 1929.

Newberger, C.M. The cognitive structure of parenthood: designing a descriptive measure. *New Directions for Child Development* 7:45-67, 1980.

Orthner, D.K.; Brown, T.; and Ferguson, D. Single-parent fatherhood: an emerging family life style. *The Family Coordinator* 25:429-437, 1976.

Powell, D.R. Strengthening parents' social networks: an ecological approach to primary prevention. Paper presented at the annual meeting of the American Psychological Association, Montreal, Canada, September 1980.

Santmire, T.E. Developmental differences in adult learners: implications for staff development. University of Nebraska, manuscript, 1979.

Schwarz, J.C. Childhood origins of psychopathology. *American Psychologist* 34:879-885, 1979.

Snow, M. A survey of parenting needs and community services. Paper presented at the annual meeting of the American Educational Research Association, Los Angeles, California, April 1981.

Sparling, J.J.; Lowman, B.D.; Lewis, I.S.; and Bartel, J.M. *What parents say about their information needs.* Progress report. Grant No. 90–C–1263, Administration for Children, Youth, and Families, 1978.

Staub, E. *Positive social behavior and morality: socialization and development,* vol. 2. New York: Academic Press, 1979.

Stevens, J.H. Jr. Parent education programs. *Young Children* 33:59–65, 1978.

White, B.L. *The first three years of life.* Englewood Cliffs, N.J.: Prentice-Hall, 1975.

Yankelovich, Skelly, and White, Inc. Raising children in a changing society. *General Mills American Family Report, 1976–1977.* Minneapolis: General Mills, 1977.

3

The Adaptations of Mothers of Toddlers to Multiple Social Roles

Elizabeth C. Ringsmuth

Motherhood exists as one role among others in the adult stage of life. Studies on the effects of different styles of parenting on the child have proliferated over the years. However, the effects of being parented have taken precedence over the effects of parenthood on parents themselves (Gutman 1975).

One effect which parenthood may have on women is the problem of adapting to multiple social roles. Besides the role of mother, women who have toddlers (children who have just begun to walk, to approximately a developmental age of three) may also experience simultaneously the roles of wife, housekeeper, wage earner, and student, as well as trying to retain a sense of self-identity.

The nature of the skills necessary to adapt to multiple social roles will vary. Mastering a series of developmental tasks within the normative stages of life may be one paradigm of an adaptive skill. Life-span theorists (Buhler and Massarik 1968; Erikson 1950; Havighurst 1972) describe normative stages in which motherhood is included but is not considered as a separate entity. Stages of motherhood have been delineated (Benedek 1970; Deutsch 1944; Friedman 1957; Galinsky 1981), but specific developmental tasks have not been addressed. However, motherhood may be viewed as a series of developmental tasks within the normative stages of life.

The developmental perspective considers the complex relationship between developmental stages and developmental tasks. The social role perspective focuses on the adaptive responses necessary to accommodate to multiple social roles.

Review of Literature

Developmental Stages of Parenthood

There are few descriptive studies on the theorized developmental stages of parenthood. Gutman (1975) argues that parenthood constitutes the pivotal

29

stage of the human life cycle, organizing the form and content of the stages which lead up to it, as well as those that succeed it.

The literature addresses four major stages of parenthood (table 3-1). The preparatory stage lays the foundation in childhood and adolescence for acquiring the attitudes and beliefs of the nature of parenthood. The primary stage is dominated by birth and the child-rearing functions of early adulthood. In the secondary stage, middle-aged parents adapt to no longer having children in the home—the empty nest. The tertiary stage finds the elderly parent becoming the child again as the roles reverse and the parent becomes dependent on the child-now-adult for support and nurturance.

Each of these four stages could cover approximately a twenty-year time period. With the changing life-styles of delayed marriage, living together, delayed child rearing, and teenage parenting, these stages cannot be considered hierarchical. A teenage mother might be taking care of her own infant and a critically ill parent at the same time. This mother would be seen as having a shortened preparatory stage, while simultaneously going through the primary and tertiary stages of parenthood. Similarly a woman in her late thirties who had delayed child-rearing, also might be taking care of a senile parent, thus being in the primary and tertiary stages simultaneously.

Developmental Tasks of Parenthood

Each of the four major stages of motherhood theoretically has inherent developmental tasks. The successful achievement of a task leads to further happiness and mastery of later tasks. Failure results in unhappiness, shame, and difficulty in achieving success with later tasks.

Broad developmental tasks analogous to the four stages of parenthood are identified by Havighurst (1972) (table 3-2). "Preparing for marriage and family life" precedes "Starting a family," "Rearing children," and "Assisting teenage children to become responsible and happy adults." The final developmental task related to parenthood is that of adjusting to aging parents. The recurrent nature of some of these tasks throughout the various stages of life must be emphasized.

Social-Role Perspective

Four stages of parenthood have been identified with at least one developmental task at each stage focused on parenting. However, the developmental tasks frequently use broad descriptors; they are recurrent at successive stages; and they cover, on the average, a twenty-year time-span. The question can be raised as to whether each stage of parenthood might have distinct phases of its respective developmental tasks.

Table 3-1
Stages of Motherhood Inferred from the Literature

Inferred Stages	Theorists				
	Erikson (1950)	Deutsch (1935)	Benedek (1970)	Galinsky (1981)	Friedman (1957)
Preparatory	Trust vs. Mistrust Autonomy vs. Shame Initiative vs. Guilt Industry vs. Inferiority Identity vs. Role Confusion	Childhood Puberty		Image-making	
Primary	Intimacy vs. Isolation	Motherhood	Early Motherhood	Nurturing Authority Interpretive Interdependent Departure	Learning the cues Learning to accept growth and development Learning to separate Learning to accept rejection without desertion Learning to build a new life, having been thoroughly discredited by one's teenager
Secondary	Generativity vs. Stagnation	Grandparenthood	Middle Motherhood		
Tertiary	Integrity vs. Despair		Late Motherhood		

Table 3-2
Stages of Motherhood and Corresponding Developmental Tasks

Stages of Motherhood	Developmental Task
Preparatory	"Preparing for marriage and family life"
Primary	"Starting a family"
	"Rearing children"
Secondary	"Assisting teenage children to become responsible and happy adults"
Tertiary	"Adjusting to aging parents"

One way to approach this question is to examine the various stages of a given social role and determine the various foci of the applicable developmental task. Rossi (1968) compares the structural ways in which the parental, marital, and occupational roles differ. She applies to these three social roles, four broad phases of a role cycle: Anticipatory; Honeymoon; Plateau; and Disengagement/Termination.

If Rossi's (1968) Honeymoon stage of the role cycle is renamed the Initial stage, then the marital role connotations are less obvious, and the role cycle might be more applicable to other social roles. An application of Rossi's (1968) four phases of a social role to the stages of motherhood could be attempted, with developmental tasks taking precedence over chronological age of occurrence (table 3-3).

This chapter addresses the beginning of the Plateau phase of the Primary stage and conceptualizes motherhood as one of multiple concomitant social roles. Mothers of toddlers do not function in their roles in isolation from other responsibilities and simultaneous social roles. Every human being usually performs several social roles at any stage of life. The life cycle of a woman involves shifts in the priorities of her roles as new roles are added or modified, and old roles dropped. The study described in this chapter examines the relationship among five concomitant roles: motherhood, marriage, self-identity, housewife, and wage earner. A sixth role, student, is seen as a commitment outside the family, which is indirectly related to parenting, self-identity, and employment.

The Mother-Toddler Study

Setting

The study was conducted in parent-toddler classes within the Los Angeles Unified School District, in the San Fernando Valley. Fourteen publicly

Table 3-3
Hypothesized Foci of the Developmental Task, "Rearing Children" for Four Stages of Motherhood and Four Phases of a Social Role

Stages of Motherhood	Anticipatory	Initial	Phases of a Social Role Plateau	Termination
Preparatory	Childhood perceptions of parenthood	Conception and early pregnancy	Late pregnancy	Birth
Primary	Symbiosis	Attachment	Individuation	Departure
Secondary	Adult-child's transition to new roles	Adult-child's commencement of new role	Adult-child's role-fruition	Adult-child's role-completion
Tertiary	Chronological aging	Physiological or psychological deterioration	Increased dependency on children	Death

sponsored and forty-one privately sponsored parent education classes for mothers of toddlers provided the settings for the data collection. These fifty-five classes were located on twenty-seven sites: eleven publicly sponsored, and sixteen privately sponsored.

Data Collection

A twenty-eight page questionnaire contained eighty-eight questions focused on six concomitant roles: mother; spouse/partner; self-identity; housekeeper; wage earner; student. After testing the questionnaire on twenty-five mothers, data collection proceeded. In fifty-five parent-toddler classes, 594 questionnaires were distributed, and 442 were completed, resulting in a return rate of 74.4 percent (public sponsors, 30.3 percent; private sponsors 44.1 percent).

Reliability for each of the responses was established through interviews. One to two weeks after the questionnaires in the parent education classes were completed, an interviewer readministered the questionnaire to fifty-one women, randomly sampled from the 249 who volunteered to be interviewed. Pearson product-moment correlations were determined for all of the 372 possible responses of the questionnaire. Overall the reliability for the responses in the questionnaire was very high.

The questionnaires were personally administered to the classes. A cover letter emphasized anonymity and confidentiality. The researcher explained the purpose of the study to the mothers in a concise and standardized manner.

The researcher stayed in the class, as a means of obtaining a high rate of return. Mothers were encouraged to complete the questionnaire in class; those not completed were taken home, brought back to class the following week, and mailed or collected personally.

Subjects

All mothers attending the parent-toddler classes on the day the questionnaires were distributed were invited to complete the survey. If fathers or other care givers were present with the toddler, they were asked to take the questionnaire home to the mother to complete.

Most of the toddlers had two parents in the household (91.4 percent); the parents were married (85.9 percent), Caucasian (91.0 percent), native-born (88.0 percent), and lived in a single-family dwelling (92.3 percent). Approximately two-thirds of the mothers were 27–33 years old (68.3 percent), did not have any help with housekeeping (63.6 percent), and were not working for wages (70.4 percent).

Most of the toddlers were 18–36 months old (81.2 percent) and qualified as natural children of their mothers (96.8 percent). There were only 4.1 percent more male than female toddlers, and almost two-thirds of the toddlers were first-born (63.6 percent).

All but one of the mothers had finished high school, and over half had a B.A. or B.S. degree or higher (51.4 percent). They were financially comfortable; just about as many mothers had family incomes over $40,001 (28.7 percent), as under $25,000 (34.6 percent).

In the San Fernando Valley, predominantly white, middle-class women attend parent-toddler classes. Consequently, the study is biased toward white, middle-class, two-parent families with educated women who do not work for wages.

Results of the Study

Three research questions were examined. The first addressed the difficulties and gratifications of mothers of toddlers; the second, overall adaptations; and the third, control variables which might affect the overall adaptations of mothers of toddlers to multiple social roles. The toddler's effect on a woman's overall adaptations to each of the social roles formed a cluster around family commitments, housekeeping, and commitments outside the family.

Family Commitments

Toddlers had a favorable effect on women in their roles as mother (93.1 percent), self-identity (84.9 percent), and wife (73.0 percent). The overall impact of the toddler on the roles of mother, wife, and self-identity tended to form a relatively cohesive relationship. The effect of the toddler between the roles of mother and self-identity (.69), mother and wife (.41) and wife and self-identity (.40) were all moderate to substantial positive associations, with chi squares statistically significant at less than the .001 confidence level. The positive adaptations to motherhood were associated respectively with the toddler favorably affecting the woman's self-identity or marriage. Likewise, when the toddler enhanced the marriage, the toddlers' effect on self-identity was also positive.

Women as Individuals

Mothers of toddlers were inclined to regard themselves as the major source of stress in their own lives. Not having enough time for themselves were frequently attributed to management skills related to time and people, as well as not having a social life of their own that was distinctly separate from social events with the spouse and/or the children.

Indirectly related to seeing themselves as the major source of stress were the women's perceptions of their own individuation, weaknesses, environmental conditions, and their fantasies of how they would spend one day all for themselves.

Three relationships involved in mothers feeling psychologically separate from their toddlers and spouses were examined (table 3-4). From the mothers' perspective, most toddlers were regarded as individuals distinct from their parents (92.8 percent). However, lower proportions of mothers did not consider themselves as individuals separate from either their toddlers (68.3 percent) or their husbands (55.7 percent). The greatest proportion of ambivalence occurred in 40.0 percent of the women, who only "sometimes" felt a sense of being individuals separate from their husbands.

While individuation is initially completed within the third year of life (Mahler, Pine, and Bergman 1975), adolescence and early adulthood may create new relationships which require additional resolutions. The underlying assumption is that most mothers are already fully individuated at an early stage of development. The high proportion of ambivalence in feeling psychologically separate from toddlers and spouse raises questions: Has individuation occurred only partially? Does individuation from parents, children, or spouse occur in qualitative different ways?

Another indirect relationship to mothers seeing themselves as a major source of difficulty focuses on the "weaknesses" the women stated in relation to their own personalities. Of the women who stated weaknesses, 75.9 percent of the responses were in the "emotional" category. "Outburst of temper" (17.3 percent) and "insecurity" (11.2 percent) were reported by

Table 3-4
Three Relationships Involved in Mothers Feeling Psychologically Separate from Their Toddlers and Spouses

Relationship	Sense of Being a Separate Individual				
	Missing Data	Sometimes	No	Yes	Total
Toddler from parents	1.1	0.0[a]	6.1	92.8	100.0
Mother from toddler	3.2	35.8	2.7	68.3	100.0
Mother from spouse	2.7	40.0	1.6	55.7	100.0

Note: N = 442.
[a]"Sometimes" was not an available response for this question.

a higher proportion of women than any other emotional weaknesses. Other weaknesses addressed such attributes as: being inconsistent, indecisive, changeable, submissive, intolerant, sarcastic, guilty, rigid, naive, and lackadaisical.

Besides relating personal attributes as sources of difficulty, environmental conditions also could be influential. Did the women have adequate child care to allow them to get away? Almost three-fourths of the mothers (73.8 percent) had help at least once a week in caring for the toddler. Of the mothers who had help at least once a week, 85.9 percent considered the source of help to be good quality child care. However, 86.8 percent of these mothers who had help once a week also felt that good quality child care needs to be more readily available.

Family income can be another influential environmental condition. When family income was controlled, the toddler's overall effect on the role of self-identity was statistically significant ($p < .01$) with a low positive strength of association ($\gamma = .16$). As family income increased from $25,001 to over $40,000, the very positive effects of the toddlers on the mothers' self-identity increased.

The realities of both personal attributes and environmental conditions could be contributing factors to the women seeing themselves as a major source of difficulty. When asked, "If you had one day all to yourself what would you do?", the highest proportion of responses focused on their role as women (86.4 percent). One inference is that most of the women would like to be nurturing themselves part of the time. Leisure activities represented the greatest proportion (29.9 percent) of the categories related to the women themselves. "Physical care" (19.2 percent), "intellectual pursuits" (15.8 percent), "social relationships" (11.6 percent), "crafts" (8.1 percent) and "just doing nothing" (1.9 percent were other areas of self-indulging fantasies).

All of these fantasies may have in fact been partial or complete realities, given the high income levels of most of the mothers in this study. While the majority of mothers cited themselves as the primary source of difficulty, they also saw themselves as a source of gratification. This is not inconsistent. An awareness of the pleasure of being an individual may exist, but at the moment, the child and spouse are seen as more gratifying than time spent alone.

Women as Mothers. Children were chosen as the primary source of gratification (97.3 percent) and the second major source of stress (68.8 percent) by mothers of toddlers. The specific examples of the kinds of stress and gratification clarify this double bind. Essentially toddlers were viewed as complicated phenomena, who provided more gratifications than difficulties.

The particular ways in which toddlers gratified their mothers varied.

"Developing language skills" (96.2 percent) and learning or "mastering new tasks (puzzles, toys)" (94.6 percent) were chosen as the primary joys of having a toddler at home. Both of these tasks are related to later achievement and are highly valued in middle- and upper-class homes (Martin 1975; Schaefer 1972). Four other ways in which toddlers gratify their mothers included "developing physical skills (walking, and the like)" (86.2 percent), "imitating family or friends" (72.9 percent), "beginning to obey and know right from wrong" (62.9 percent), and "exploring behaviors (opening, touching, and so forth)" (57.2 percent).

The difficulties that a toddler created also varied. Accepting limits from the care giver was the problem most frequently cited by the mothers of toddlers (57.9 percent). Temper tantrums was the second major problem related to stress with children. A cluster of seven other toddler experiences also emerged, including: exploring behavior (31.9 percent); saying "no" (29.9 percent); diapering/toileting (28.3 percent); crying when the parent leaves (27.8 percent); sharing toys (27.6 percent); eating (26.5 percent); and bedtime (23.5 percent). Preferring one parent (14.0 percent), enduring fears (12.4 percent), and illnesses (9.7 percent) were the problems of toddlers with which these mothers were having relatively less difficulty.

The similarities and differences of the physical characteristics and temperaments between the mothers and toddlers was another area potentially affecting the mother-child relationship. A higher proportion of mothers regarded themselves as similar to, as opposed to different from, their toddlers in physical characteristics (57.7 percent), temperament (65.2 percent), and other characteristics (11.1 percent).

All mothers have expectations for their toddlers. One way mothers' expectations are reflected is through making wishes for their children. Most of the wishes for the toddlers referred to personal attributes, rather than worldly possessions. The three wishes made by the highest proportion of mothers were: happiness (67.2 percent); health (59.5 percent), and success (45.0 percent).

A high proportion of mothers indicated advances in communication to be the toddlers' accomplishment that would be remembered most (85.1 percent), as well as the greatest immediate joy (96.2 percent). For those mothers who did believe there might be a delay in their toddlers' milestones, the area of communication skills was also the greatest concern (35.6 percent). Similar parallels between the memorable milestones and joys of a toddler were found in the mothers' second and third choices: "gross motor skills," and "mastery of new tasks."

Over four-fifths (80.5 percent) of the mothers did not believe there were other milestones which the toddler should have, but in fact had not, reached. This assumption of normality could have contributed to children being seen as the mothers' greatest source of pleasure. Being able to take pride in and to acknowledge the accomplishments of their offspring was one way in which these mothers might be measuring their success at motherhood.

Women as Wives. The impact of a child on the marriage may be a contributing factor to a lowered satisfaction in the marriage (Burr 1970; Rollins and Feldman 1970). The data in this study support this thesis. The spouse was perceived as a secondary source of gratification (87.3 percent) to the primary source of the toddler (97.3 percent). However, less than half of the women (42.1 percent) saw their husbands as a major source of difficulty. Three sources of stress in the marriage focused on spouse-related problems: disciplining the children (37.3 percent); sharing the child rearing (39.1 percent); and spending enough time with the children (21.0 percent).

What were the conditions of the marriages that may have contributed to such a high level of intact families (95.9 percent)? The greatest proportion (47.7 percent) of the mothers had been married to or had lived with the child's father for four to seven years before having their first child.

The number of couples who had waited four to seven years to have children was positively related with the time before having children as being "just right." The greatest proportion of mothers who had been married less than three years before their first child was born considered the time to be "too short," and mothers married over eight years considered the time to be "too long."

A positive relationship existed between planning the pregnancy and the time before having children as being "just right." Unplanned pregnancies were positively related to the time being too short. Two-thirds of the toddlers in this study were first-borns. Many, but not all, of those mothers probably want to have more children. As reported by the parent education teachers, 31.5 percent of the mothers were pregnant at the time the questionnaire was completed. When asked what their reactions would be if they were told right now that they couldn't have any more children, nearly half (45.0 percent) expressed negative feelings. A comparable percentage of the mothers (44.9 percent) indicated that they would be "O.K." or pleased.

Two other areas which tend to support the finding that the spouse was a greater source of pleasure than of difficulty were the amount of time parents devoted only to themselves, and the congruence of parents in two child-rearing practices. Over four-fifths (82.2 percent) of the mothers responded that they were able to spend one to two hours a week away from the house and children, doing something with their husbands.

While the number of hours per week was not significantly related to the toddler's effect on the marriage, there was an indication that a vacation of two or more days with only the spouse was positively related to the toddler's overall effect on the marriage.

A high proportion (67.6 percent) of mothers responded that they and their husbands used similar methods of disciplining (67.6 percent) and agreed when talking about their toddlers (71.9 percent) most of the time.

Housekeeping Commitments

Problems related to housekeeping were the third major source (47.7 percent) of stress for mothers of toddlers. Housekeeping was defined as "shopping, preparation and clean-up after meals, washing, mending, and folding of clothes, cleaning, daily picking up of family belongings, budgeting and bookkeeping, and house and yard maintenance."

Across the six roles, the unfavorable effects of the toddler were felt by 43.1 percent of the women in the role of housekeeper. The overall effect of the toddler on the role of housekeeper was significant and positively related to the comparable relationships in the role of mother and wage earner.

When the toddler's effect on the role of housekeeper was controlled by the mothers' age, a low negative strength of association emerged. As mothers became older, the toddlers' effect on housekeeping became more unfavorable. The toddlers had an unfavorable effect on the greatest proportion of women over 34 years of age (56.9 percent), as compared with 27–33 years (42.2 percent) and under 26 years (32.4 percent).

The toddlers' effect on the role of housekeeper was significantly related to roles represented in both commitments within and without the family. The emphasis on order and cleanliness could facilitate or hinder family harmony. Likewise the emphasis on shopping, preparation of meals, maintenance of house, yard, and car could affect the time available for commitments outside the family.

Approximately one-third (34.8 percent) of the mothers did all the housekeeping themselves. Help with the housekeeping included family members—the spouse (44.8 percent) and older children (7.2 percent)—and paid employees, part-time (33.3 percent) or full-time (12.0 percent). When each of these areas of help with housekeeping was examined in relation to the toddlers' overall effect on each of the six adult social roles, three areas of significance were found.

Help from a spouse was inclined to affect favorably the toddler's influence on how the women regarded themselves. A higher proportion of women who had help with the housekeeping from their husbands (89.6 percent), as compared to no help (79.3 percent) found the toddler to affect favorably the womens' feelings about themselves.

Housekeeping help from older children in the family was negatively related to the toddlers' effect on the women as students. A higher proportion of women who had help with the housekeeping from their older children (77.8 percent), as compared with no help (35.8 percent) regarded the toddler as a negative influence on their studies. The toddler was a positive influence only for the proportion of the mothers (32.1 percent) who had no housekeeping help and no help from older children (0.0 percent). The toddler did not make any difference to the studies of a higher percentage of women who had no housekeeping help (32.1 percent), as compared with help from older children (22.2 percent). The quality of "help" from older children could be inferred to complicate more than help the relationship of studying and housekeeping.

Housekeeping employees were seen as not making any difference on the toddlers' overall effect on the mothers' role as housekeeper. A higher proportion of women who had either or both part-time and full-time paid help (44.5 percent), as opposed to no help (28.9 percent) regarded the toddlers as not making any difference to their housekeeping.

In the interviews, as compared to the self-administered questionnaire, a higher proportion of women acknowledged their husbands' help with the housekeeping. Some mothers would have liked the help to be more extensive and were somewhat reluctant to acknowledge any help.

Over three-fifths (62.3 percent) of the mothers had toddlers who "helped" with housekeeping tasks, such as picking up the family belongings, cleaning, shopping, and cooking. Housekeeping for these mothers was a means of facilitating the role of parent.

The time spent in housekeeping tasks was viewed as a possible influence on the toddlers' effect on the housekeeping role. When the toddlers were asleep, only 10.0 percent of the mothers indicated they did nonhousekeeping tasks. On the surface, it would appear that this time of the day would be ideal for pursuing the mother's interests, particularly since time for self was stated as a major source of stress. However, organizing one's time for maximum efficiency was cited as a difficulty for 26.5 percent of the mothers. Management of the mothers' time may be a reason why more mothers did not use the time for themselves when their toddlers were asleep.

When asked how they would choose to spend their time, if the time now spent in housekeeping tasks could be used differently, 39.1 percent of the mothers chose "personal interests." The theme of more time for mothers' own interests was prevalent throughout the study.

Commitments outside the Family

Women as Wage Earners. A comparable proportion of women regarded their employment as a source of difficulty (15.6 percent) or as a source of pleasure (17.0 percent). The overall unfavorable effects of the toddler were felt by 32.5 percent of the women in their role as wage earner. The overall effect of the toddler on the role of wage earner was negatively related to the effect of the toddler on the role of mother. The role of wage earner can be considered from at least three perspectives: women who had previously been employed; women who were presently employed either full- or part-time; and women who planned to be employed in the future.

A slightly higher proportion of women (92.1 percent) had worked at some time after having their first child, as compared with women who had worked for wages before having any children (89.1 percent). The main pattern of responses indicated that working only during their pregnancies was the choice of the highest proportion of women (52.1 percent).

Twenty-four percent of the 442 mothers were currently employed: full-time, 3.4 percent; part-time, 20.6 percent. Because some women had more than one job, there were 121 job descriptions for the 108 women who were working. The greatest proportion of women were teaching (28.9 percent), followed by business (21.5 percent), and office management (19.8 percent).

On the average, about half (52.8 percent) of the working mothers were employed one to two days per week. While some of the mothers were not able to do any of their work at home (43.5 percent), others could do part (38.2 percent) or all (17.6 percent) of their work at home.

Future employment was anticipated by 81.3 percent of the 336 mothers who presently were not working because they wanted to be at home with their toddlers. Of the mothers who expected to work in the future, the greatest proportion wanted to return to work when the youngest child was five to six years old (32.8 percent).

The greatest proportion of mothers who expected to work in the future could qualify with existing training (49.1 percent), but some would need to be retrained (17.3 percent). Studying for retraining is but one of several reasons for taking classes and adapting to the additional role of student.

Women as Students. A higher proportion of women found their studies to be a source of pleasure (11.3 percent), rather than a difficulty (5.9 percent). The effect of the toddler on the women's overall adaptations were most unfavorable to the role of student.

Classes other than parent education were attended by 22.2 percent of the mothers. The most frequently chosen reasons for attending classes were for personal reasons—personal enrichment (84.7 percent), to get away from the routine of daily living (43.9 percent), to meet new people (31.6 percent)—as opposed to achievement reasons—certification (26.5 percent) or degrees (15.3 percent). About half (50.7 percent) of the women expected to enroll in classes other than parent education in the future.

Ironically, the highest proportion of women stated that time for themselves was their greatest source of stress. Yet, in getting out and taking a class for purely personal reasons, approximately half (52.9 percent) of the women considered the toddler as hindering their role as student. The gain of personal enrichment may be traded for feelings of inadequacy or mediocrity as a student.

Parent education classes were attended for a variety of reasons: finding friends for their toddlers (77.6 percent), learning more about child development (73.5 percent), and meeting other mothers (71.9 percent). While the women regarded themselves as the major source of stress in their lives at that time, discussing personal shortcomings was not given as a major reason for enrolling in the class.

However, the group aspect appeared to have an attraction. Close to one-fourth (24.4 percent) of the mothers were enrolled in more than one mother-toddler class. For these women, as compared with mothers attending classes only once a week, the need to be away from the house at least two mornings a week, may have slightly different or more intense meaning.

Implications of the Study

For Research

In addition to replicating the study with women who reflect a broader diversity of backgrounds, several research questions might be asked:

1. Can the difficulties and gratifications of a particular stage of parenthood be considered developmental tasks?
2. What is the relationship between developmental tasks specific to mothers of toddlers, and the tasks of other developmental stages of parenthood?
3. Why does the toddler affect some roles more favorably than others?
4. What are the variables which intervene in the overall affect of the toddler on one role, as compared with other roles?
5. What are the longitudinal findings from studying parents through all stages of parenthood?

For Education and Public Policy

Education for parents of infants and toddlers is growing rampantly in the nation, especially for middle- and upper-class families. Parents are asking for more classes that meet more than once a week. Changes in the character of contemporary families represent potential difficulties and gratification for women experiencing multiple social roles. Participants in parent education see these changes in the American family structures in different ways.

These changes impinge upon the social milieu of parent education and should be reflected in its programs.

Parent education must be broadly conceptualized to meet the variety of needs manifest in the multicultural, multilingual, multieconomic, and multieducational levels of our society. Through both public and private sponsors, adult education must meet the needs of parents other than the white middle class. Early childhood education must place equal importance on the effects of parenthood on the parents themselves, as well as the effects of parenting on the children.

Early childhood education must be seen as taking place twenty-four hours a day, in the home as well as in institutional settings. Child care must be easily accessible at any time of the day, with low adult-child ratios, and well-planned programs. Administrators must provide for staff development, benefits, and professionally competitive salaries. Parent education must be regarded as an integrated component, not a supplemental enrichment, and must be based on a theoretical rationale that is compatible with the children's program. A developmental perspective considers principles of human development to be basic for any curriculum designed to facilitate learning.

The implications for mothers in parent education, based on the findings of this study, are presented within the developmental framework which guided the rationale for the research. This approach includes the assumptions that: (1) development takes place in a social setting; (2) parents and children influence each other mutually; and (3) families deal with their total environment in a continual interaction of constitutional and learning factors in ways that might be called self-generative (Johnson 1976). A logical emphasis of this approach would be to help parents learn problem-solving skills.

Brim (1965), Pickarts and Fargo (1971), Auerbach (1968), and Slavson (1958) have all advocated problem-solving approaches to parent education based on value-free premises. Common to this approach is the perspective that there is more than one way to solve a problem and that there is not any one right answer in parent education.

Guidelines for implementing a developmentally based parent education program would include:

1. Determine the mothers' strengths and areas of greatest gratification;
2. Determine the area of greatest concern to the mother;
3. Use the strengths and areas of gratification to overcome the obstacles and resolve the difficulties;
4. Acknowledge the interrelationship of concomitant roles;
5. Generalize the problem-solving skills to difficulties in other roles related to motherhood; and

6. Use a variety of techniques to initiate discussion that allows for self-reflection.

Informal as well as formal, individual as well as group, educational as well as therapeutic approaches must all be considered when developing public policy about parent education and parent development.

References

Auerbach, A.B. *Parents learn through discussion: principles and practices of parent group education.* New York: Wiley, 1968.

Benedek, T. Parenthood during the life cycle. In *Parenthood: its psychology and psychopathology,* ed. E.J. Anthony and T. Benedek. Boston: Little, Brown, 1970.

Brim, O.G. *Education for child rearing.* New York: Free Press, 1965.

Buhler, C., and Massarik, A., eds. *The course of human life: a study of goals in the human perspective.* New York: Springer, 1968.

Burr, W.R. Satisfaction with various aspects of marriage over the life cycle: a random middle class sample. *Journal of Marriage and the Family* 32: 29–37, 1970.

Deutsch, H. *The psychology of women,* vols. 1 and 2. New York: Grune and Stratten, 1944.

Erikson, E.H. *Childhood and society.* New York: Norton, 1950.

Friedman, D.B. Parent development. *California Medicine,* 36:25–28, 1957.

Galinsky, E. *Between generations: the six stages of parenthood.* New York: Times Books, 1981.

Gutman, D. Parenthood: a key to the comparative study of the life cycle. In *Life span developmental psychology: normative life crises,* ed. N. Datan and L. Ginsberg. New York: Academic Press, 1975.

Havighurst, R.J. *Developmental tasks and education.* 3rd ed. New York: McKay, 1972.

Johnson, D.L. *Houston parent child development center. Final report.* Houston, Texas: University of Houston, 1976. (ERIC Document Reproduction Service No. ED 135 459).

Mahler, M.S.; Pine, F.; and Bergman, A. *The psychological birth of the human infant.* New York: Basic Books, 1975.

Martin, B. Parent-child relations. In *Review of child development research,* vol. 4, ed. F.D. Horowitz. Chicago: University of Chicago Press, 1975.

Pickarts, E., and Fargo, J. *Parent education: toward parental competence.* New York: Appleton-Century-Crofts, 1971.

Rollins, B.C., and Feldman, H. Marital satisfaction over the family life cycle. *Journal of Marriage and the Family* 32:20–28, 1970.

Rossi, A. Transition to parenthood. *Journal of Marriage and the Family,* 30:26–39, 1968.

Schaefer, E.S. Parents as educators: Evidence from cross-sectional-longitu-dinal and intervention research. In *The young child: reviews of research,* ed. W. Hartup. Washington, D.C.: National Association for the Education of Young Children, 1972.

Slavson, S.R. *Child-centered group guidance of parents.* New York: International Universities Press, 1958.

4 Children in Violent Families: Direct and Indirect Victims

Mildred Daley Pagelow

> *Now I lay me down to sleep;*
> *I pray the Lord my soul to keep.*
> *If I should die before I wake,*
> *I pray the Lord my soul to take.*

A child at night, tucked into bed after saying the old, familiar prayer that was probably said by his or her parents and grandparents, creates a warm, glowing image of family life. Security, rest, tranquillity—safe from the troubled and troubling world outside the home, surrounded by people who love each other—that is what comes to mind when we picture the family and home. But is it an accurate picture?

No, say the experts, with massive evidence to support their claim. In fact, home may be the most dangerous place, and family members may be more violently aggressive toward each other than toward strangers. Children may face more dangers from their own families than they possibly can meet outside the front door.

Introduction

This chapter explores the incidence of violence[1] in the home and looks at the effects of abuse directed at child victims as well as victimization of children living in homes where mothers are beaten by fathers or father-figures.[2] It is suggested that children send some "signals" to adults outside the home. By dispelling common misconceptions and by gaining some understanding of what goes on in the lives of children, sensitive and perceptive adults beyond the family unit may be prepared to identify child victims of violence and respond appropriately. The focus here differs from others that approach the topic of child abuse only from the viewpoint of the direct victimization of children (Fontana 1973; Gelles 1979; Gil 1970; Helfer and Kempe 1968; Steele and Pollock 1968). As for indirect victimization of children through seeing abuse of their mothers, most writers focus on the adult violence; children, when and if they are mentioned, are peripheral (Dobash and Dobash 1979; Martin 1976; Pagelow 1981a, 1981b; Pizzey 1977; Walker 1979).

Extent and Direction of Violence in the Home

Most writers agree that it is difficult, if not impossible, to gauge with accuracy the amount of violence that occurs in the household, particularly in a society such as ours that venerates "The Sanctity of the Home and the Integrity of the Family" (Kremen 1976). Another writer says that the family is a true microcosm of our violent society and insists that there is more violence in the privacy of the family than in the outside world (Freeman 1979, p. 1).

The child who murmurs the bedtime prayer may not become one of the estimated five to seven hundred children killed by parents each year in this country (Fontana 1973; Gil 1970). The exact number of homicides is unknown, largely because they are part of a social process in which doctors, courts, and coroners participate, and only those relatively few cases of all child victims that are positively identified as homicide and purposeful fatal injury become part of the official record (Freeman 1979, pp. 17–21). Freeman gives an example of children whose deaths are classified as due to pneumonia, yet they contracted the disease while suffering the effects of nonaccidental injury.

Violence toward children may be viewed as a continuum, with homicide at one extreme and parental force for disciplinary purposes at the other. Most children experience some type of physical violence from parents such as slapping, punching, or beating with belts and other objects, and kicking—"for the child's own good"—because 84 to 97 percent of all parents in this country approve, and use, physical punishment (Blumberg 1964; Erlanger 1974; Gelles 1979; Stark and McEvoy 1970). It is probably true that many of the parents interviewed in studies are referring to socially approved use of corporal punishment to discipline children but from the point of view of small children hit by persons who tower far above them, they may indeed be far more violent and traumatic than adults can imagine. From the perspective of this writer and in agreement with Gelles (1979) and others, slapping or hitting children is violence, regardless of the adult rationalizations accompanying the act. In fact, ". . . [some] acts parents carry out on their children in the name of corporal punishment or acceptable force, could if done to strangers or adults, be considered criminal assault" (Gelles 1979, p. 79).

Since the focus here is on both direct abuse (in which the child is the recipient of physical force) and indirect abuse (in which the child is exposed to physical force against a loved one) of children in violent homes, the question immediately arises—who are the most frequent abusers and who are their most frequent victims? What are the probabilities of a child's direct or indirect victimization? The best source of information for some answers are provided by Dobash and Dobash (1978, 1979). These sociologists analyzed police and court records in Edinburgh and Glasgow, Scotland, for a year; they found that in all types of violent crime, males and females are about equally likely to be victims, but over 91 percent of the perpetrators are males.

Because more of the Dobash and Dobash findings are relevant here, it seems best to compare data they obtained from official records in Scotland and see if they are unique to that country or compatible with records in the United States. The best source for American data is the Staff Report to the National Commission on the Causes and Prevention of Violence (Mulvihill and Tumin 1969) (table 4–1). In seventeen large American cities 2,424 violent crimes were committed where the sex of the offender and victim was recorded; Dobash and Dobash were able to identify the sex of offender and victim in 2,872 violent crimes. In table 4–1 the percentages for each category are shown, with the Dobash and Dobash percentages in parentheses, for ease of comparison.

Table 4–1 shows that whether the aggressors or victims are Scottish or American, violence by males is not only much greater but also disproportionately directed against females by males than the reverse. While the proportions of male/female aggressors are the same in both countries, there are two notable differences. The proportion of American male aggression against women is higher than in Scotland, and when American females are the aggressors, their rate of aggression against men is twice as high as against other women. Scottish women assault other females somewhat more often than they assault men. One possible reason for this may be the easier availability of firearms in the United States, which some have called the "equalizer" (Martin 1976). Usually smaller and less muscular, women may

Table 4–1
Sex of Victim and Offender in All Cases of Violent Crime
(percent)

	Victim		
Offender	Male	Female	Total
Male	55	36	91
	(51)	(40)	(91)
Female	6	3	9
	(4)	(5)	(9)
Total	61	39	100
	(55)	(45)	(100)

Source: Computed from Mulvihill and Tumin (1969, pp. 210–215) and Dobash and Dobash (1978, p. 436).
Note: Figures in parentheses are from Dobash and Dobash.

be unlikely to act aggressively toward men unless they have the advantage of a weapon, such as a gun. From victimization reports we know that approximately twice as many crimes are actually committed than are reported, and that the rate for reporting criminal victimization is about the same for males and females (U.S. Government Sourcebook 1977, 1981). In the United States, men commit three times the assaults on women than the reverse, and for all crimes of violence combined, violence against women by men is approximately six times greater than that of women against men (Mulvihill and Tumin 1969).

Dobash and Dobash further analyzed their data by cases of violence between all family members (1978, p. 436). Within the family, females were victims in almost 95 percent of all cases where the sex of victim and offender was known; in less than 3 percent of almost 900 cases was the offender female. Most important to this discussion, these researchers itemized the assaults according to the family position of the victim. From this (Dobash and Dobash 1978, p. 437) it is clear that the two most common forms of violence in the family are wife assault (in which children are indirect victims) and child assault (direct victimization). Out of a total of 1,044 assaults occurring between family members, 791 (76 percent) were assaults against wives; 112 children (11 percent) were assaulted by parents; and 50 children (7 percent) were assaulted by siblings. According to these data, children are seven times more likely to live in a home where mothers are beaten by fathers or father-figures than they are to be themselves beaten by a parent (or five times as likely, if we include assaults by siblings). This chapter addresses first the direct victimization of children through parental physical abuse, then indirect victimization, and finally, double victimization.

Direct Victimization

We do not have any reliable figures on the number of children who are physically abused in families in the United States. Most studies are restricted to samples obtained through public social services, law enforcement or medical agencies, and most researchers recognize that cases that become publicly identified probably represent only a tiny number of the many actual occurrences of child abuse each year. One of the most serious handicaps in trying to estimate the incidence of child abuse stems from the fact that there is no consensus on a definition of child abuse. The Child Abuse Prevention and Treatment Act of 1973 subsumes neglect in its definition, as well as emotional and sexual abuse, together with the most commonly identified form, physical abuse. In addition, there is the problem of vague terminology such as "maltreatment," "harm," or "threatened harm," used in the official definition as noted by Gelles (1979, p. 45).[3]

Another problem is the issue of "selective labeling" (Gelles 1979, p. 46), despite "Good Samaritan" laws mandating reporting of suspected cases of abuse. A number of physical abuse cases come to the attention of outsiders that never become part of the public record, for example, family doctors are more likely to accept parents' explanations and record suspicious injuries and evidence of trauma as accidental (Gelles 1979, pp. 60–63; Sussman 1974, p. 245). Least likely to report suspected cases of child abuse are teachers and school administrators; somewhat more likely to report are the clergy; and in between in willingness to report are social workers, according to a study by Viano (cited in Gelles 1979, p. 60). Estimates range from 60,000 (Helfer and Kempe 1968), 250,000 (Nagi 1975), 500,000 (Light 1974), to 1.5 million children abused in families each year (Fontana 1973; Gelles 1975). Drawing from the Straus et al. (1980) national probability sample of 2,143 intact couples, Gelles found there were 1,146 families who had children between the ages of three and seventeen living at home and 63 percent of the parents admitted at least one violent episode in the survey year; 73 percent reported at least one violent occurrence in the entire course of raising the child (1979, pp. 80–81). Whatever the true incidence of physical child abuse, it is clear that the problem is immense.

When it comes to direct violence toward children, some studies repeatedly state that the majority of primary abusers in their samples are mothers; three frequently cited have relatively small samples. These are: the ten cases studied by Bennie and Sclare (1969) that found seven abusing mothers; the sixty cases studied by Steele and Pollock (1974, p. 89) revealed that 83 percent of the abusers were mothers; and the study by the National Society for the Prevention of Cruelty to Children in Great Britain cited by Freeman (1979, p. 16) investigated seventy-eight cases and found that 54 percent of the abusers were mothers. Gelles cites a 1971 report by Zalba which identified abusers evenly divided between mothers and fathers (1979, p. 33).

Data from the national study of family violence in which Gelles was a coinvestigator reveal that 68 percent of the mothers and 58 percent of the fathers reported at least one violent act during the survey year. When addressing the question of *ever* using violence, the ratio of mothers and fathers narrowed to 76 and 71 percent respectively. However, when it came to the most dangerous and potentially injurious acts of violence, the men used these modes more than the women. These were "threatening with a knife or gun," or "used knife or gun" (1979, p. 84). Gil's national survey found mothers the primary abusers in 50 percent of the cases compared to 40 percent abused by fathers (1970). As Freeman notes, "His cases did, however, have a predominance of female-headed households and where the homes were headed by fathers, the father was the abuser two-thirds of the time" (1979, pp. 28–29). In fact, almost a third of the homes were headed by females; therefore the fathers had a higher involvement rate than the mothers (Chase 1976, p. 106). A review of the literature suggests that homes with fathers present much of the time due to unemployment, illness and so forth, are more likely to contain abusing fathers than homes from which fathers are absent for the greater part of the day.

A number of these studies have serious problems too complicated to detail here, involving definitions, methodology, sample selection and sample size, as well as other shortcomings.[4] Despite cultural insistence on stereotyping mothers as always loving, gentle, nurturant, and forgiving, mothers are often identified by researchers as abusers. This certainly calls into question the myth of "maternal instinct," or the Udry claim in the mid-1970s that "certain fundamental sex-differentiated behaviors are androgen-programmed," for example: "Females have a greater predisposition to care for infants" (1974, p. 48).

If the majority of child abusers are mothers, particularly those in single-parent homes, one of the most logical explanations for this can probably be found in the factor "time at risk" (Gelles 1979, p. 13; Straus, Gelles, and Steinmetz 1976, p. 17). Straus and his colleagues listed characteristics of the family that contribute to making it a setting for violence, or a "violent-prone institution" (Gelles 1979, p. 13). Mothers are primary caretakers of children in this (and most) societies; thus they spend proportionately more time in close interaction with children and usually bear the greater responsibility for their daily needs. Even in two-parent families, if a child is sick at night, it is the mother who is expected to render care; if both parents are employed, it is usually the mother who is called by the school when a child is ill or in trouble. Additionally, single-parent families headed by women have the lowest median incomes of all family categories and one-third are below the poverty level.[5]

These facts are introduced here because they may have a relationship with factors leading to child abuse. If time at risk is compounded by lack of alternatives and responsibilities without relief, this suggests some ideas for corrective measures to be introduced later.

Indirect Victimization

Estimates of the number of women beaten by spouses (legal or quasi-legal husbands) also vary widely, and of course not all of these unions include resident children exposed to the violence. Walker (1979) estimated that half of all women in this country are likely to be battered by spouses at least once. The Straus et al. study (1980) from which Gelles drew his subsample of parents mentioned above, asked about violent acts between spouses in

1975 and found that 3.8 percent of their respondents admitted to one or more physical attacks. Specific violent acts performed during the survey year were reported almost equally by men and women, although once more, men had higher rates in the most dangerous and injurious forms and they used them more frequently (Straus 1978, pp. 448–449). Respondents were also asked about any violence that occurred in the relationships—28 percent had experienced at least one violent incident; however these data do not reveal which persons were victims and which were assailants (Straus 1978, p. 446). Straus concluded that the extent of the violence was greatly under-reported and underestimated and stated that: "These considerations . . . suggest that *the true incidence rate is probably closer to 50 or 60 percent of all couples than it is to the 28 percent who were willing to describe violent acts in a mass interview survey"* (1978, p. 447).

What is known is that there are more than 47 million married couples in the United States; 52.4 percent live together with children under the age of eighteen (Reiss 1980, pp. 365–366); therefore there are almost 25 million cohabiting couples with legally dependent children. There are 62,938,000 children under eighteen in the U.S. population (U.S. Government Statistical Abstract 1980, p. 34), 80 percent of whom live with two parents, biological or social (Light and Keller 1979, p. 379). This means that over 50 million children are in the "at risk" group for exposure to intraparental violence. If the estimates of Straus (1978) and Walker (1979) on incidence rates of wife abuse are correct, there may be more than 25 million children in this country who suffer the trauma of living in violent homes. These figures may be low because they do not allow for many reconstituted or quasi-legal marriages that are missing from census data; nor do they include the great amount of abuse that takes place only *after* separation or divorce occurs. Once more, we can only estimate how many children live in homes where they may hear or see (or both) the horror of their father beating their mother, but there can be little doubt that their numbers are in the millions.

Some persons will argue that children who live in violent homes are unaware of what actually occurs, because it usually happens during the night. This is probably correct for many of them, particularly infants and very young children. However, the author has observed children as young as one year begin to regress into states later diagnosed as "mental retardation" when they were exposed to parental hostilities that never went beyond the verbal level of abuse. Symptoms of retardation rather quickly disappeared after the combatants separated. The psychologist Patrick Clark believes there is a direct effect on children's behavior and learning patterns from anxiety levels in their immediate environments (1981: personal communication).

Young children's worlds are small—usually confined to the family residence and expanded to only a few select "outsiders." Children, regardless of age, are extremely perceptive about mood changes, attitudes, and emotions. Is there any full-time mother who has not noticed, when she has a particularly bad day, that there is a concurrent "bad day" with her children? Regardless of her intention and determination to go about her daily chores without letting her personal feelings show, it seems that children—even tiny babies—sense this diminished capacity and respond with restlessness, crying, or other manifestations of upset.

Between 1976 and 1980, I conducted a study of woman battering, using a variety of research techniques that included in-depth interviews with hundreds of women and some of their children in this country and abroad; a survey questionnaire was also completed by 350 American women. There were 306 mothers in the survey sample who had a total of 735 children (an average of 2.9 children), ranging in age from birth (one mother came to a shelter directly from a hospital) to over eighteen years.

Many of the interviewed women felt confident that at least the youngest children had neither witnessed nor heard their beatings, yet a few minutes of observation or conversation revealed that the young ones usually had some knowledge of what had been going on and were affected by it. One very young mother of two sons returned to a shelter for a group meeting on an evening when her husband was out of the state. She explained that she had returned from the shelter to her batterer because, as far as she could see, she had no real alternative. She was a high-school dropout with no job skills; she could not even drive a car. She told the group that her husband was a "very good father" to the children, despite the extreme violence he unleashed against her. She needed to provide food, clothing, and a "good home" for her sons which she could not do alone. While she was talking, the older child, a two-year-old, bit her leg when he wanted her undivided attention and was unable to get it. This was an unusual tactic for him; normally, he would kick his mother's legs or hit his one-year-old brother.

Dobash and Dobash asked a sample of 109 battered women about the violent events they had experienced: the first, worst, last, and typical attacks (1979, p. 97). They found just over half of all the first attacks occurred with no witnesses, but for the last violent episode, 75 percent reported that at least one other person was present, usually their children (1979, p. 112). These researchers also heard the often-repeated phrase from battered mothers that they stayed with the men who beat them as long as they did "for the sake of the children" (1979, p. 148). Not only do the women know that their children will suffer from the lack of material necessities but they fear the stigma attached to children from "broken homes," and believe that having a father—any father—is better for their children than having no father at all. They usually fail to see the damage being done to their children until either they are confronted with the knowledge that the children do see and hear the violence or the children become direct targets of abuse (accidentally or deliberately).

Of the 306 mothers in the author's survey sample, 233 (76 percent) said there was a child or children present when their beatings occurred and 158 of these women said the observers were *all* their children (the others said the observer was a particular child, say, the eldest). But during interviews, many mothers admitted that they believed their children were unaware of what was going on until the first time they saw a horrified face outside the bedroom door or when their own screams (which they tried to muffle) brought terrified children running into the living room. Sometimes the youngsters asked pointed questions the following morning that let mothers know the terrible "secret" had been exposed. On the other hand, some mothers said they were fairly sure the children knew what was happening but there seemed to be an unspoken agreement not to discuss it.

Frequently mothers keep insisting to themselves that their children are not being harmed until they are directly involved in the abuse. As one mother said, "It was one thing, him beating me, but when he hit me that last time, my baby was in my arms and we both hit the floor. My baby could have been killed! I couldn't take the chance of that ever happening again, so I left."

In a society that encourages females in self-sacrifice, deference, and service to others in the family, it is not surprising that so many women devalue their own rights and needs but will take strong action to protect their children. Dobash and Dobash's study also found many victims who left their abusive situations only after becoming aware that staying is *not* good for the children (1979, pp. 148–152). Some mothers they interviewed told them that their batterers would deliberately see to it that the children witnessed the violence (Dobash and Dobash 1979, p. 151), whereas in other families the children were put out to play or would be asleep when their mothers were beaten. But Dobash and Dobash conclude: "Nevertheless, concealment is very difficult, if not impossible, to keep up. In this sense, the child's primary role in the violence is that of witness to it" (1979, p. 150).

Double Victimization

There is a greater probability that children are indirect victims of violence in the home but unfortunately, some children are both recipients and observers of violence. Some men not only batter their wives but one or all of the children as well. The author's own study of woman battering revealed that while some of the abusers never or seldom used any kind of physical force on their children,[6] the violence sometimes spilled over to include the children as well. One of the items on the survey instrument asked if their children were ever battered by the men who beat them. Of the 306 mothers in the sample, 109 (one-third) said yes, and 75 women said the children's beatings were moderate to severe. About half of the battered children appeared to have been hit because they somehow happened to be caught in the middle of the parental violence—being too close to their mother when the attack occurred or intervening on their mother's behalf. However, only 36 mothers said that the child beating was *directly* connected with their own beatings and 26 mothers said that at least one child required medical attention or hospital care—all cases except one were for injuries administered by fathers or father-figures. In sixteen cases the children's injuries were serious and one later died.

The case of the fatal attack occurred just after the youngest child was born and the oldest of the five children was ten years old. Their father, according to the mother, was extremely violent with the entire family and abused the children with straps, fists, and choking. The abuse culminated in his beating their second child to death. The statement written for the mother on the quesionnaire by a staff member of a Florida shelter reveals that the boy:

> had head split open—took to hospital—[boy's name] beaten until blood splattered all over the walls. . . . She pressed charges—police got him—he went to court, pleaded not guilty. She and children would have had to testify against him in court. . . . They were afraid to testify because he threatened [the eldest son] that if his mother pressed charges he would kill son and mother.

Another family revealed during interviews that the batterer not only beat his wife who was dying from a degenerative disease but made a particular target of the youngest of their three daughters *after* it was discovered that the child had a chronic illness. The child's older sister wrote a letter to the researcher that said in part:

> When my little sister got sick [diabetes] and kept needing water and needing to use the "necessary" room, he kept hitting her and make [sic] her wet her pants even worse . . . . When I first noticed the "conflict" between my parents, I just thought, "They're at it again!" later it was, 'There he goes." . . . Before my mom got sick, he tried a few things on her, but he didn't get far. . . . And when my mom got sick, that's when everything went to hell. She can barely hobble around and he knows she can't defend herself. Her hips are really sore and he would drive her around in the car slamming on the brakes—which is agony for her. . . . He was always telling me how my mother was brainwashing me and how she was breaking up the family, but all I could think was that I want the family broken up (or him broken off) and that if my mother was brainwashing us, she was doing the best job of it I had ever seen. . . . The worst thing about him is that he's so smart. We went to family counseling once and he drove the poor psychiatrist up the wall by sending the conversations around in circles as well as scaring him to death.

The mother of the three girls, aged from eight to twelve, succumbed to her disease while they were still residents of a shelter. All the children were terrified of their father and wanted desperately to go to another state to live with their mother's relatives, which she had arranged for just before her death. However, before they could board the plane, their father secured legal help and deputies picked up the girls and returned them to their father's custody, despite their protests.

During an interview—after extended retrospection of her life with a violent husband—one mother suddenly came to the realization that her husband basically was a child abuser since all of her own beatings were direct results of her intervention on behalf of the children. It had not occurred to her previously that she was never beaten except when her husband had initially been engaged in attacking their children; when she tried to save them from harm, the fury and abuse were directed at her. She recalled that the worst beating she ever received culminated in a kick, as she bent over the abused child, that resulted in hospitalization and extensive surgery. At the time of the interview, that same child had reached the age of twenty and had bragged to the mother that she was her own father's "lover." The young woman confronted her mother with this information, saying that she was a much better sexual partner than her mother had been because she received expensive gifts from her father rather than the beatings her mother had suffered. More will be said later about this type of occurrence.

Effects of Violence on Children

It is difficult to state with any degree of confidence exactly what the effects of direct child abuse are on victims because there is no way of knowing what happens to the majority of victims—the ones who are never publicly identified. In addition, most researchers and writers indicate that, because of the privacy in which abuse occurs and the reluctance of many outsiders to report, the cases that do come to light are frequently the most severe (Chambers 1980, pp. 215–251; Chase 1976, pp. 64–91).

Finally, there are no large-scale longitudinal studies to show whether early symptoms noted by outsiders continue into adulthood. However, enough cases have come to the attention of official agencies and researchers so that some common features can be detected. Clues for identifying victims of child abuse and neglect have been gathered into lists; many of these clues are indicative of the apparent immediate effects of child abuse on victims. One of these lists has been widely distributed by the Child Abuse Registry of the Orange County Human Services Department in California. Most of the characteristics listed were obtained from a booklet published by the federal Department of Health, Education, and Welfare (DHEW) (U.S. Government 1975, vol. 1, pp. 4–8). Besides alerting readers to physical signs of abuse, they set forth a number of behavior patterns that reveal differential effects on abuse of children.

Abused children's behavior seems to go to one extreme or the other and it may be that this is what causes or is directly related to some of the other problems abused children are reported to experience later in life (Chase 1976; Gil 1970). Some immediate effects may act as triggers that propel children from one problem to the next; they are stigmatized and labeled and this in turn leads to a self-fulfilling prophecy of defeat. Some of these extremes are:

1. crying often or crying very little;
2. being excessively fearful or fearless of adult authority;
3. being extremely aggressive and destructive or unusually passive and withdrawn;
4. being hungry for affection but unable to use appropriate methods of obtaining it, or being apprehensive and fearful of affection or physical contact;
5. being very disruptive or very withdrawn and shy;
6. arriving late for school and having many absences, or arriving early and staying late after school (DHEW, 1975).

If children react to abuse by these extreme behaviors, it is obvious why many are later described by researchers and others as disturbed, maladjusted, or even criminal (Bolton 1977; Chase 1976; Lewis 1976). Any extremes in behavioral patterns are likely to bring punitive social sanctions since most American institutions, particularly schools, value highly both conformity and obedience from children. Children who are nonconformists, whether they are extremely passive or extremely aggressive, are likely to meet with disapproval from agents of socialization. Disapproval and negative sanctions may well reinforce already low self-esteem and feelings of unworthiness, exacerbating the problem. Considering that the children he studied were publicly identified victims of parental abuse, it seems surprising that Gil found only 29 percent had problems in social interaction and general functioning the year preceding the abusive incident that received attention of the authorities (1970). However, perhaps it was then too soon to determine the extent of the long-term effects of child abuse on victims.

It is likely that there is a circular effect of negative feelings that, if uncorrected by positive reward and approval, continue to grow and result in more seriously maladaptive behavior. A DHEW report says that long-term physical effects can include mental retardation, loss of hearing or sight, lack of motor control, and speech defects, and in addition,

Child victims of abuse and neglect have also been found to have learning behavior, and habit disorders. . . . Some maltreated children experience problems such as drug abuse, obesity, teenage pregnancy, and delinquency in later life (1975, p. 13).

Effects on children who witness paternal violence against mothers should be addressed at both the early aftermath and later levels. When entering shelters with their mothers, some children appear to have either been unaware of or to have learned to cope with the violence in their families. For others, immediate effects are visible: insecurity is demonstrated by clinging, crying, nervousness, or demanding to know where their mothers are and what they are doing at all times. Some seem to be susceptible to minor infections, colds, sore throats, bed wetting, insomnia or fitful sleep, and frantic play activities, others passively avoid group activities and games. Dobash and Dobash (1979, p. 151) observed the same reactions among children in the United Kingdom, noting that some "were prone to hysterics at the first indication of an altercation, or grew very resentful toward their father."

It is true that some children become extremely attached and even protective toward their mother and bitterly resentful toward their father, but sometimes they seem to turn in the other direction. Occasionally, the children resent being taken from their homes and friends and insist that the "problem" was their mother's, not theirs. Some observers believe that there is a sex-specific effect of living with violent fathers that shows up in shelters, that is, girls appear to be passive and withdrawn, whereas boys may be more aggressive than average (Pizzey 1977). Whether this effect is short-term or permanent is uncertain. Many observed behaviors of children in shelters may be partly the result of being taken away from everything familiar to them: home, neighborhood, friends, and school, and suddenly being exposed to communal (usually overcrowded) living conditions with adult females and other children of all ages. Most shelters have child-care specialists who make special efforts to work with the children, particularly those who exhibit behavioral or emotional disturbances. Those with the most serious problems are placed in community child-guidance centers whenever possible.

Most of the children in shelters seem to make remarkable recovery from symptoms of disturbance in a relatively short time, bouncing back to normal behavioral patterns. The safety, security, supportive and nonviolent atmosphere of shelters seems to be the most effective "medicine" for the vast majority of the young victims of violence.

When parents separate, even in the best of circumstances and unrelated to violence, children frequently are confused, resentful, and unhappy. Often they go through a period of self-blame, feeling that somehow the fault is theirs because if they had been "good enough," Dad and Mom would still be together. Add to these feelings the strange surroundings (since usually battered women must leave the family residence for safety) together with their previous experiences of intraparental violence, and it is not surprising that many children exhibit behavioral or emotional upset when they arrive at shelters. The feelings many of these children have had are eloquently described by Del Martin in relating her grandson's reaction to seeing his mother hit by a family acquaintance. The eight-year-old saw impending danger as a menacing man approached, so he ran to a car and locked himself in, and with horror watched the man "give his mother a couple of hard slaps." The effects of that one violent event were immediate and intense and had an emotionally devastating effect upon the child who "had been scared; he hadn't known what to do and felt guilty about that" (Martin 1976, p. 22).

The feelings of pain, terror, and guilt these children feel sometimes are resolved by learning to hate the abusing parent. Some learn to hate both parents. This point was brought home sharply by one of the women I interviewed whose husband suffered double victimization: he was severely abused by his father to a point where it could only be described as torture, and he also witnessed his mother's beatings. As an adult, he not only beat his first but also his second wife *and* his own aging mother after his father died. Certainly this case seems to give support to the often-repeated (but seldom substantiated) claim that abused children grow up to be adult abusers. However, this case history reveals that this double victimized man was the eldest of five children, all of whom were abused, albeit the others less severely. Yet *not one* of this man's siblings is violent with a spouse or children. They seemed to have gone to the other extreme of total nonviolence.

On the other hand, there was a young male medical student who, in a chance meeting, shared some of the pain of his indirect victimization. He was an only child who spent his entire youth in a home where his father beat his mother. He described his horror, pain, and helplessness at being an unwilling witness to brutality. He recalled vividly his younger years—into adolescence—when he begged his mother to leave his father:

> I'd plead with her so we could go somewhere, anywhere, just so the beatings would stop! But she'd tell me she couldn't leave because she couldn't make a home for me by herself. She said we had to stay. I'd tell her I'd help out—I'd rather live anywhere but there! I could never understand why we couldn't go. There was nothing I could do to stop him—he was too big and strong. I was hurting so much . . . torn between two people I loved. It was easy to learn to hate my father but finally I had to learn to hate her, too. I had to hate both of them so I could shut them out or it would have killed me. I hated him for hurting her and I hated her for hurting me by letting him hurt her. Do you understand what I mean? It was all I could do to protect myself until I could get out. . . . I don't think I'll *ever*

get married. Oh, I date now, but not much and not seriously. I don't ever want to marry because I'm afraid I'd be like my father. I can't take that chance.

This fear of the "cycle of violence" seems to worry a number of adults who were victimized by violence in childhood. The assumptions that violence is transmitted intergenerationally are well known and popularly accepted as fact. Many young men and women fear marriage because they do not want to be abusers or victims as their role models were, and some fear parenthood because they are afraid they will become abusers as they were abused. These issues of possible long-term effects are important and must be addressed.

Is There a "Cycle of Violence"?

Attention is first focused on the "cycle of violence" theory as it pertains to direct victims of child abuse. One case of someone fearing motherhood was a young woman, pregnant with her first child, who had been beaten by her husband and fled to a shelter. During an interview, she expressed great fear and concern that she was certain to become an abuser of her child, since she had been abused as a child. She said she had seriously considered putting up her child for adoption so she could never do it harm until she found that there was a home in a nearby community where she could go to await the birth of her child and continue residency for six months afterward to learn parenting skills and to adjust to motherhood. She asked the researcher, "What exactly are the chances that I'll become an abuser? How many abusers were abused when they were children?"

This seemed like a reasonable question to ask. A search of the literature reveals that many writers repeat the claim, but few produce any sound empirical evidence to support it (Chambers 1980; Chase 1976; DHEW 1975; Gelles 1979). Most writers have done no original research but gather reports in the field and repeat findings and assumptions from secondary sources. There is a detailed critique of many of these reports in Freeman (1979, p. 21-32) that objects to the lack of scientifically sound research methods, small and nonrepresentative samples (frequently cases that happened to become part of a case load), retrospective data, unsupported generalizations of findings, researcher bias, and studies that begin and end with "relatively untested commonsense assumptions" (Freeman 1979, p. 29, quoting Spinetta and Rigler). In essence, many writers seem to report impressions, informal observations, opinions, and ideas as fact without strong empirical evidence to support them.

A notable exception is a very large national study of almost 13,000 cases which found that 11 percent of the parents who abused children were themselves victims of abuse in their own childhood (Gil 1970). This hardly seems sufficiently strong evidence of a "legacy of abuse" to convince a troubled young mother to relinquish her child for adoption. The Steele and Pollack study (1974) that is frequently cited in the literature as providing evidence that the abusing parent was an abused child was a report on sixty cases that came to the attention of two psychiatrists. These doctors recognized the limitations of their work and warned against generalizing their findings beyond the particular sample they studied by stating:

> Our study group of parents is not to be thought of as useful for statistical proof of any concepts. It was not picked by a valid sampling technique nor is it a "total population." It is representative only of a group of parents who had attacked children and who came by rather "accidental" means under our care because we were interested in the problem (1974, p. 90).

Nowhere in their report is there strong evidence to support the "cycle of violence" thesis. They found abusing parents came from families that could be described as authoritarian, demanding, unrewarding, and in which they were deprived of warm, loving, supportive relationships (Steele and Pollock, 1974, pp. 97–98). A good question to ask is, "How many nonabusing parents came from homes like that?" Or to put it another way, "How many of us had *ideal* parents?"

It seems that others have lifted out of context what these authors said and used it to support popular assumptions. For example, Steele and Pollock say, "Without exception . . . there is a history of having been raised in the same style which they have recreated in the pattern of rearing their own children" (1974, p. 97). However, the following sentence reveals their findings regarding actual abuse; they state: "Several had experienced severe abuse in the form of physical beatings from either mother or father; a few reported *'never having had a hand laid on them'*" (emphasis added) (1974, p. 97). "Several" hardly seems conclusive evidence to support widespread insistence that one need only look at the abused child's parent to see another abused child.

Since this popular assumption seems to be based on a rather shaky foundation, why do so many service providers and agency people seem to find that abusers were abused? We do tend to find what we expect to find; we know which questions to ask. If professionals assume that abusers were abused, is it too large a stretch of the imagination to suggest that adults suspected or accused of abusing their children are not also aware of this common assumption? The author suggests that—until we have more, bigger, better, and replicated studies, including some longitudinal research—it would be advisable to approach the topic of effects of violence intergenerationally without bias and with an open mind.

The "cycle of violence" theory has frequently been invoked regarding indirect victimization through observing parental abuse (Gelles 1979; Steinmetz 1977; Straus 1978; Straus et al. 1980), yet a simple and direct linkage may also be questioned (Pagelow 1981c). In his article on why abused wives stay with their abusers, Gelles posited that "the more a wife was struck as a child by her parents, the more likely she is to stay with her abusive husband" (1976, p. 659). Gelles's hypothesis was tested with data from the author's study; they offered no support for his proposition (Pagelow 1981c). In fact, these data show that women who had been abused as children were likely to leave violent relationships somewhat sooner than women who were inexperienced in violence. There were, however, some interesting differences in homes of orientation of the sample women and their spouses. There were large and statistically significant differences between the men and women on measures of both direct and indirect victimization. In essence, the men much more frequently came from homes where they were abused or their mothers were beaten by their fathers. In addition, there was a statistically significant difference between the persons who administered the punishment these people received: the women's punishers were equally likely to be either parent or parent-figure; the men's punishers were far more likely to be fathers or father-figures than mothers or mother-figures. These findings suggest that some boys with violent fathers may follow their same-sex role model's behavior in adulthood, but the "cycle of violence" appears to have little or no explanatory value for girls. For a more detailed critique of the theoretical assumptions expressed by Gelles, see Pagelow (1981c).

Analysis of the Effects of Violence
Victimization on Children

It is possible that by seeing immediate effects of violence on children we assume that their early pain, fear, and guilt last a lifetime and are directly responsible for their behavior in adulthood. To a strong supporter of the teachings of social learning theory (Akers 1977; Bandura 1973; Pagelow 1978c), it seems almost heretical to suggest that there is not a causal connection. However, it must be remembered that learning is a lifelong process (Dobash and Dobash 1981). People tend to behave in ways that meet with success and are rewarded by positive reinforcement; they adjust their behavior patterns to meet life circumstances and social environments as they mature. For example, men who never saw themselves as killers, can be resocialized by a few weeks of military training into becoming unquestioning killers (albeit not without problems in becoming nonviolent civilians again later).

The problem of later life maladjustment of abused children should be reexamined, taking into consideration some ideas addressed here. In the first place, abused children's later behavioral problems may be more directly related to negative social reactions to their early behavior patterns than to the abusive treatment. It may not be the *abuse* they suffered earlier that directly leads to adult maladjustment but rather their early maladaptive *behavior patterns themselves* that spiral into more problems.[7]

In the second place, it should be emphasized that persons who become identified as child abusers are only a small fraction of the actual abusers in our society. Identified abusers are likely to view their early childhood experiences in retrospect as abusive to meet expectations of many professionals with whom they come in contact. This is where definitional problems become important. It would be impetuous to jump to the conclusion that abused children grow up to become abusing parents until social agents reach some consensus on what "abuse" is, know how many people in the population were abused as children, and know how many who were abused fall into the abusing and nonabusing categories. The "cycle of violence" theory seems questionable when it comes to the matter of bequeathing child abuse from one generation to the next. We need more and stronger evidence before we use this theoretical assumption with confidence.

However, there is some evidence that there may be sex-specific differences in accepting violence as appropriate behavior. As noted elsewhere (Pagelow 1978c), ours is a violent culture but it is one in which males are traditionally socialized into aggressiveness and competition as appropriate sex-role behavior. Females, on the other hand, are discouraged from those behavior patterns and are socialized into passivity and compliance. Table 4-1 shows that males are far more likely to be accused of violent crimes than females are. Men are more likely to be positively reinforced for aggressive behavior than women are, regardless of whether their targets are men, women, or children, based on their size and muscular strength, compared to women. Learning to use and to repeat certain behaviors depends on successful outcome and reward; as Stark explains, *"The type of behavior that is most frequently and consistently reinforced by people will be the one most often exhibited"* (1975, p. 506).

Approval to use force and violence has been given to men—but not to women—in this society, and persons whose behavior runs counter to social norms are likely to receive negative sanctions or punishment. There is also the important concept of *modeling* in social learning theory. Tests show that both boys and girls are likely to imitate aggressive acts especially when performed by male adult models, although the girls require rewards before they reach an imitation level almost equal to the boys (Bandura 1973, p. 80). In addition, boys are three times more likely than girls to imitate a *familiar* aggressive model, although a nurturant relationship with the model has no effect on either sex. Bandura explains that if the model's behavior appears to have functional value, observers have strong incentives to practice and learn them, and therefore "Conditions of observational learning combining repeated exposure with opportunities for overt practice and symbolic rehearsal ensure more or less permanent retention of modeled activities" (1973, p. 78).

There is no better place than a child's home for observing behaviors performed repeatedly by familiar models and to learn them most thoroughly. In addition, the behavior of models who possess the highest status in "prestige, power, and competence hierarchies is more likely to be successful and therefore to command greater attention from others than the behavior of models who are [lower in status]" (Bandura 1973, p. 70).

In the hierarchical structure of the traditional patriarchal family, the husband-father position carries highest status in prestige and power (Dobash and Dobash 1979). Boys are particularly likely to imitate the behavior of their same-sex role models, especially when that behavior is rewarded. Girls are also likely to imitate fathers' behavior because they are higher in the family hierarchy but daughters are less likely to be rewarded for it. This may partially explain why some children identify with the abusing father and turn against the mother. Some women return to shelters after having left abusive husbands only to find that their adolescent sons take up where their fathers left off. As some writers note, people in our society admire winners and scorn losers and we tend toward "victim blaming" (Ryan 1971). The blaming is not necessarily vicious but there is social psychological evidence that experimental subjects are more hostile toward victims than they are toward aggressors (Wrightsman 1977, p. 224). When girls identify with the power of fathers, they are especially vulnerable to using whatever means are available to win their favors, as in the case of the young women mentioned earlier who became her formerly abusive father's "lover." Boys who strongly identify with violent fathers are more likely to court their approval through imitative "super-macho" behavior.

Summary and Suggestions

The preceding may help to explain why the "cycle of violence" theory has more relevance for boys than it has for girls in violent families. Social learning theory also helps explain why some persons—both men and women—who were raised in violent families do *not* physically abuse spouses or children, since Bandura says: "Discrepancies between learning and performance are most likely to arise under conditions in which the acquired behaviors have limited functional value or carry high risk of punishment" (1973, p. 65).

It is suggested that unknown millions of people in our society are non-violent with other family members because they do not value power and control over others by force or because such behavior is likely to result in more punishment than reward. If we want to stop the recurrence of violence in families, we must begin to remove social approval of "masculine" violence. Little boys need standards of sex-appropriate behavior that allow them to express themselves and obtain approval through nonaggressive ways.

When children have been identified as direct or indirect victims of parental violence in the home, special emphasis should be placed on a relearning process with rewards for nonviolent behavior so that they can replace old norms with new. Boys may require even more attention than girls to encourage them away from violence. They particularly need to develop close relationships with nonaggressive adult male role models so they can imitate a new model of appropriate behavior.

On a long-term basis for societal change, several suggestions are offered here that may make the family a less violence-prone institution as well as reduce social approval of violence. Concerned Americans can apply what we have learned through research and do everything possible—individually and collectively—to eliminate violence in our society by becoming activists for:

1. Classes in family living—including sex education, parenting, and interpersonal relations—at least by the junior high school level, if not earlier. We need to educate future parents so they will not go into it as totally unprepared as most past and present parents have.
2. Effective parenting courses for parents at local high schools in evenings and on weekends.
3. Hotlines with an available resource of "family helpers" who make home visits to give on-the-job training to parents in need.
4. Programs to provide a way of "dropping off" children when parents need respite from continuous and total responsibility for them.
5. Quality child care at neighborhood schools—after the regular school day, on Saturdays, and school holidays—supervised by professionals in order to reduce the problem of "latch-key" children.
6. Help from medical professionals and clergy to prepare young couples for what lies ahead by strongly recommending that they take courses in effective parenting *before* they marry or give birth to their first child.[8]
7. Nonviolent training of children—no physical punishment for children at home or in the schools—"people are not for hitting."
8. Nonsexist care and treatment of children from infancy. Promote the best characteristics of both feminine and masculine in children, regardless of sex, as well as discourage the damaging characteristics of

both, such as aggressiveness in boys, dependency/passivity in girls. Abolish sex-role stereotypes in homes, preschools, schools, and all social institutions.

9. Reexamining our own gender prejudices and discarding anything we do that supports inequality between males and females; demanding equal pay for work of equal value and supporting the Equal Rights Amendment.

10. Federal gun control: representative polls show that 70 to 77 percent of Americans favor some form of handgun control.

11. Elimination of violence in the media by protesting to sponsors and boycotting products such as violent movies, magazines, books, record covers, advertisements, television programs (including cartoons), and toys that are symbols of violence and promote violent play.

12. Boycotting extremely violent sports such as boxing and wrestling; and protesting excessive violence in others such as football and hockey.

13. Elimination of capital punishment; demand life sentences without possibility of parole.

14. Turning aggressive behavior around by teaching assertion and better communication skills.

15. Youth diversion programs, community programs, and groups like the PTA, and neighborhood associations.

16. Birth control education, free abortion on demand, rights to use contraceptives, and the development of new and better methods of contraception. Research shows that a high percentage of women are battered by husbands when they are pregnant; too many children in families cause additional stress; and there is a high incidence of abuse of unwanted children.

17. Educating others, exchanging information, and supporting more conferences such as this one.

18. Courses on family violence to be required for credentials in the following professional fields: counseling, teaching, human services, psychology, psychiatry, nursing, medicine, law, social work, law enforcement, and the ministry. None of these disciplines has institutionalized training in the identification, intervention, or services for members of violent families, yet the people who work in these career fields are the ones most likely to come in contact with troubled families.

19. Lobbying Congress for a domestic violence bill.

Present and future generations could be helped in many other ways. Adopting some of these ideas could go a long way toward *preventing* violence against children rather than merely trying to correct the problem *after* it occurs. What we need to do now is to help the current generation of victims in the best ways possible and at the same time, devote time, energy, and resources in a intensive program for prevention.

Notes

1. For clarity of focus, "violence" refers to overt and deliberate acts of physical force employed by parent or parent-figures, either toward the children or one of the parents. To narrow our focus to manageable proportions, other forms of direct child abuse are excluded, such as psychological abuse and neglect, sexual abuse, and physical neglect. While undeniably hurtful and damaging, they are not included in the definition of violence used herein for a number of reasons. For example, some persons (but not the author) would argue that since sexual abuse of children seldom involves the overt use of physical force or battering, it need not be classified as "violent." There are other reasons, but because each form of child abuse is so different—although some children suffer more than one type of abuse—the causes, indentifying features, consequences, and corrective measures vary widely. In essence, victimization of children through violence as referred to here is restricted to physical violence which is objectively measurable and most visible, thus most identifiable and consequently, most researched.

2. The question of which parent is most likely to be victim or aggressor in cases of spouse abuse will be discussed later. Substantial evidence exists to show that in cases of direct assault against a spouse who may or may not attempt self-defense, the victims are most likely to be female. The "battering" addressed here is the (usually) one-way aggression of husbands against wives noted by Steinmetz and Straus as "one-sided aggressive acts" (1974, p. 11). Battering is sometimes confused with and sometimes undifferentiated from "mutual combat" engaged in between couples equally bent on inflicting the greatest damage on each other, usually within informal, mutually acceptable limits (for a further discussion of this activity, see Pagelow 1978a, 1978b, 1978c, 1981a). For other responses to the grossly exaggerated claim of the "battered husband syndrome," see Dobash and Dobash (1981), Fields (1978), Gelles (1979), and Pleck et al. (1978).

3. The definition in the Child Abuse Prevention and Treatment Act of 1973 states:

Child abuse and neglect means the physical or mental injury, sexual abuse, negligent treatment, or maltreatment of a child under the age of eighteen by a person who is responsible for the child's welfare under circumstances which indicate that the child's health or welfare is harmed or threatened thereby.

On the other hand, some definitions are specifically directed at one form of child abuse and are quite brief, such as: "A basic definition of physical abuse is the nonaccidental injury of a child. Injury may be the result of a single episode of abuse or may occur repeatedly and can range in severity from minor to fatal" (McNeese and Hebeler 1977, p. 3).

4. For example, the Conflict Tactics Scale (CTS) used in the nationally representative research project conducted by Straus et al. (1980) contains an item that asks: "Did you hit or try to hit [spouse, child, etc.] with something?" (item "o," pp. 10, 12, 18). Reports of the findings show data for a category identified as "Hit with something" (Gelles 1979, p. 84; Straus et al, 1980, p. 61). Unfortunately, it is not made clear *why* the phrase "or try to hit" was deleted. It seems to me there is an important difference in trying to do something and accomplishing the act—in fact, when the issue is violent behavior—there can be a life or death difference. Respondents may have answered this question with an assumption that there was a significant difference and might be surprised to learn that the question they answered was later changed in reports.

There are numerous other problems with the CTS scale, one of which is that there was no search to identify the "something" respondents used. Again, there is a substantive difference between hitting with a pillow or other soft, light object and hitting with a stick, belt, or potentially lethal object. The category "threw something" has the same lack of identity of the object(s) and there is the haunting question whether these respondents who threw some (unknown) subject actually *hit* their targets. Again, there can be a life or death difference. Finally, there was no attempt to measure the extent of the injuries sustained (if any) by the targets of the aggressive behavior. For other inadequacies of the CTS scale, see Dobash and Dobash (1981, p. 16).

5. When women are single parents heading a family, their average family income in 1977 was only $7,765 compared to $14,535 for families headed by men (or $17,720 for husband-wife families) (National Commission on Working Women, n.d.). According to the same source, 8.2 million (14.4 percent) of all American families were female-headed whereas only 1.6 million (3 percent) of them were headed by men only in 1978.

6. Some men who batter their wives not only are totally nonviolent with their children but sometimes forbid their wives to use any physical discipline. One women told of slapping her eighteen-month-old son after he bit her, whereupon her husband gave her a beating for punishment. The boy was unusually large for his age and was observed behaving aggressively with other children his age and older.

7. For example, if children miss many school days or frequently arrive late they are very likely to make slower progress than their peers. They may eventually be labeled slow learners and through tracking become stigma-

tized (Light and Keller 1979). As teachers expect less and less of them, their original feelings of worthlessness are increased and school performances decrease in a continuing downward spiral. By a process of social labeling, they become "deviants" (Lemert 1972).

8. A friend recently mentioned hearing about an obstetrician who refuses to take a new patient until she and the unborn child's father agree to take a parenting course. This is a fine example of concern for both patient and child; it might be well if more doctors followed this innovative method to prevent possible child abuse.

References

Akers, R.L. *Deviant behavior: a social learning approach.* 2nd ed. Belmont, Calif.: Wadsworth, 1977.

Bandura, A. *Aggression: a social learning analysis.* Englewood Cliffs, N.J.: Prentice-Hall, 1973.

Bennie, E., and Sclare, A. The battered child syndrome. *American Journal of Psychiatry* 125:975–979, 1969.

Blumberg, M. When parents hit out. *Twentieth Century* 173:39–44, 1964.

Bolton, F.G. Delinquency patterns in maltreated children and siblings. *Victimology* 2:349–357, 1977.

Chambers, M.J. The murder of Robbie Wayne, age 6. *Reader's Digest,* November, 1980, pp. 215–251.

Chase, N.F. *A child is being beaten.* New York: McGraw-Hill, 1976.

Dobash, R.E., and Dobash, R. Wives: The "appropriate" victims of marital violence. *Victimology* 2:426–441, 1978.

Dobash, R.E., and Dobash, R. *Violence against wives.* New York: Free Press, 1979.

Dobash, R.E., and Dobash, R. Social science and social action: the case of wife beating. *Journal of Family Issues* 2(4):439–508, 1981.

Erlanger, H. Social class and corporal punishment in child-rearing: a reassessment. *American Sociological Review* 39:68–85, 1974.

Fields, M. Wife beating: facts and figures. *Victimology* 2:643–647, 1978.

Freeman, M.D.A. *Violence in the home.* Westmead, England: Saxon House, 1979.

Fontana, V. *Somewhere a child is crying: maltreatment—causes and prevention.* New York: Macmillan, 1973.

Gelles, R.J. Abused wives: why do they stay? *Journal of Marriage and the Family* 38:659–668, 1976.

Gelles, R.J. *Family violence.* Beverly Hills: Sage, 1979.

Gil, D. *Violence against children: physical child abuse in the United States.* Cambridge: Harvard University Press, 1970.

Helfer, R., and Kempe, C., eds. *The battered child.* Chicago: University of Chicago Press, 1968.

Kremen, E. The "discovery" of battered wives: considerations for the development of a social service network. Paper presented at the annual meeting of the American Sociological Association, New York, August 1976.

Lemert, E.M. *Human deviance, social problems, and social control.* Englewood Cliffs, N.J.: Prentice-Hall, 1972.

Lewis, D.O. Diagnostic evaluation of the juvenile offender. *Child Psychiatry and Human Development* 6:198–213, 1976.

Light, D., and Keller, S. *Sociology.* 2nd ed. New York: Knopf, 1979.

Light, R. Abused and neglected children in America: a study of alternative policies. *Harvard Educational Review* 43:556–598, 1974.

Martin, D. *Battered wives.* San Francisco: Glide, 1976.

McNeese, M.C., and Hebeler, J.R. The abused child: a clinical approach to identification and management. *Clinical Symposia* 29, 1977.

Mulvihill, D.J., and Tumin, M.M. *Crimes of violence.* Staff report to the National Commission on the Causes and Prevention of Violence. Washington, D.C.: U.S. Government Printing Office, 1969.

Nagi, R. Child abuse and neglect programs: a national overview. *Children Today* 4:13–17, 1975.

National Commission on Working Women. "An overview of women in the work force." Data sheet. Washington, D.C.: National Commission on Working Women, n.d.

Pagelow, M.D. Secondary battering: breaking the cycle of domestic violence. *Domestic violence, 1978.* Hearings before the Subcommittee of Child and Human Development, U.S. Senate. Washington, D.C.: U.S. Government Printing Office, 1978a.

Pagelow, M.D. Battered Women: a new perspective. *Domestic violence, 1978.* Hearings before the Subcommittee of Child and Human Development, U.S. Senate. Washington, D.C.: U.S. Government Printing Office, 1978b.

Pagelow, M.D. Social learning theory and sex roles: violence begins in the home. Paper presented at the Ninth World Congress of Sociology in Uppsala, Sweden, August 1978c.

Pagelow, M.D. *Woman battering: victims and their experiences.* Beverly Hills: Sage, 1981a.

Pagelow, M.D. Secondary battering and alternatives of female victims to spouse abuse. In *Women and crime in America,* ed. L.H. Bowker, pp. 277–300. New York: McMillan, 1981b.

Pagelow, M.D. Factors affecting women's decisions to leave violent relationships. *Journal of Family Issues* 2:391–414, 1981.

Pizzey, E. *Scream quietly or the neighbors will hear.* Short Hill, N.J.: Ridley Enslow, 1977.

Pleck, E.; Pleck, J; Grossman, M; and Bart, P. The battered data syndrome: a reply to Steinmetz. *Victimology* 2:680–683, 1978.

Reiss, I.L. *Family systems in America.* 3rd ed. New York: Holt, Rinehart and Winston, 1980.

Ryan, W. *Blaming the victim.* New York: Random House, 1971.

Stark, R. *Social problems.* New York: Random House, 1975.

Stark, R. and McEvoy, J. Middle class violence. *Psychology Today* 4:52–65, 1970.

Steele, B. and Pollock, C. A psychiatric study of parents who abuse infants and small children. In *The battered child,* eds. R. Helfer and C. Kempe. Chicago: University of Chicago Press, 1968 (2d ed., 1974).

Steinmetz, S.K. *The cycle of violence: assertive, aggressive, and abusive family interaction.* New York: Praeger, 1977.

Steinmetz, S.K., and Straus, M.A., eds. *Violence in the family.* New York: Harper and Row, 1974.

Straus, M.A. Wife beating: how common and why? *Victimology* 2: 443–458, 1978.

Straus, M.; Gelles, R.J.; and Steinmetz, S. Violence in the family: an assessment of knowledge and research needs. Paper presented at the annual meeting of the American Association for the Advancement of Science, Boston, February 23, 1976.

Straus, M.; Gelles, R.J.; and Steinmetz, S. *Behind closed doors.* New York: Doubleday, 1980.

Sussman, A. Reporting child abuse: a review of the literature. *Family Law Quarterly* 8:245–313, 1974.

Udry, J.R. *The social context of marriage.* 3rd ed. New York: Lippincott, 1974.

U.S. Government Printing Office. *Sourcebook of criminal justice statistics—1976.* Washington, D.C., 1977, 1981.

U.S. Government Printing Office. *Child abuse and neglect,* vol. 1. Washington, D.C.: Department of Health, Education, and Welfare, 1975.

U.S. Government Printing Office. *Statistical abstracts, 1980.* Washington, D.C., 1980.

Walker, L.E. *The battered woman.* New York: Harper and Row, 1979.

Wrightsman, L.S. *Social psychology.* Monterey: Brooks/Cole, 1977.

5

Psychoeducational Needs of Minority Children: The Mexican American Child, a Case in Point

Richard R. Valencia

In this chapter several psychoeducational research needs concerning minority children are identified. Discussed also are the policy implications of these research needs. The focus is on the Mexican American child because of historical circumstances and changing demographic patterns.

Nationally, ethnic minority groups are increasing at significant rates. Demographers predict that by 1990 the nation's Hispanic population—two-thirds of whom are Mexican American—will surpass blacks to become our country's largest ethnic minority. For example, Foote, Espinosa, and Garcia (1978), who specialize in educational demographics, have analyzed California public school enrollment projections by ethnicity. Based on the 1967–1977 trends, these writers project that by 1990 the combined ethnic minority school population will become the majority, and Mexican Americans will be the predominant ethnic minority group. In short, a radical change will occur in less than a decade; the white student population in California, now the majority, will become the minority.

As we enter the 1980s, the outlook for improvement of the quality of life for minority children and their families seems dismal. It is likely that the conditions of alienation and disenfranchisement presently characterizing minority groups will be exacerbated. Repressive policies and actions concerning education have already been set in motion as indicated by massive resistance to school desegregation and the mounting opposition to bilingual education.

An attempt will be made here to sensitize researchers and policymakers to several psychoeducational research needs of minority children with particular emphasis on the Mexican American child. Given the contemporary sociopolitical climate and the sharp increase in minority populations, it is critical that these needs be addressed. Psychoeducational research has been selected for analysis for the following reasons: (1) research in this area has generated the most debate with respect to minority children; (2) it is an area into which "requests for proposals" by government agencies are largely

73

being directed; (3) the mandate of Public Law 94–142 is forcing more attention to the issue of nondiscriminatory psychoeducational assessment and services for culturally diverse children; and (4) research in this area has the clearest potential for making improvements in the schooling process and outcomes for minority children, especially limited- and non-English-speaking children. In order to understand some current research needs, as identified in this chapter, it is important to provide a historical context.

A Brief History of Intelligence Testing

Before about 1960, psychoeducational research on Mexican American children was dominated by studies which investigated the performance of Mexican American pupils on standardized intelligence tests. The major finding was that Mexican Americans compared to white subjects or to standardization norms, performed about two-thirds of a standard deviation lower. In the earliest studies, many researchers argued that the poorer performance of Mexican Americans could largely be attributed to genetic inferiority (for example, Garretson 1928; Terman 1916). In contrast to these genetic inferiority explanations, several early and many recent investigators have concluded that environmental factors—particularly the limited English language skills of Mexican American children—were more adequate explanations for the depressed IQ scores of Mexican Americans (for example, Carlson and Henderson 1950; Chandler and Plakos 1969; Christiansen and Livermore 1970; Davenport 1932; Jensen 1961; Palomares and Johnson 1966; Rapier 1967; Sanchez 1932, 1934; Valencia and Sheehan 1981a).

Valencia (1979) reviewed the available literature on intelligence testing of Mexican Americans, and argued that the lower scores of Mexican American children—as a group—were largely a result of methodological issues and not substantive ones. In almost every study there was a failure to control for one or more influential variables linked to intellectual performance. Specifically, Valencia pointed to three major control problems: failure to control for socioeconomic status (for example, Carlson and Henderson 1950; Garretson 1928); failure to control for limited English language proficiency of Mexican Americans by not providing instructions and test content in Spanish (for example, Rieber and Womack 1968; Sheldon 1924); failure to control for the white, middle-class cultural content of standardized IQ tests (for example, Garth 1923; Rieber and Womack 1968).

Notwithstanding these methodological and research issues, the history of intelligence testing vis-à-vis Mexican Americans and the educational system has been overshadowed by tragic social consequences. The intelligence testing of Mexican American pupils has, on a large scale, contributed to the perpetuation of Mexican American school failure (Valencia 1981). The mechanism of testing has resulted in classification practices (within-class-room ability grouping and between-classroom ability grouping, commonly referred to as *tracking*), curricular differentiation (nonacademic course work such as vocational education; low-level academic work), and differentials in schooling outcomes (low-level scholastic attainment; early leaving). Valencia (1981) analyzed the oppressive role of the testing mechanism by discussing three interrelated aspects—the nature of testing instruments and performance, the criteria for sorting and selection, and the agents of decision making in the sorting and selection process. For a history of the oppressive uses of intelligence testing in general, see Kamin (1974).

The Educable Mentally Retarded Controversy

Ethnic minorities historically have been disproportionately assigned to classes for the educable mentally retarded. This has created psychological hardships and led to diminished learning opportunities for the pupils involved. The subsequent lawsuits by parents have had some positive results. We have seen clearer identification of issues in the psychoeducational assessment of minorities, the development of plaintiffs' legal arguments, and steps toward the resolution of such issues (Henderson and Valencia, in press). In fact, if it were not for the efforts of minority parents working in conjunction with lawyers and advocates of children's rights, Public Law 94-142, the Education for All Handicapped Children Act of 1975 (Federal Register 1977), would not have been developed. Although the influences that have helped shape the special education movement as applied to nondiscriminatory assessment and services for handicapped and minority children are complex and varied, the outcomes (identification of issues) and resolutions (PL 94-142) can be viewed as radical changes in the ways such children have historically been perceived and treated.

The litigation efforts by minority parents have been one of the most powerful influences that have molded, and continue to mold, guidelines for psychoeducational assessment and services, as well as research needs. "Right-to-placement" lawsuits (suits asking for exclusion from inappropriate special-class placement such as educable mentally retarded classes) have largely involved ethnic minority parents (Theimer and Rupiper 1975, cited in Henderson and Valencia, in press). The concerns brought forth in such cases (for example, *Diana* v. *Board of Education* 1970) can be stated as follows:

1. Language assessment practices are discriminatory.
2. Tests (such as IQ tests) are discriminatory.
3. Psychologists are often poorly trained and insensitive.

4. Minority children are overrepresented in special education classes.
5. There are no systematic evaluations of children assigned to special education classes.
6. There is a lack of consultation with parents regarding the placement and progress of their children in special education classes.
7. There are limited data sources and information in making placement decisions (Oakland 1974–1975, cited in Henderson and Valencia, in press).

Issues raised in such litigation plus the influence of professional organizations helped to bring about legislative mandates to deal with the problem of discriminatory psychoeducational assessment and services. A number of these legislative features—in the form of PL 94–142—have direct implications for improving assessment and services for minority children. Concerning the identification of research needs, some of the more significant provisions are as follows:

1. Testing and evaluation instruments must not be racially and culturally biased.
2. Safeguards of informed consent and due process are required.
3. Assessment in the child's native language is required.
4. Tests are to be validated for specific use.
5. Multiple data sources must be used in classification and placement decisions.
6. Assessment and placement will involve a multidisciplinary team (Reschly 1979, cited in Henderson and Valencia, in press).

The next section will discuss how some of these provisions plus other identified areas can be targeted and conceptualized as psychoeducational research needs.

Psychoeducational Research Needs

In this section, three areas in which research concerning minority children should be encouraged are identified and discussed. These research areas should be regarded as representative of some of the major research trends and issues. The areas are: validation of standardized testing instruments for specific use; multiple data sources in assessment; and familial and sociocultural factors in intellectual functioning of children.

Validation of Instruments for Specific Use

The provision of PL 94–142 that mandates assessment instruments used for children from linguistically and culturally diverse populations be validated for specific use has implications not only for special needs of minority children but also for the assessment of normal minority children. This is particularly evident in the case of standardized achievement testing of limited- and non-English-speaking pupils. For Mexican American pupils, the validation for specific use notion is a pressing area for research because of the very high percentage of these children who begin school with limited or no proficiency in English.

Valencia (1982a) has pointed out that only a limited number of research studies have investigated the concurrent and predictive validity of standardized intelligence and achievement tests with Mexican American pupils (for example, Davis and Rowland 1974; Davis and Walker 1976; Dean 1977; Hurt and Mishra 1970; Kent and Ruiz 1979). Studies investigating the reliability of standardized measures are even fewer in number. For the available validity studies, the findings are mixed. Valencia (1982a) suggested that the major reason for these inconclusive findings is that the language status of the children was not controlled either in the assessment or in the statistical analyses. For example, Dean (1977) compared the performance of white and Mexican American pupils referred for psychological evaluation; the tests administered were the Wide Range Achievement Test (WRAT), WISC-R, and the Peabody Individual Achievement Test (PIAT). It was found that concurrent validity was generally adequate between the PIAT and the WRAT and between IQ and achievement for both ethnic groups. This finding of psychometric soundness and equivalence for both groups should be interpreted with caution, since all of the Mexican American children were tested in English. It is likely that some of these children had limited English. If so, the language proficiency of the Mexican Americans might have confounded the observed intercorrelations among the three measures. There is some evidence for this speculation as the Mexican Americans compared to the white subjects scored significantly lower on WISC-R Verbal IQ. This is a typical finding in previous studies (for example, Christiansen and Livermore 1970).

Examples of two studies that have attempted to gather validity and reliability data in a more reasonable manner on a standardized test are the investigations of Valencia (1981a, 1982b). The major focus of the studies was to investigate the psychometric properties of the McCarthy Scales of Children's Abilities (MSCA; McCarthy 1972) for Mexican American children. The McCarthy, a cognitive battery, is competing favorably with the well-known and widely used WPPSI, WISC, WISC-R, and Stanford-Binet tests. In a review of nearly a decade of research on the MSCA, Kaufman (in press) has concluded that in preschool assessment the McCarthy appears to be stable and reliable, correlates highly with the Wechsler and Binet scales,· correlates significantly with school achievement and has good construct validity. Finally, there is some evidence that the MSCA may be nondiscriminatory in the assessment of ethnic minority children, particularly black preschool and kindergarten-age children.

The study by Valencia (1982a) was designed to gather criterion-related validity data of the MSCA for Mexican American children by seeing how well the McCarthy predicts reading and mathematics achievement. The primary focus was on monolingual English-speaking children because the conventional McCarthy was standardized only on English-speaking children (a small percentage of Mexican American children were included in the standardization sample). However, a subsidiary focus of Valencia's (1982a) study was to gather exploratory data on monolingual Spanish-speaking children by using a carefully translated version of the MSCA. Since it is likely that a Spanish standardized version of the MSCA will be developed in the future, exploratory research can be valuable at this time. The subjects in the Valencia and Sheehan (1982a) study were thirty-one English-speaking Mexican American second graders. The criteria variables were total raw reading and mathematics performance on the Comprehensive Tests of Basic Skills (CTBS 1974). The predictor variables were the General Cognitive Index (GCI) and the other MSCA scale scores [Verbal (V), Perceptual-Performance (P), Quantitative (Q), and Memory (M)]. The results showed that the GCI had a reasonably high correlation with total reading ($r = .74$) and a moderate one with total math ($r = .44$). The exploratory analyses for the Spanish-speaking youngsters ($n = 43$) showed low rs of .36 and .31 between GCI and reading and math, respectively. The Spanish-speaking children were administered the Spanish translated version of the MSCA and the Spanish standardized version of the CTBS (CTBS Español 1979).

In a similar study concerned with the validation for specific use provision of PL 94–142, Valencia (1982b) designed a one-year test-retest investigation. The MSCA was administered to forty-two monolingual English-speaking and forty-two monolingual Spanish-speaking preschool Mexican American children. One year later, the eighty-four children (enrolled in kindergarten) were retested on the MSCA (language status did not change over the one-year period). Correlations were computed for the test-retest scores for the General Cognitive Index and the other MSCA scale scores (Verbal, Perceptual-Performance, Quantitative, and Memory) for the English-tested and Spanish-tested groups. The observed rs for the scales ranged between .63 and .85 and .43 and .62 for the English-tested and Spanish-tested groups, respectively. For the General Cognitive Index, the test-retest rs for the two groups were .85 and .57 respectively. The major conclusion was that the MSCA yielded good test-retest reliability for the English-tested children but poor reliability for the Spanish-tested group.

In conclusion, the two Valencia investigations are examples of the kind of research that needs to be continued in the area of validation of tests for specific use. The findings of research such as this appear to be helpful in ensuring that limited- and non-English-speaking children are evaluated with psychometrically valid instruments that allow these children the widest opportunities to demonstrate competency.

Multiple Data Sources in Assessment

The use of multiple informed sources (medical, psychometric, parent, teacher) provides a rich data base and also improves the credibility of these data. Applying multiple data sources for the psychoeducational assessment of ethnic minority children is an important strategy because it allows for cultural diversity in the assessment process. As Reschly (1979) has pointed out, the diagnostician's assessment of culturally and linguistically diverse children may be biased in several ways—in instrumentation (content bias), in the testing situation (atmosphere bias), and in how test results are used (bias in use). A multidisciplinary evaluation system has potential to minimize, perhaps eliminate, these forms of bias.

Multiple data sources in assessment challenge a major assumption in the evaluation process. Gradel, Thompson, and Sheehan (1980) pointed out that the three major sources of data (diagnostician, teacher, and parent) are assumed to fall on a continuum of credibility. The trained diagnostician, who uses or has access to information based on a wide range of sources (for example, standardized tests, informal tests, structured and unstructured interviews, observations, cumulative records, medical records) is regarded as the most credible. The parent, on the other hand, who has an entire developmental history on which to draw plus daily observations of the child in his or her natural setting, is assumed nevertheless to be the least credible in providing data about the child. The teacher as a data source is perceived to be somewhere between diagnostician and parent regarding credibility.

There is growing evidence that the assumption that mothers cannot provide credible data about their children is largely unsupported. The investigation of parents' perceptions and assessments of their children's behavior has been of interest to social scientists and educators for some time. Over twenty-five years ago, clinical psychologists began to study how the degree of accuracy of parents in making evaluations of their children's mental retardation was related to acceptance or realization of the child's retardation (Ewert and Green 1957). However, only recently has multiple data sources research expanded to include normal and culturally diverse populations (for example, Blair 1970; Colligan 1976; Hunt and Paraskevopoulos 1980; Valencia and Cruz 1981). Taken together, the multiple data sources in assessment research have included a variety of assessment paradigms, purposes, age levels, and intellectual functioning of children. Although it is well beyond the scope of this chapter to review the available literature, two major and rather consistent findings can be summarized. First, the assessments that parents (mothers have primarily been studied) make of their children are fairly credible. That is, using a variety of indexes to compute accuracy of maternal estimations of their children, mothers' assessments are fairly accurate, and in some studies, they are extremely accurate compared with more traditional data sources (trained diagnosticians and teachers). Second, reliable differences do exist between mothers and traditional data sources. There is a consistent pattern of maternal overestimation. This phenomenon is so common that it holds across age levels (infants, preschoolers, young elementary school children), intellectual functioning (normal and handicapped), and ethnicity (Anglo and Mexican American). Gradel, Thompson, and Sheehan (1980) and Valencia and Cruz (1981) hypothesized that a plausible explanation for the maternal overestimation phenomenon is that the professional or trained diagnostician's data reflect an underestimation of the child's performance. They have argued that mothers, when estimating their children's performance, might be operating from a generic or "macro" frame of reference. That is, perhaps mothers, compared to diagnosticians, possess a larger and more representative data base from which to assess their children's behavior because of the quality and quantity of contact time they have with their children. If "maternal overestimation" is actually a more accurate indication of a child's behavior, then this concept may need to be looked at more critically. Perhaps traditional assessment instruments, such as IQ tests, are so narrow in what they measure that "diagnostician underestimation" may be a more meaningful notion. It is important to have further research on the issue of overestimation.

What are the implications of multiple data sources in assessment for research with Mexican American children and their parents? In the only known investigation in which Mexican American families were studied, Valencia and Cruz (1981) asked 261 Mexican American mothers to estimate (on an item-by-item basis) their preschool children's actual performance on the MSCA. As in the general literature in which white parents were asked to assess their children's performance, the Mexican American mothers also overestimated. On all scale scores of the MSCA, the mothers' estimations of their children's actual MSCA performance were significantly higher. For example, on the MSCA General Cognitive Index, the mean estimation of the mothers was 112.38 and the actual mean score of the children was 95.44 (the standardization mean is 100). In brief, it was found that mothers who estimated their children's intellectual performance to be significantly higher were characterized as mothers who were born in the United States (versus born in Mexico), English-speaking (versus Spanish-speaking), younger (versus older), had higher schooling attainment (versus lower), schooled in the United States (versus Mexico), and were of higher socioeconomic class (versus lower). Concerning accuracy (as defined by mean score differences between maternal estimations and children's performance), it was found that mothers did not differ significantly on the above demographic variables. As a group, the mothers' estimations on the different scales of the MSCA correlated significantly with the children's actual performance (for example, correlation of .55 on the General Cognitive Index), indicating fairly good accuracy of the mothers.

In conclusion, the major value of the Valencia and Cruz maternal estimations investigation is that data are now available on Mexican American families, and such data indicate that Mexican American mothers are very much like other mothers in that they overestimate but yet are relatively accurate. The observed demographic findings in the Valencia and Cruz study should be taken into consideration in future research on multiple data sources in assessment. Given the economic and psychometric advantage of including parents in prescreening techniques (for example, Frankenburg et al. 1976) and the need to accommodate cultural diversity in the assessment procedure, Mexican American and other minority parents should be included in future multimeasurement efforts that attempt to address the issue of across-setting validity.

Familial and Sociocultural Factors in Intellectual Functioning

This third and final research area is characterized as being more toward the basic than the applied end of the research continuum. Compared to the general state of the art regarding psychoeducational research, such research on minority children and their families is an impoverished area. More studies of the relation between the minority home environment to the intellectual development and school achievement of minority children and youth are woefully needed. Longitudinal studies are virtually nonexistent. The focus of this section is to discuss recent research on the relation between familial and sociocultural factors to the intellectual performance and development of Mexican American children. For an excellent discussion of the general state of the art regarding the relation between home environment factors and children's performance on intelligence tests and school achievement, see Henderson (1981).

The work by Valencia and associates (Valencia, Henderson, and

Rankin 1981; Valencia, Rankin, and Henderson 1982) has been an attempt to investigate the relation between family constellation variables (family size and birth order) and sociocultural variables (language of parents and child, schooling attainment and country of schooling of parents, and socioeconomic status) to the intellectual performance of Mexican American children. The subjects in the Valencia, Henderson, and Rankin (1981) study, were 190 Mexican American preschool children and their mothers from low-income families. It was found that the single most powerful predictor of the children's intellectual performance (as measured by the MSCA) was a language/schooling factor. This factor was loaded with language of child and parents and the educational attainment and country of schooling of the parents. The second most significant predictor was socioeconomic status; this was factorially separated from educational attainment. Family constellation, consisting of family size and birth order, constituted a clearly separate and distinct factor. It contributed less than 3 percent of the variance in MSCA performance. The observed relation among the three factors indicated that the most intellectually competent children who were tested in English rather than Spanish, came from homes in which English, not Spanish, was the dominant language, had parents who had the highest educational attainment levels, and were educated in the United States rather than in Mexico. In a follow-up investigation, Valencia, Rankin, and Henderson (1982) tested 77 of the 190 children on the MSCA one year later. The factor scores served as the independent variables in both original and follow-up studies. A major result of this one-year longitudinal investigation was that the family constellation factor—contributing little to MSCA variance in the original sample—actually decreased in its contribution to predicting intellectual performance in the follow-up. Another important factor was that the language/schooling factor, ranking first in relative contribution in the original sample, shifted to second place in importance. Socioeconomic status, ranking second in the original study, shifted to first in the follow-up study. Several hypotheses were advanced to explain these shifts as predictors of intellectual performance. Because the timing of the testing period for the follow-up coincided with the children's entry into public school (kindergarten), it is likely that the Spanish-speaking children had increased opportunities to interact with their English-speaking peers. Another possible explanation is that the children's teachers held different expectations of their academic performance, based on personal characteristics of the children. For the children in the follow-up study, it is likely that teachers' expectations were more influenced by socioeconomic factors than by language or ethnicity.

It is recommended that more studies of this nature be done. Research designs should include different criterion measures, varied age groups, and specific independent variables such as the intellectual climate of the home.

The policy implications of the work by Valencia and his associates appear to be somewhat sensitive. The research was designed to address some of the criticisms of the confluence model proposed by Zajonc and Markus (1975). The confluence model argues that the intellectual development of children is largely influenced by the intellectual environment of the family. The home intellectual environment is basically defined as the sum of the intellectual levels of all members of the family, divided by the number of family members. In a gross sense, the model postulates that the more children a family has and the closer the spacing, the less intelligent are the children. The confluence model has been criticized for a number of reasons and by many investigators (see Henderson 1981). The investigations by Valencia and his associates were largely designed to address issues related to their concerns that (1) the confluence model cannot be generalized to culturally diverse groups; (2) the model uses an aggregated data analysis approach which is not very meaningful to understanding within-family patterns, and (3) longitudinal data are not available.

Although the policy implications of the confluence model are unclear, one can surmise that serious ethical ramifications could arise in the contentious area of family planning. This is a very sensitive issue, particularly in Mexican American families where large families are common and tend to be valued. The research by Valencia and his associates on the confluence model concerning the cognitive development of Mexican American children fails to support the predictions of the confluence model. This research on Mexican Americans suggests that the improvement of educational opportunities for parents and their children may serve as more productive means of intervention as opposed to the strategy of altering orientations and values about family size. This should be clearly understood by policymakers, particularly given the dramatic increase in the Mexican American population.

Implications for Researchers and Policymakers

Policymakers should be aware of at least two possible scenarios that would not be in the best interests of minority children. One might be a return to the use of inappropriate tests by school psychologists. In *Larry P.* v. *Wilson Riles* (1979), the judge called for a moratorium on the use of the Stanford-Binet and WISC-R tests in placing minority children into educable mentally retarded and learning disabled special education classes. Consequently, some school districts have begun to use other tests (for instance, Peabody Picture Vocabulary Tests) which are reputed to be discriminatory against minority children. A second possible scenario is that some schools may declare self-imposed moratoriums on testing altogether when minority children are suspected of being candidates for special education classes. In these cases, the rationale for the moratorium might be based on a school district's fear of being sued by parents for discriminatory assessment and placement.

There is a definite need for further research concerning familial and sociocultural factors in intellectual performance. Given the chronic school failure among Mexican American pupils, some people might be tempted to blame the victim. That is, one might argue that large families create impoverished intellectual climates which in turn cause poor school performance. In fact, this link has been argued in much of the literature on Mexican Americans that deals with socialization practices (such as the "deficit" model, pervasive in the 1960s). Researchers and policymakers should not only be aware of the methodological and ideological biases of the deficit model, but they should become aware of research that provides alternative hypotheses.

It is important that school psychologists provide feedback to researchers regarding their needs for appropriate assessment measures and strategies for nondiscriminatory services. Likewise, researchers should take the initiative to observe the real world of the school and the home environment to develop ideas for applied research. Finally, policymakers should become aware, if they are not already, that whenever services are mandated by courts or legislation (as in PL 94-142), substantial gaps between the mandates and the level of knowledge and technology will occur.

Policymakers might consider two aspects to decrease the gap and expedite a direct link in policy between what is right and what will work. This can be done by including more social scientists, practitioners, and parents as advisors and as policy analysts. Second, policymakers must allow more money for research. Although the federal role in granting research money is more prominent compared to state and local governments, the percentage of federal research funds is minuscule.

In the final analysis, the future of the research needs outlined in this chapter rests to a large degree in the hands of policymakers. The push for more and better quality basic and applied research can possibly be expedited if policymakers embody the qualities discussed by Max Weber who in 1918 described the prominent qualifications of a policymaker—passion, a feeling of responsibility, and a sense of proportion (Weber 1946; cited in Graham 1980).

References

Blair, J. A comparison of mother and teacher ratings on the Preschool Attainment Record of four-year-old children. *Exceptional Children* 37: 299–300, 1970.

Carlson, H.B., and Henderson, H. The intelligence of American children of

Mexican parentage. *Journal of Abnormal and Social Psychology* 45: 544–551, 1950.

Chandler, J.T., and Plakos, J. Spanish-speaking pupils as Educable Mentally Retarded. *Integrated Education* 1:28–33, 1969.

Christiansen, T., and Livermore, G. A comparison of Anglo-American and Spanish-American children on the WISC. *Journal of Social Psychology* 81:9–14, 1970.

Colligan, R.C. Prediction of kindergarten reading success from preschool report of parents. *Psychology in the Schools* 13:304–307, 1976.

Comprehensive Tests of Basic Skills, Level C, Form S: Examiner's Manual and Technical Bulletin No. 1. Monterey, Calif.: CTBS/McGraw-Hill, 1974.

Comprehensive Tests of Basic Skills Español and SERVS: Technical Report. Monterey, Calif.: CTBS/McGraw-Hill, 1979.

Davenport, E.L. The Intelligence Quotients of Mexican and non-Mexican siblings. *School and Society* 36:304–306, 1932.

Davis, E.E., and Rowland, T. A replacement for the venerable Stanford-Binet? *Journal of Clinical Psychology* 30:517–521, 1974.

Davis, E.E., and Walker, C. Validity of the McCarthy Scales for Southwestern rural children. *Perceptual and Motor Skills* 42:563–567, 1976.

Dean, R.S. Analysis of the PIAT with Anglo and Mexican-American children. *Journal of School Psychology* 15:329–333, 1977.

Diana v. *Board of Education,* Civil Action No. C–70–37 (N.D. Cal. 1970).

Ewert, J.C., and Green, M.W. Conditions associated with the mother's estimate of the ability of her retarded child. *American Journal of Mental Deficiency* 62:521–533, 1957.

Federal Register. *Education of handicapped children.* Regulations implementing the Education for All Handicapped Children Act of 1975, August 23, 1977, pp. 42474–42518.

Foote, T.H.; Espinosa, R.W.; and Garcia, J.O. *Ethnic groups and public education in California.* San Diego State University: The California School Finance Project and the California Association for Bilingual Education, 1978.

Frankenburg, W.K.; Van Doorninck, W.J.; Liddell, T.N.; and Dick, N.P. The Denver Prescreening Developmental Questionnaire. *Pediatrics* 57: 744–753, 1976.

Garth, T.R. A comparison of the intelligence of Mexican and mixed and full-blood Indian children. *Psychological Review* 30:388–401, 1923.

Garretson, O.K. A study of causes and retardation among Mexican children in a public school system in Arizona. *Journal of Educational Psychology* 19:31–40, 1928.

Gradel, K.; Thompson, M.S.; and Sheehan, R. Parental and professional agreement in early childhood assessment. *Topics in Early Childhood Special Education* 1:31–39, 1981.

Graham, P.A. Historians as policymakers. *Educational Researcher* 9: 21–24, 1980.

Henderson, R.W. Home environment and intellectual performance. In *Parent-child interaction: theory, research and prospect,* ed. R.W. Henderson. New York: Academic Press, 1981.

Henderson, R.W., and Valencia, R.R. Nondiscriminatory school psychological services: beyond nonbiased assessment. In *School psychology in contemporary society,* ed. J.R. Bergan. Columbus, Ohio: Merrill (in press).

Hunt, J.McV., and Paraskevopoulos, J. Children's psychological development as a function of the inaccuracy of their mothers' knowledge of their abilities. *Journal of Genetic Psychology* 136:285–298, 1980.

Hurt, M., and Mishra, S.P. Reliability and validity of the Metropolitan Achievement Tests for Mexican-American children. *Educational and Psychological Measurement* 30:989–992, 1970.

Jensen, A.R. Learning abilities in Mexican-American and Anglo-American children. *California Journal of Educational Research* 12:147–159, 1961.

Kamin, L.J. *The science and politics of IQ.* Potomac, Md.: Laurence Erlbaum Associates, 1974.

Kaufman, A.S. An integrated review of almost a decade of research on the McCarthy Scales. In *Advances in school psychology,* vol. 2, ed. T.R. Kratochwill. Hillsdale, N.J.: Erlbaum (in press).

Kent, J., and Ruiz, R. IQ and reading scores among Anglo, Black, and Chicano third- and sixth-grade school children. *Hispanic Journal of Behavioral Sciences* 3:271–277, 1979.

Larry P. v. Wilson Riles, Superintendent of Public Instruction, California. Opinion C–71–2270 RFP U.S. District Court, San Francisco, October 16, 1979.

McCarthy, D. *McCarthy Scales of Children's Abilities.* New York: Psychological Corporation, 1972.

Oakland, T. Assessment, education and minority-group children. *Academic Therapy* 10:133–140, 1974–1975.

Palomares, U., and Johnson, L. Evaluation of Mexican-American pupils for Educable Mentally Retarded classes. *California Education* 3:27–29, 1966.

Rapier, J.L. Effects of verbal mediation upon the learning of Mexican-American children. *California Journal of Educational Research* 18: 41–48, 1967.

Reschly, D.J. Nonbiased assessment. In *School psychology: perspectives and issues,* ed. D.J. Reschly and G.D. Phye. New York: Academic Press, 1979.

Rieber, M., and Womack, M. The intelligence of preschool children as related to ethnic and demographic variables. *Exceptional Children* 34: 609–614, 1968.

Sanchez, G.I. Group differences and Spanish-speaking children: a critical review. *Journal of Applied Psychology* 16:549–558, 1932.

Sanchez, G.I. Bilingualism and mental measures. *Journal of Applied Psychology* 18:765–772, 1934.

Sheldon, W.H. The intelligence of Mexican children. *School and Society* 19:139–142, 1924.

Terman, L.M. *The measurement of intelligence.* Boston: Houghton Mifflin, 1916.

Theimer, R.K., and Rupiper, O.J. Special education litigation and school psychology. *Journal of School Psychology* 13:324–334, 1975.

Valencia, R.R. Comparison of intellectual performance of Chicano and Anglo third-grade boys on the Raven's Coloured Progressive Matrices. *Psychology in the Schools* 16:448–453, 1979.

Valencia, R.R. Synthesizing a theoretical perspective on Chicano school failure: the testing mechanism. Paper presented at the Ninth Annual Meeting of the National Association for Chicano Studies, University of California, Riverside, April 2–4, 1981.

Valencia, R.R., and Cruz, J. *Mexican American mothers' estimations of their preschool children's cognitive performance.* Final technical report (contract 90-C-1777) submitted to the Administration for Children, Youth, and Families, Office of Human Development Services, U.S. Department of Health, Education, and Welfare, 1981.

Valencia, R.R.; Henderson, R.W.; and Rankin, R.J. Relationship of family constellation and schooling to intellectual performance of Mexican American children. *Journal of Educational Psychology* 73:524–532, 1981.

Valencia, R.R.; Rankin, R.J.; and Henderson, R.H. *Longitudinal stability of familial and sociocultural factors as predictors of intellectual performance among Mexican American children.* Manuscript submitted for publication, 1982.

Valencia, R.R. *Predicting academic achievement of Mexican American children: Preliminary analysis of the McCarthy Scales.* Manuscript submitted for publication, 1982a.

Valencia, R.R. *Stability of the McCarthy Scales of Children's Abilities over a one-year period for Mexican American children.* Manuscript submitted for publication, 1982b.

Weber, M. Politics as vocation. In *From Max Weber: essays in sociology,* ed. H.H. Gerth and C.W. Mills. New York: Oxford University Press, 1946, 1976.

Zajonc, R., and Markus, G.B. Birth order and intellectual development. *Psychological Review* 82:74–88, 1975.

6

Infant–Caretaker Vocalization: The Foundations of Language

Alan L. Ziajka

Long before they speak their first words, infants communicate with people around them. The antecedents of what will later become sophisticated communicative patterns involving language and various nonverbal modes can be seen in this early communication between infants and the significant adults in their lives. One of the most salient options used by infants to communicate with others is nonverbal vocalization. This chapter will review the existing literature regarding how prelinguistic infants use nonverbal vocalization to communicate with their parents and others, and analyze the findings of a longitudinal study of communicative interaction between six infants and their mothers in home settings.

The first vocal option available to the infant is the cry. Spectrographic analysis (Dale 1976; Smart and Smart 1973) reveals that the basic cry of the newborn consists of a characteristic rhythm of cry, rest, inhalation, and rest and usually has a rising and falling frequency contour. Brain-damaged infants have a distinctive cry, more shrill and piercing than a normal cry (Smart and Smart 1973). The cry is present at birth and temporarily prevails as the only vocal choice at the infant's disposal. The infant cries, and the caretaker regards the infant's sounds as a request for action on his or her part. This is the natural beginning of two-way communication.

The infant's cry has received considerable research attention in the last two decades. Bowlby (1958), for instance, designated crying as an important attachment behavior because of its predictable outcome in bringing the mother or other care giver to the child. In his longitudinal work, he found that of the various communication modes of early infancy, crying was one of the most effective in promoting proximity to the mother. In another study, Wolff (1969) analyzed the crying of fourteen babies whom he observed from ages three to six months. He used taped records to supplement his observations and analyzed the tapes by means of sound spectrographs. Using these spectrographs, he differentiated several types of cries,

This research was part of a larger study of prelinguistic communication conducted by the author in 1979. The complete study can be found in the author's book, *Prelinguistic Communication in Infancy*, Praeger Publishers, 1981. Printed with permission.

coordinated these with his observations, and concluded that some cries meant hunger, others indicated pain, and still others seemed to be associated with gastrointestinal upset. Wolff also found that mothers could usually distinguish among these different types of cries on the basis of sound alone. The mothers came rushing to the sound of a pain cry, but responded to a hunger cry less quickly, depending on their personal child-rearing styles. Wolff also found that picking up the infant was consistently effective in terminating crying.

In a longitudinal study of twenty-six infant–mother pairs, Bell and Ainsworth (1972) found that during the first three months crying occurs more often when the mother is out of sight than when she is nearby, and least frequently when infant and mother are in actual physical contact. They also found that picking up and rocking the infant or even just holding the child is the most frequent maternal response to crying. Such a maternal response, they discovered, is the best way to end the infant's cries; it is over 85 percent effective throughout the first year. Bell and Ainsworth also noted that mothers who promptly responded to a crying baby during the child's first few months of life had infants who cried less at the end of the first year than did infants whose mothers were unresponsive to the baby's crying signals. Moreover, they discovered that maternal responsiveness was associated with the development of more elaborate noncrying communication, such as vocalization, smiling, and gesture. Infants who cried less also tended by the end of the first year to use a greater variety of other, more subtle modes of communication that clearly invited and sustained contact.

By the age of one or two months, infants use cooing to interact with the significant adults in their environment. Spectrographic analysis (Lenneberg 1967) of cooing reveals a clear distinction between this mode of communication and crying. Physiologically, crying is the blowing of air for a variable length of time along the vocal cords with little articulation, whereas a distinct coo lasts for approximately half a second, the tongue moves, and vowel-like sounds, acoustically similar to back vowels (frequently exemplified by the [u] sound), are produced.

Research regarding infant cooing and the vocal interplay that develops as infants use this option to interact with adults reveals a communication synchrony in existence long before the onset of speech. For example, in his longitudinal research, Wolff (1963, 1969) found that as early as four weeks of age infants begin to respond to the human face and voice with gurgling and cooing sounds accompanied by smiles. By five weeks, Wolff observed, infants can engage in "conversations" consisting of from ten to fifteen vocalizations when their vocalizations are imitated by adults. Between the ages of six and eight weeks, vocalization expands and is used more frequently both in vocal play and in social transactions. According to Wolff, the human infant demonstrates a significantly greater amount of vocalization when the adult "talks" than when that partner is silent. When an adult introduces low-pitched sounds that are part of the infant's repertory, for example, infants imitate these vocalizations and produce their own versions of the low-pitched sounds.

Wolff also found, as did White (1975), that a mother's voice more effectively elicits vocalizations from her infant than does the voice of an outside observer. Further, according to White, by four to five months of age the infant can distinguish the mother's voice from others by its unique sound qualities, irrespective of the words she uses.

Cooing, like other early vocalization, can be both sustained and increased in frequency by a socially responsive environment. The young infant learns to use the vocal option to interact with significant others, and very early in the infant's life vocalizations become differentially directed to specific persons, to those adults who have responded most frequently and effectively to previous vocal behavior.

Laughing is another vocal option used by infants and caretakers to initiate and maintain contact during children's first months of life. Studies (Washburn 1929; Ambrose 1963; Sroufe and Wunsch 1972; Sroufe and Waters 1976) show that infant laughter first appears at approximately four months of age and that its major elicitors are tactile, auditory, and visual stimulation by significant others, especially the mother. In a cross-sectional laboratory study of ninety-six infants aged four to twelve months and their mothers, Sroufe and Wunsch (1972) found that a vigorous kissing of the stomach or a tickling of the ribs by the mother or a vocal "I'm gonna get you" accompanied by a looming approach by the mother produced laughter in one-third of the four-month-olds. Five-month-old infants additionally laughed at a loud "boom, boom, boom" vocalization coming from the mother. By six months of age, one-third of the infants laughed at a loud "aah" sound with an abrupt cut-off, when they were gently tickled under the chin, and when the mother approached with her face covered by a cloth. By eight months of age, one-third of the infants in the sample laughed at peek-a-boo (without sound) and when the mother crawled on the floor, shook her hair, or pulled a dangling cloth from her mouth. By age twelve months, infants laughed most frequently at visual stimuli such as the mother walking like a penguin, sucking on the baby's bottle, sticking out her tongue and then pulling it in as the baby reached for it, and stuffing a cloth back into her own mouth. For many of the infants, this last behavior produced the loudest laughs of all. Overall, the researchers found an increase with age in the amount of laughter that could be elicited by the mothers, with a cross-age average of 10 percent, 37 percent, and 43 percent for the four-to-six-, seven-to-nine-, and ten-to-twelve-month age groups respectively. The researchers concluded that, "like the social smile, laughter may have a positive effect on caretaker–infant interaction" (Sroufe and Wunsch 1972, p. 1340).

Babbling, which appears at approximately five or six months, is another means infants use to initiate and maintain contact with others in the social world. In contrast to cooing, infant babbling includes consonant and vowel syllables drawn directly from adult language. Oller (1976), for example, noted that the babbling of infants between six and eight months of age exhibited many of the same phonetic elements, such as initial and final consonant sequences, found in the speech of older children and adults. The infant's phonetic production, Oller believes, is clearly an important precursor of later language. Rebelsky, Starr, and Luria (1967) described the babbling stage as the time during which infants practice and play with the phonemes typical of the language of their particular culture and minimize or drop the phonemes not used by their culture's language. Among American infants, for example, repetitions of the "ba," "ma," "da," and "ta" sounds are characteristic of babbling.

Babbling can also be viewed as a sophisticated option used by the prelinguistic infant to interact with significant adults in the social and cultural milieu. Several researchers have pointed out how infants use babbling for this end. In his research, Bowlby (1969), for example, found that both the sight of a human face and the sound of a human voice elicited infant babbling. Moreover, he noted, a baby's babbling usually elicits babbling by the mother and a more or less long chain of interchange in which "each partner seems to be expressing joy in the other's presence and the effect is certainly one of prolonging their social interaction" (1969, p. 246). Similarly, Papousek and Papousek (1977) found that parents often imitate infant babbling, responding to the pauses between individual bursts of babbling and "thus giving the interaction the semblance of a dialogue, pleasing to both partners" (p. 80).

Bruner (1975, 1977) observed that infant babbling during the first year is often integrated with other options, such as looking, that are used by infants to interact with adults. An infant may, for example, simultaneously pick up an object and show it to the mother, look at the mother, and babble, thus using the resources at his or her disposal to "comment" on a topic and interact with an important adult. According to Bruner, by age ten or eleven months the infant has developed vocalization and other options into a highly polished give-and-take game to be played with significant adults. This game might involve objects, passed from infant to mother or from mother to infant and back again, as "topics of exchange." Also, not only does the infant babble during the game, but the total interaction exhibits the basic characteristics of a dialogue in that it ascribes roles, turn-taking, initiating, and responding.

In another study of infant babbling, Ninio and Bruner (1978) recorded the exchanges of a mother and her eight-month-old infant while they read a picture book together. The infant's babbling vocalizations, as well as the child's smiling, reaching, and pointing, all evinced the infant's understanding of the social rules for achieving dialogue. According to the researchers, this child "very early and very strongly conformed to the turn-taking structure of conversation" (1978, p. 6).

Some researchers (Bzoch and League 1971; Leitch 1977; Gesell and Amatruda 1947) have described another preverbal mode of communication, "jargoning," that emerges toward the end of the child's first year of life. In the tenth or eleventh month of life, infants have been observed vocalizing to persons in what sound like meaningfully inflected sentences, but without using actual words (Bzoch and League 1971). "Jargoning" is defined as a continuous utterance containing four or more different phonemes and a tonal inflection pattern drawn from the surrounding linguistic community. (Babbling, on the other hand, is an utterance of less than four different phonemes and that, more important, lacks sophisticated intonation such as stress, pitch, and juncture.) "Jargoning" is thus characterized by some of the paralinguistic options described by Trager (1964) and Smith (1969) that accompany mature speech patterns. Both Bruner (1975) and Dore (1975), for example, noted that by the end of the first year, infants begin to mark vocalizations differentially with the stress and intonation patterns which later will form the paralinguistic component of their expressive language. Similarly, Stark, Rose, and McLagen (1975) concluded that the earliest examples of suprasegmental linguistic features such as stress, pitch, and juncture exist during this stage of infant vocal behavior.

Halliday (1975) also proposed that children under one year of age begin to use sound patterns to interact with individuals in the surrounding environment, particularly with the mother and other important adults. According to Halliday, before the child is a year old, he or she has a set of options that "embody the child's need for human contact" (1978, p. 259). By age 10½ months, Halliday's subject, Nigel, possessed three distinct sounds that were used for the interactional, or "me and you," function. One such sound pattern ("ihng! ng! ng!") was interpreted by Halliday to mean "Nice to see you, and why weren't you here before?" Halliday characterized this as an impatient and intensified greeting not mediated by any joint action. Nigel also possessed another distinct sound pattern which directed adults' attention to a particular object and then was "used as the channel for interacting with this other person" (1975, p. 23). Finally, Nigel possessed a response form used when another person initiated verbal interaction with him. Halliday concluded that before Nigel reached his first birthday, he possessed the vocal resources of sound articulation and intonation (rise and fall in pitch) to express meaning distinctions. According to Halliday, the young child "may have a well-developed semantic system long before he begins to combine words, in fact long before he has any words at all" (1978, p. 256).

Adults play an important role in fostering infants' use of various vocalization instruments available during the first months of life. For example, Rheingold, Gewirtz, and Ross (1959), in their study of three-month-old institutionalized infants, found that infants' vocalizations can be increased if an adult responds to them. In their study, each time the baby vocalized, the observer immediately responded by smiling, vocalizing, and touching the baby. The researchers noted that infant vocalization increased significantly during this treatment period and decreased when adults did not respond. Similarly, Weisberg (1967) found that the vocalizing rate of three-month-old infants could be increased in an experimental setting by social reinforcers provided by the experimenter (briefly touching the infant's chin, smiling, and talking to the infant) but not by nonsocial reinforcers (the ringing of a door chime) or by the mere presence of an inactive adult. A study by Anderson and Vietze (1977) of twenty-four three-month-old infants and their mothers revealed greater infant vocalization, to a statistically significant degree, when the mother spoke to the infant than when she was silent. These researchers suggested that a complex vocal interaction takes place between infant and mother in which the infant's vocalization affects the mother's talk, and the mother's speech affects the infant's vocalization. The same conclusion was reached in a study of fifty-one mothers and their 2½-month-old infants (Vietze, Strain, and Falsey 1975) and in a study of eight infants from their third to fourth month of life (Stern et al. 1975). The latter study revealed a pattern of "coactive" vocalizations: the infants tended to vocalize when their mothers were vocalizing, and the mothers tended to vocalize when their infants were vocalizing. In their home-based observation of forty-one five-month-old black infants and their mothers, Yarrow, Rubenstein, and Pedersen (1975) also found a significant positive correlation between maternal speech directed toward the infant and the infant's vocalization. Brazelton, Koslowski, and Main (1974), Newson and Newson (1976), and Lewis and Freedle (1973) all also have noted the conversationlike nature of vocal exchanges between young infants and their mothers and the tendency of infants to vocalize more when their mothers pause in the "conversation" and for mothers to reserve their utterances for intervening pauses.

Adult vocalization directed toward the young infant is also related to the child's eventual acquisition of language. Studies of children raised in orphanages and other institutions in which the infants' opportunity to hear adult language is minimal were found to be grossly retarded in language development (Dennis 1973; Skeels 1966; Spitz 1945). In normal home environments, the child's acquisition of language also appears to be in part related to adult vocalization patterns. Tulkin and Covitz (1976), for example, in their study of thirty middle-class and thirty working-class children, found a significant positive correlation in the middle-class group between the amount of time the mothers vocalized to their ten-month old infants and the childrens' scores on the Illinois Test of Psycholinguistic Abilities (ITPA) at age six. The researchers also found a significant positive correlation between the amount of mother–infant reciprocal vocalization when the infants were ten months of age and the childrens' ITPA scores at six years. Within the lower-class group, the correlations were also positive, though not statistically significant. By comparison, a study by Clarke-Stewart (1973) of thirty-eight lower-class infants and their mothers revealed a significant positive correlation between the total amount and variety of maternal speech directed toward infants when they were eleven to thirteen months old and the infants' expressive and receptive language development at seventeen months.

Cross-cultural differences have been observed in the amount of vocalizing infants engage in during the first year of life, suggesting that the culture in which an infant matures can have a significant impact on early vocalization patterns. Caudill and Weinstein (1970, 1972), for example, found vocal differences between thirty Japanese and thirty American three-to-four-month old infants and their mothers. American mothers stimulated their infants vocally more often than did the Japanese mothers, a difference that significantly correlated with the greater rate of vocalization among American infants than among Japanese infants. Similarly, Kagan, Kearsley, and Zelazo (1978) found that a group of thirty-three Chinese infants, when tested at nine to eleven months of age, vocalized significantly less than a matched group of Caucasian infants. Evidently, it is through the dynamics of infant–caretaker social interaction that a culture's communication patterns are transmitted to the young child.

The influence of the child's sex upon infant–caretaker vocalization patterns also has been the focus of some research. In a home study of thirty-two three-month-old infants and their mothers, for example, Lewis (1972) found that mothers of girls vocalize significantly more to their children than do mothers of boys. A laboratory study of sixty-four six-month-old infants (Goldberg and Lewis 1969) also revealed that mothers vocalize to girls significantly more than to boys. By contrast, however, a home study of twenty-four three-month-old infants and their mothers (Anderson and Vietze 1977) revealed no significant sex-based differences in the pattern of reciprocal vocalization. Likewise, Will, Self, and Datan (1976), in their laboratory research, and Yarrow, Rubenstein, and Pedersen (1975), in their home study of forty-one black infants (twenty-one boys and twenty girls) aged five to six months and their mothers, found no significant sex-linked differences in the amount of talking mothers engaged in with their children. Because of the conflicting results of existing research, conclusions about differences in maternal vocalization depending on the sex of the infant cannot be made with any assurance of accuracy.

The results are similarly equivocal when the sex of the parent is used as the independent variable. Thus, the eight-month-old infants in a study conducted by Lamb (1976) vocalized more to their fathers than to their mothers in a natural play situation in the home, and one-year-olds in laboratory studies by Ban and Lewis (1974) and Feldman and Ingham (1975) vocalized more to their mothers than to their fathers.

The impact of social class upon infant–caretaker vocalization has also been investigated by researchers. Tulkin and Kagan (1972), for instance, conducted a study in the homes of thirty middle-class and twenty-six lower-class Causasian mothers and their infants in which all of the infants were ten months old, first-born, and female. The middle-class mothers in the study were significantly more verbal with their infants than the lower-class mothers were. No class differences were found, however, in the amount of time the mothers spent in close proximity to their infants or in the frequencies of kissing, holding, touching, or active physical contact. Kagan (1971) also conducted a longitudinal study of 180 infants in which the children were assessed twice in a laboratory setting, once at eight months and again at thirteen months. Kagan found significant vocalization differences related to social class among the eighty-nine girls in his sample. Girls high in vocalization at both eight and thirteen months were more likely to come from upper-middle-class than from lower-middle-class families; further, vocalization of the upper-middle-class girls increased by 50 percent during the five-month period, while vocalization of lower-middle-class girls showed almost no change. The possible origins of these differences, according to Kagan, can be found in mother–infant interaction in the home. For half of his sample, Kagan conducted a four-hour home observation when the infants were four months of age. He found that upper-middle-class mothers engaged in more face-to-face vocalization with their daughters than less well educated mothers did. He found, however, no comparable difference among the mothers of sons.

Notwithstanding the sizable amount of research that has been conducted regarding infant–caretaker interaction through the vocal mode, there are several areas in need of further illumination. First, there is a need to describe more fully changes over time in the use of *all* of the major vocal tools—crying, cooing, babbling, laughing, and jargoning—by a group of infants in a natural setting. Most previous studies have been conducted in the laboratory, have focused on a large group of infants but used only one or two observations of the infants, or have followed one or two infants over time in their use of only one or two vocal options. Second, there is a need to explore the possible covariance between each of the infant's major vocal options using data gathered from a large enough number of observations and infant–caretaker dyads to optimize the potential for significant and meaningful correlations.

A Study of Infant–Caretaker Vocalization

In this study, conducted by the author, six infants and their primary caretakers were each observed monthly on seven consecutive occasions, a total of forty-two observations. The study sought to answer these questions:

1. What is the overall pattern of vocalization among the six infants in the sample and their primary caretakers?
2. Are there significant differences by age in the infants' use of various nonverbal vocal modes?
3. Are there significant differences in the caretakers' use of various vocal modes as the infants mature?
4. Are there significant correlations among the caretaker–infant pairs in the use of various vocal modes?

Method of the Study

Subjects. The sample consisted of six infants (four girls and two boys) and their mothers (primary caretakers) recruited through contacts made by the researcher. The contacts were made through an intermediary (a friend, relative, or work colleague) known to both the researcher and the parents. In five of the six cases, the researcher did not personally know the parents before the study began. In one case, the researcher and the parents had met once, about a year before the first home observation. In none of the cases had the infants been seen by the researcher before the beginning of the study.

All the families were intact, white, and middle-class; the infants were between six and twelve months of age.

Procedures. Seven visits were made to the home of each of the six infant-caretaker dyads. Observations were rescheduled if an infant was ill or if a mother reported any major departures from the daily routine.

Identical procedures were followed during each home visit. The observer arrived at the home at a time prearranged with the mother in order to increase the probability that the infant would be awake. An attempt was made, however, to schedule visits to sample different times of day in each home. Before the first observation, the researcher told the mother that he wanted to observe the infant for about one to two hours during a normal daily routine. The mother was also instructed to try to ignore the presence of the observer and to act in as customary a fashion as possible. After arriving at the home, the researcher talked briefly with the mother, asked about the infant's health, and again mentioned to the mother that he was there to observe the infant during a typical set of daily activities and that he would be following and observing the infant throughout the home.

To remain unobtrusive while recording, the observer stood or sat quietly at least five feet from the infant; did not move quickly when changing location or position; did not speak at, smile at, or otherwise interact with the infant; and, to the extent possible, did not interact with any of the other individuals in the environment. The observer was always in the presence of the infant, so if the mother left the infant and went into another room, the observer remained behind. After a fifty-minute observation period, the researcher talked freely with the mother, answered any questions she had, and also responded to any overtures made by the infant.

The study used a modified time-sampling method of observation with precoded observational categories. The observer recorded, at defined intervals, infant vocalization (crying, cooing, babbling, laughing, jargoning) directed at the primary caretaker, caretaker vocalization (prelinguistic sounds, laughter, words) directed at the infant, and infant–caretaker mutual vocalization. Each time-sampling cycle was sixty seconds long (marked by the sound of a timer in an inconspicuous earphone), during which time a decision was made as to the occurrence or nonoccurrence of infant vocalization at caretaker, caretaker vocalization at infant, or mutual vocalization, though observation was discontinued if the infant fell asleep. Observations were recorded on forms containing twenty-five vertical columns, each representing a sixty-second cycle. One complete observation form thus represented twenty-five minutes. One home observation covered two observational forms, or fifty minutes. In the complete study, a total of 2,100 sixty-second observational cycles were recorded (fifty observational cycles × seven home visits × six infant–caretaker dyads).

Interscorer Reliability. An important part of any time-sampling observational study is the establishment of interscorer reliability: Two observers must agree about the presence of a category of behavior in exactly the same observational cycle. To test interscorer reliability in this study, a second observer accompanied the primary researcher on four of the fifty-minute home visits, and the primary researcher and second observer sat within two feet of each other and recorded parallel but independent accounts of infant and caretaker vocalization. The passage of sixty-second observational cycles was monitored by the primary researcher, who alerted the second observer by a tap on the shoulder when it was time to move to a new observational cycle.

Interscorer reliability ratings, expressed as percentages of agreement between observers, were obtained by dividing the number of agreements (both observers recording the same behavior in the same cycle) by the number of agreements and disagreements (the observers recording a behavior differently). The formula was thus: number of agreements/(number of agreements + disagreements). The interscorer reliability percentages ranged between .78 and .92 for the various vocal modes observed.

Results of the Study

The mean number of observational cycles during which infants vocalized to their caretakers increased only slightly during the course of the six-month study. This increase was not statistically significant. Notwithstanding the relatively consistent pattern of overall vocalization by infants between ages six and twelve months, the specific vocal tools used by infants to initiate and maintain contact with their caretakers did change during this time period. The mean number of observational cycles during which the infants cried, for example, gradually decreased between six and twelve months, although this decrease did not prove to be statistically significant. Similarly, although the infants' use of laughter to initiate and maintain contact increased somewhat between six and twelve months, this change was not significant. Infant cooing, by comparison, occurred in 48 percent of the observation cycles at six months but by ten months had disappeared completely. The sharpest decline occurred between seven and eight months, a decrease that was statistically significant ($t = 4.62$, $df = 5$, $p < .002$). At the same time that the nonculturally specific sounds of cooing were making their sharpest decline in the infants' repertoire of nonverbal contact tools, the culturally specific sounds of babbling were being used with increasing frequency. A *t*-test comparison between the seven- and nine-month means revealed a significant increase in babbling during this two-month period ($t = 3.45$, $df = 5$, $p < .01$). Infant babbling continued to increase until the infants' eleventh month and then declined during the twelfth month. This decrease in infant babbling between the eleventh and twelfth months was statistically significant ($t = 2.83$, $df = 5$ $p < .05$). As babbling declined, a new vocal tool, nonverbal jargon, was rising rapidly, though by twelve months infants still used it less than babbling to initiate and maintain contact with their caretakers.

Nonverbal jargon was first used by one child at ten months and by two more at eleven months. The means during the tenth and eleventh months were so skewed, therefore, that *t*-tests to measure the significance of the change would have produced spurious results. For the same reason, the few words employed by three of the infants at eleven months and by two more of the infants at twelve months do not lend themselves to statistical analysis. The appearance of these tools, however, does mark the beginning of the children's use of verbal instruments to interact with the surrounding social world. The overall pattern of infant vocalization is depicted in figure 6-1.

There was little change in the mean number of observational cycles during which caretakers vocalized to their infants during the course of the six-month study. A *t*-test using the six- and twelve-month means revealed no statistically significant change during this period.

Three important vocal modes were used by caretakers to initiate and

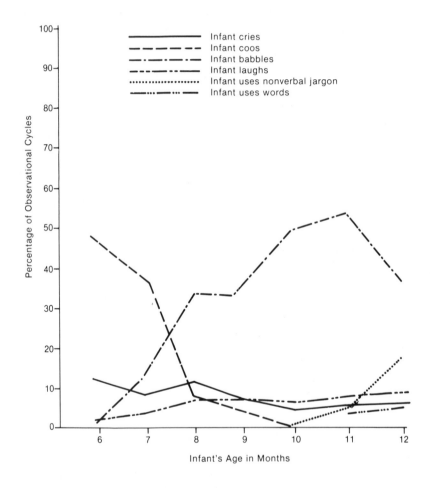

Figure 6-1. Infant Vocalization to Caretaker

maintain contact with their infants: prelinguistic sounds, laughter, and talk. The mean number of observational cycles during which the caretakers made prelinguistic cooing or babbling sounds to their infants remained relatively constant over the six-month period. A t-test using the six- and twelve-month means revealed no significant change in the caretakers' use of this option. Similarly, although the mean number of observational cycles during which the caretakers in the sample laughed at their infants increases slightly over the six-month period, this change was not significant. The caretakers in the sample talked to their infants during an average of 52 percent of the observational cycles when their children were six months of age, and this percentage never fluctuated more than six points either way during the next six months of the study. A t-test comparison of the six- and twelve-month means revealed no statistically significant change during this time period. The mother's use of vocalization is presented in figure 6–2.

To illuminate the pattern of infant–caretaker contact through the vocal mode, Pearson product-moment correlation coefficients were computed using the following paired variables: infant vocalizes to caretaker and caretaker vocalizes to infant; mutual vocalization and infant vocalizes to caretaker; and mutual vocalization and caretaker vocalizes to infant. Table 6–1 presents the correlation coefficients. All three correlations were positive, and two of the three were statistically significant. Infant vocalization to caretaker and caretaker vocalization to infant correlated moderately, though not to a statistically significant degree. The positive correlation between infant vocalization to caretaker and mutual vocalization, however, was statistically significant ($r = .75$, $p < .05$). Caretaker vocalization to the infant also correlated significantly with mutual vocalization ($r = .74$, $p < .05$). These findings indicate that infant-caretaker pairs in which each partner frequently independently vocalizes to the other also tend to engage frequently in mutual vocalization. Only a moderate covariance, however, exists between independent vocalization by a caretaker and independent vocalization by an infant.

An additional fifteen Pearson product-moment correlation coefficients were computed using various pairs of specific vocal instruments used by the infants and caretakers in the sample to initiate and maintain contact. Table 6–2 reveals three positive signficant correlations: between infant cooing and caretaker making prelinguistic sounds ($r = .72$, p $< .05$), between infant laughing and caretaker laughing ($r = .87$, $p < .05$), and between infant using jargon and caretaker making prelinguistic sounds ($r = .76$, $p < .05$). These findings indicate substantial covariance in the nonverbal vocal mode: caretakers who frequently use prelinguistic sounds to initiate and maintain contact with their infants have children who likewise frequently use the nonverbal vocal tools of cooing and jargon to interact with their caretakers. Moderately high, though not significant, positive correlations were found

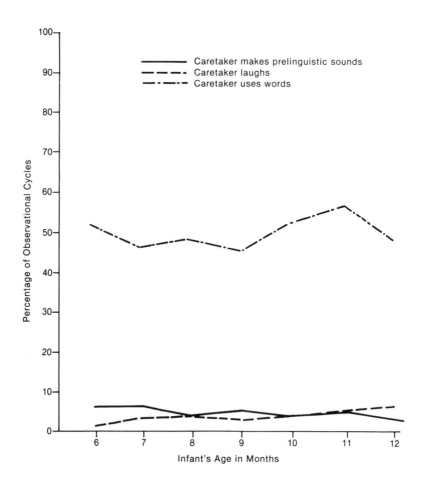

Figure 6-2. Caretaker's Vocalization to Infant

between infant babbling and caretaker prelinguistic vocalizing and between infant "jargoning" and caretaker speaking. Additionally, caretaker laughing negatively correlated with infant crying, though this correlation was not statistically significant. This negative correlation, in conjunction with the significant positive correlation between caretaker and infant laughing, indicates that caretakers who frequently initiate and maintain contact by laughing have infants who also frequently laugh and who seldom cry.

Table 6-1
Correlations between Infant and Caretaker Vocalizing

	Caretaker Vocalizes to Infant	Mutual Vocalizing
Infant vocalizes to caretaker	.47	.75[a]
Mutual vocalizing	.74[a]	—

[a]$p < .05$, one-tailed test.

Table 6-2
Correlations between Infant and Caretaker Vocal Communicative Instruments

	Caretaker		
Infant	Uses Prelinguistic Sounds	Laughs	Uses Words
Cries	− .06	− .63	− .26
Coos	.72[a]	.30	− .20
Babbles	.69	.19	.31
Laughs	.01	.87[a]	.27
Jargon	.76[a]	.23	.45

Note: N = 6 pairs
[a]$p < .05$, one-tailed test.

Discussion of the Study

Considerable individual differences among infants existed in the use of various vocal options to initiate and maintain contact with caretakers. Even so, however, many significant group patterns did emerge. The infants' uses of nonculturally specific cooing sounds for contact with their caretakers, for example, underwent a statistically significant decrease between the time the infants were seven and eight months of age, at the same time that the infants' uses of culturally specific babbling sounds to interact with caretakers was undergoing its most significant increase. Likewise, infant babbling significantly declined (between the infants' eleventh and twelfth months) just as a new vocal contact option, jargon, was making its appearance and some of the infants were using their first words. By comparison, the caretakers' uses of various vocal choices (prelinguistic sounds, laughter, words) to initiate and maintain contact with their infants remained quite constant throughout the study, as none of the mothers' vocal tools used for this end underwent any significant increase or decrease. Correlational analyses revealed significant covariance between the following pairs of infant–caretaker vocal instruments: infant's cooing and caretaker's use of prelinguistic sounds, infant's laughing and caretaker's laughing, and infant's jargoning and caretaker's use of prelinguistic sounds. Moderately high, though not significant, covariance also was found between infant's babbling and caretaker's use of prelinguistic sounds, and between infant's jargoning and caretaker's use of words. This pattern of shared variance denotes that caretakers who frequently use their vocal tools for contact have infants who reciprocate more frequently than do caretakers who less frequently employ their vocal tools for this end.

The findings in this study are consistent with previous research regarding infant–caretaker vocalization patterns. Laboratory research by Rheingold, Gewirtz, and Ross (1959); Weisberg (1967); and Anderson and Vietze (1977), and a home-based study by Yarrow, Rubenstein, and Pedersen (1975) revealed positive correlations between caretaker and infant vocalization. All of these studies, however, involved infants under six months of age. The present study indicates that the shared variance between the caretaker's use of the vocal mode and its employment by the infant exists during the second half of the first year as well. This study also revealed, however, that within the overall category of vocalization, certain options used by caretakers covary with the choices made by their infants, but others do not. Previous research has not detailed these various options nor looked at their possible correlations with the same specificity as the present study. The significant positive correlations found in this study between infant and caretaker laughing, for example, provides evidence of communicative interaction through an important channel not previously examined.

This study of infant–caretaker communicative interaction was in certain respects limited. First, six months is a relatively short period for a longitudinal study. To a one-year-old infant, however, six months is half a lifetime. Moreover, the numerous significant changes in the communicative interaction between infants and caretakers and the development of communication modes in infants during this period of time adds validity to the longitudinal claims made for this study. A longer study, in which observations are spaced across greater time intervals, should be conducted, however, to describe more fully the developmental changes that occur in infant–caretaker interaction.

A second limitation of this study is the small size of the sample and the degree of causality that can thus be inferred from correlational analyses; in this case, the degree to which the caretaker's choice of communication modes influenced the child's development of these same options. In a strict sense, of course, a direct causal relationship can never be posited from a correlation, and although the covariance found between many measures in this study suggests the powerful role of the caretaker in influencing the infant's choice of communication options, this statistical utilization of observational data does not permit inference of a causal relationship with the same level of confidence as might multivariate techniques and a greater number of infants and caretakers. Future research using a much larger sample, for instance, could employ stepwise multiple regression analysis to determine whether statistically significant interactions occur among *combinations* of communication instruments used by infant–caretaker dyads. Ultimately, statistical procedures are needed that are capable of handling many variables that interact with each other in many complex ways.

A third limitation is that the data in this study were derived from only intact middle-class families. Generalizations to other groups, therefore, can only be made with extreme caution. This study has provided, however, a body of longitudinal data that can be used comparatively with data obtained from children of the same age but from different social or cultural groups and with data gathered from children who posses one or more communication handicaps. The data gathered in the current study can also be used as a foundation for research in which important variables such as sex or birth order are held constant as well as in cross-sectional studies of older and younger children.

Several methodological implications can also be derived from this study. In the field of special education, for example, the need for analytical systems to identify the strengths and weaknesses of handicapped children is underscored by both federal legislation (Education for All Handicapped Children Act of 1975, Public Law 94–142) and state legislation (California's AB 1250). These laws mandate that educators at every level must become more sensitive to the various communication strategies used by handicapped children and must develop ways for integrating handicapped children into the "least restrictive" educational environments to the "maximum extent" possible. The methodology used in this study can help practitioners describe, diagnose, and provide remediation for infants and young children with special needs. The system can be employed to identify, through rigorous empirical analysis, a handicapped child's communication instruments and the functions those tools serve; to document and compare the relative frequencies of various instruments and functions among normal and handicapped populations; and to assess any interpopulation and intrapopulation differences in communicative modes and their uses. Thus, the system can help educators better understand differences among infants and young children with the same or different handicaps. By analyzing the various verbal and nonverbal instruments chosen by handicapped children, profiles of individual children can be more accurate. These profiles can then be used to create optimal environments for handicapped children and thus enhance their opportunities and prospects for the future.

The methodology is also of value in studying how individual communication patterns develop and how they are influenced by the surrounding world. The observational grid can be employed, for example, for a better understanding of how parents' uses of communication options are intimately linked to the development of communication modes in their children. The system can be used to create comprehensive individual profiles of infants from different families or from the same family by distinguishing those tools that are unique to the child and those that are more reflective of patterns of communication within the family.

Although experimental methodology and the methodology employed in this study are quite different, the two are not necessarily incompatible. Data gathered in the natural environment of the home and community can be used as a basis for generating hypotheses that may be tested in more controlled experimental settings. The approach used in this study is of value, for example, in supplying researchers with categories of naturally occurring communication options, the context and conditions under which these modes are normally used, and the preferences of individuals from a specific social or cultural group. Knowledge of this repertoire of instruments provides a background against which the use of communication choices under experimental conditions can be evaluated. The laboratory, by comparison, is an important diagnostic tool, and has considerable value for testing theoretical models, and for conducting research when intervening variables need to be controlled. Causal hypotheses thus could be tested by employing a combination of experimental methodology and the methodology described in this study with infants in settings such as foster homes, hospitals, and infant-care centers. The researcher could, for example, use the observational grid to discover if the rate of vocalizing among infants can be significantly increased by having the substitute caretakers markedly increase the use of these communication options while interacting with the children.

In summary, the approach employed in this study can make a valuable contribution to research regarding infant–caretaker patterns of interaction. First, it offers a system of analysis that facilitates the identification, description, and organization of the options used by infants and adults as they interact in natural settings, and examines the functions of those instruments in the life of the developing child. Second, it is an adaptable system because it does not assume a priori the type of infant–caretaker interaction that should be taking place and thus facilitates the construction of new observational categories and the refinement of old ones. Third, it is an accessible system that can be employed by educators, students of child development, parents, and others without special research facilities or extensive training. Fourth, it facilitates the understanding of the ontogeny of individual communication patterns, which can be the basis for the creation of comprehensive individual profiles.

Studies of early vocal interaction between infants and adults strongly suggest the antecedents of the reciprocal pattern of vocal interaction that characterizes adult conversation. Preverbal dialogues between infants and adults are distinguished by some of the same characteristics that are found in later communication situations involving speech. One of the most important of these characteristics is the exchange of speaking turns that normally occurs in conversation. The prototype for this exchange of turns may, according to Bruner (1975, 1977), be learned in infancy as the infant exchanges vocalizations with the adult in his or her environment. Through mutual vocalization, Bruner contends, the infant learns to take turns in vocal exchanges and to read another person's signals regarding the beginnings and ends of turns. Turn-taking is thus one aspect of the rich exchange that occurs between infants and adults as the framework for further communication development is established.

The vocalization that occurs between preverbal infants and their caretakers is thus a prototype for later linguistic interaction. Mutual vocalization engaged in by child and parent involves a to-and-fro dialogue and, although it may be nonverbal in nature, provides the infant with an opportunity to exchange social meanings with an adult while learning the most effective means of bringing about such exchanges. Before infants speak their first meaningful words they possess sophisticated vocalization patterns. The development of language in the second and third years of life is related to the infant's ability to participate in sequences of interaction in the course of the first year. Through this participation the infant learns to achieve such ends as contact, expression, and play—ends that will later be served by language.

References

Ambrose, J.A. The age of onset of ambivalence in early infancy: indications from the study of laughing. *Journal of Child Psychology and Psychiatry* 4:167–187, 1963.

Anderson, B.J. and Vietze, P.M. Early dialogues: the structure of reciprocal infant-mother vocalization. In *Child development: contemporary perspectives,* ed. S. Cohen and T.J. Comiskey. Itasca, Ill.: Peacock, 1977.

Ban, P.L., and Lewis, M. Mothers and fathers, girls and boys: attachment behavior in the one-year old. *Merrill-Palmer Quarterly* 20:195–204, 1974.

Bell, S.M. and Ainsworth, M.D. Infant crying and maternal responsiveness. *Child Development* 43:1171–1190, 1972.

Bowlby, J. *Attachment and loss,* vol. 1. London: Hogarth, 1969.

Bowlby, J. The nature of the child's tie to his mother. *International Journal of Psychoanalysis* 39:350–373, 1958.

Brazelton, T.B., Koslowski, B.; and Main, M. The origins of reciprocity: the early mother-infant interaction. In *The effect of the infant on its caregiver,* ed. M. Lewis and L.A. Rosenblum. New York: Wiley, 1974.

Bruner, J. The ontogenesis of speech acts. *Journal of Child Language* 2:1–19, 1975.

Bruner, J. Early social interaction and language acquisition. In *Studies in mother-infant interaction,* ed. H. R. Schaffer. London, Academic Press, 1977.

Bzoch, K.R., and League, R. *Assessing language skills in infancy: a handbook for the multidimensional analysis of emergent language.* Gainesville, Fla.: Tree of Life Press, 1971.

Caudill, W., and Weinstein, H. Maternal care and infant behavior in Japanese and American urban middle-class families. In *Families in East and West: socialization process and kinship ties.,* ed. R. Hill and R. Konig. The Hague: Mouton, 1970.

Caudill, W., and Weinstein, H. Maternal care and infant behavior in Japan and America. In *Readings in child behavior and development,* ed. C. Lavatelli and F. Stendler. New York: Harcourt and Brace, 1972.

Clarke-Stewart, K.A. Interactions between mothers and their young children: characteristics and consequences. *Monographs of the Society for Research in Child Development* 38: serial no. 153, 1973.

Dale, P. *Language development: structure and function:* New York: Holt, 1976.

Dennis, W. *Children of the creche.* New York: Meredith, 1973.

Dore, J. Holophrases, speech acts and language universals. *Journal of Child Language* 2:21–40, 1975.

Feldman, S.S., and Ingham, M.E. Attachment behavior: a validation study in two age groups. *Child Development* 46:319–330, 1975.

Gesell, A., and Amatruda, C. *Developmental diagnosis.* New York: Harper, 1947.

Goldberg, S., and Lewis, M. Play behavior in the year-old infant: early sex differences. *Child Development* 40:21–31, 1969.

Halliday, M.A.K. *Learning how to mean.* London: Arnold, 1975.

Halliday, M.A.K. Meaning and the construction of reality in early childhood. In *Modes of perceiving and processing information,* ed. H. Pick and E. Saltzman. Hillsdale, N.J.: Lawrence Erlbaum, 1978.

Kagan, J. *Change and continuity in infancy.* New York: Wiley, 1971.

Kagan, J., Kearsley, R.B., and Zelazo, P.R. *Infancy: its place in human development.* Cambridge: Harvard University Press, 1978.

Lamb, M.E. Interactions between eight-month-old children and their fathers and mothers. In *The role of the father in child development,* ed. M.E. Lamb. New York: Wiley, 1976.

Leitch, S. *A child learns to speak: a guide for parents and teachers of preschool children.* Springfield, Ill.: Thomas, 1977.

Lenneberg, E. *The biological foundations of language.* New York: Wiley, 1967.

Lewis, M. State as an infant-environment interaction: an analysis of mother-infant interaction as a function of sex. *Merrill-Palmer Quarterly* 18:95–121, 1972.

Lewis, M., and Freedle, R. Mother-infant dyad: the cradle of meaning. In *Communication and affect: language and thought,* ed. P. Pliner, L. Krames, and T. Alloway. New York: Academic Press, 1973.

Newson, J., and Newson, E. On the social origins of symbolic functioning. In *Piaget, psychology, and education,* ed. P. Varma and P. Williams. London: Hodder and Stoughton, 1976.

Ninio, A., and Bruner, J. The achievement and antecedents of labelling. *Journal of Child Language* 5:1–15, 1978.

Oller, D. Infant babbling and speech. *Journal of Child Language* 3(1):1–11, 1976.

Papousek, H., and Papousek, M. Mothering and the cognitive Head-start: psychobiological considerations. In *Studies in mother-infant interaction,* ed. H.R. Schaffer. London: Academic Press, 1977.

Rebelsky, F.G.; Starr, R.H.; and Luria, Z. Language development: the first four years. In *Infancy and early childhood,* ed. Y. Brackbill. New York: Free Press, 1967.

Rheingold, H.L.; Gewirtz, J.L.; and Ross, H.W. Social conditioning of vocalization in the infant. *Journal of Comparative and Physiological Psychology* 52:68–73, 1959.

Skeels, H.M. Adult status of children with contrasting early life experiences: a follow-up study. *Monographs of the Society for Research in Child Development* 31, serial No. 105, 1966.

Smart, M.S., and Smart, R.C. *Infants: development and relationships.* New York: Macmillan, 1973.

Smith, H.L. Language and the total system of communication. In *Linguistics today,* ed. A. Hill. New York: Basic Books, 1969.

Spitz, R. Hospitalism: an inquiry into the genetics of psychiatric conditions in early childhood. *Psychoanalytic Study of the Child* 1:53–74, 1945.

Sroufe, L.A. and Waters, E. The ontogenesis of smiling and laughter: a perspective on the organization of development in infancy. *Psychological Review* 3:173–188, 1976.

Sroufe, L.A., and Wunsch, J.P. The development of laughter in the first year of life. *Child Development* 43:1326–1344, 1972.

Stark, R.; Rose, S.; and McLagen, M. Features of infant sounds: the first eight weeks of life. *Journal of Child Language* 2:205–221, 1975.

Stern, D.N.; Jaffe, J.; Beebe, B.; and Bennett, S.L. Vocalizing in unison and in alternation: two modes of communication within the mother-infant dyad. *Annals of the New York Academy of Sciences* 263:89–100, 1975.

Trager, G.L. Paralanguage: a first approximation. In *Language in culture and society: a reader in linguistics and anthropology,* ed. D. Hymes. New York: Harper and Row, 1964.

Tulkin, S., and Covitz, R. Mother-infant interaction and intellectual functioning at age-six. *Educational Resources Information Center,* ED 111 514, 1976.

Tulkin, S., and Kagan, J. Mother-child interaction in the first year of life. *Child Development* 43:31–41, 1972.

Vietze, P.M.; Strain, B.A.; and Falsey, S. Contingent responsiveness between mother and infant. In *Child development: contemporary perspectives,* ed. S. Cohen and T.J. Comiskey. Itasca, Ill.: Peacock, 1975.

Washburn, R.W. A study of the smiling and laughing of infants in the first year of life. *Genetic Psychology Monographs* 6:396–537, 1929.

Weisberg, P. Social and non-social conditioning of infant vocalizations. In *Behavior in infancy and early childhood,* ed. Y. Brackbill and G. Thompson. Glencoe, Ill.: Free Press, 1967.

White, B. *The first three years of life.* New York: Prentice-Hall, 1975.

Will, J.; Self, P.; and Datan, N. Maternal behavior and perceived sex of infant. *American Journal of Orthopsychiatry* 46:135–139, 1976.

Wolff, P.H. Crying and vocalization in early infancy. In *Determinants of infant behavior* IV, ed. B.M. Foss. London: Methuen, 1969.

Wolff, P.H. Observations on the early development of smiling. In *Determinants of infant behavior* II, ed. B.M. Foss. London: Methuen, 1963.

Yarrow, L.; Rubenstein, J.; and Pedersen, F. *Infant and environment: Early cognitive and motivational development.* New York: Wiley, 1975.

7

Quality of Care Received by Infants in Community Group-Care Centers

Sylvia Ann White

During the 1970s, group daytime care for infants grew from experimental, model programs in university settings to a common service for parents in both public and private child-care programs. With this growth of group day care has come concern by parents and professionals about their effect on the development of infants.

In the early 1960s, Provence and Lipton (1962) published a report based on a five-year research study of institutionalized infants. Their report showed clearly that children in institutions are affected adversely under certain conditions of inadequate mothering. These researchers emphasized that it is difficult or impossible to adequately meet the multiple and complex needs of infants under conditions of group care.

The needs of infants in the 1980s and 1990s are still, and will continue to be, multiple and complex. Although residential group care of infants is virtually nonexistent today, increasing numbers of infants are being cared for in group-care programs ten or more hours a day while their parents are working or in school. As a result of their study, Provence and Lipton urged professionals to help infant care givers understand what is involved in the process of development and how the care environment influences this process. This continues to be a crucial task for professionals today as they themselves pursue the study of the intricate and complex process of development and how it is affected by early experiences in infancy.

In the past ten years research has attempted to measure and study the effect on infants of long hours in group day-care programs. Previous research on institutionalized children spurred concern that separation of the child from his mother would impair the development of infant–mother attachment and thus adversely affect the child's emotional development. In a critical review of the day-care research, Belsky and Steinberg (1978) noted that ". . . . experience in high-quality center-based day care . . . is not disruptive of the child's emotional bond with his mother" (p. 929). However, as the authors noted, the majority of studies conducted were in university-based day care, not representative of the day-care environments of most infant group-care programs.

111

In the first published study of the effects of group day care, Caldwell, Wright, Honig, and Tannenbaum (1970) reported their systematic, empirical research with infants cared for in the Syracuse University Children's Center. They found no differences between the center children and home-reared children at thirty months of age in relationship to their mothers or in their affiliation, nurturance, hostility, happiness, or emotionality. Ricciuti (1974) studied infants attending the Cornell Experimental Nursery and found the relationship the infants formed with their care givers did not replace or supersede the child's emotional bond with its mother. Ferran and Ramey (1977) studied black infants of a low socioeconomic class attending the Frank Porter Graham Child Development Center at the University of North Carolina. These infants preferred to be near and to interact with their mothers rather than their center care giver, and favored the former over the latter when they needed help with a mildly difficult problem. Kagan, Kearsley, and Zelazo (1977) studied Chinese and Caucasion infants who attended a Harvard research-administered day-care center. Data gathered when the children were twenty and twenty-nine months revealed little difference between day care and home-reared children in cognitive functioning, language, attachment, separation protest, and play tempo. The high standards, dedication and training of workers, and high adult-to-child ratios in these programs are not often available in the public and private community programs in which many infants are placed. Few studies have evaluated the impact upon infants of typical day-care programs within a community. Little is known about which aspects of a group-care program may adversely or positively affect the development of infants.

Experimental day care researchers suggest that staff-child ratio is extremely important for children, especially those under three years of age in full day-care programs. The Syracuse program had a ratio of 1:4, one adult to four children (Caldwell et al. 1970); the Ferran and Ramey study (1977) reported a 1:3 ratio for infants and 1:4 for toddlers and the Kagan et al. study (1977) reported a high adult-to-child ratio "... not representative of typical infant day care in the United States" (p. 117). The proposed Federal Interagency Day Care Staffing Requirements for infants and toddlers is 1:5 (U.S. Department of Health, Education, and Welfare 1970). For many reasons, including objections by large numbers of center administrators to the cost of providing such a high ratio, these regulations are not, and probably will not be, put into effect. Many infants are being cared for in programs with ratios much lower than in the university based centers where most of the day-care research has occurred.

The Importance of Feeding in Infant Care

Many studies which have examined the affective behavior of a mother toward her infant have rated the mother's behavior in the feeding situation

(Hock 1980; Vaughn, Taraldson, Crichton, and Egeland 1980). Characteristics evidenced during feeding are seen as predictive of interaction seen in other settings.

Freud and Erikson have theorized about the significance of feeding in an infant's early emotional development. Provence and Lipton (1962) provided detailed descriptions of the feeding experience of the institutionalized infants they studied. During the first year of life, feeding is a biologically and psychologically crucial experience around which there are many communications between mother and baby. These researchers felt that this experience represented a major difference in the lives of institutionalized infants compared with family-reared infants.

Ainsworth and Bell (1969) found feeding to be an important index of the mother's relationship with her infant. During observation in the home, these researchers rated mothers on the dimensions of timing of feeding in accordance with baby's rhythms, determination of amount of food and the end of the feeding, handling of the baby's preferences in food, and synchronization of the mother's rate of feeding to the baby's pace of intake. Ainsworth and Bell found it important that the feeding satisfy the infant, regulate his rhythm, and allow him to partake actively in the meal, instead of accepting it passively. Mothers of infants later rated as securely attached were found to feed their babies in manners which allowed for these conditions and thus led to harmonious interaction between mother and infant. The researchers hypothesized that the mother's favorable response to the various signals, actions, and communications of the infant permit him to have confidence in his capacity for influencing the events happening to him, and this sensation of effectiveness leads to a feeling of competence.

Brody (1956) gave support to feeding as the most central activity through which to observe the mother's handling of the infant. The activities of feeding, cleaning, moving, touching, offering objects, and speaking were found by Brody to exemplify the range of behavior observed in thirty-two mothers of infants. Of these observed behaviors, feeding was the behavior most often accompanied by one or more of the other five behaviors.

Brody and Axelrad (1970) conducted a research project to replicate Brody's 1956 study with a larger sample and a longitudinal design. Their study of 122 infant–mother pairs began with prenatal interviews of the mothers and continued through observations of the mothers and infants when the infants were thirty-two weeks old. Data were gathered through interviews with the mothers and through 2½- to 4½-hour observations of the mothers with their infants which included filming the mother feeding the infant. Seven types of maternal behaviors were indentified using a statistical analysis of the ratings of the mothers' handling and feeding of their infants. Each of three qualities, empathy, control, and efficiency, was rated on a five-point scale. The ratings of these qualitative variables correspond, to some degree, to the five rating points of Brody's 1956 General Scale of Maternal Response (Brody and Axelrad 1970). Brody devised the original scale in order to measure the sensitivity with which a mother responded to the needs or wishes of her infant. The scale is based on a continuum of maternal behavior which ranges from maternal passivity to hyperactivity, or from meeting the infant's needs because they cannot be ignored to behavior that is a response to the mother's own needs or wishes (Brody 1956, p. 244).

The General Scale of Maternal Response consists of five positions. The midpoint of the scale represents behavior of the mother or care giver which best accommodates to the infant due to her awareness of the infant's affective state. At both extremes of the scale, positions 1 and 5 would show that a serious lack of harmony existed in the interaction between the mother and her infant (Brody 1956, pp. 244–245). This continuum of care is illustrated in table 7–1.

The descriptions of each scale position are as follows: The mother, or care giver:

1. Answers the infant's needs after delay, or reluctantly, or perfunctorily.
2. Adequately does what is logically acceptable or desirable, in a neutral manner or without particular regard for the infant's affective state.
3. Accommodates to the infant smoothly and effectively, in response to minimal cues from him and as a result of her own steady awareness of his affective state.
4. Mildly stimulates or restricts the infant in keeping with her own tension, concern, or educative demand.
5. Controls or dominates the infant against his inclinations or disrupts his activity or condition.

An Investigation of the Quality of Infant Care

In an investigation of infant–mother attachment and two measures of care received by infants in group day-care programs, White (1975) rated the care

Table 7–1
Continuum of Care from the General Scale of Maternal Response

Scale Positions and Abbreviated Descriptions of Care				
1	2	3	4	5
Delayed, reluctant, or perfunctory care	Adequate care given in neutral manner	Accommodates to infant smoothly	Mildly controls infant for own needs	Controlling, dominating, or disrupting care

Source: Adapted from S. Brody, *Patterns of Mothering* (New York: International Universities Press, 1956).

giver's sensitivity of response to fourteen middle-class Caucasian infants in feeding episodes using the General Scale of Maternal Response. Observations took place in seven infant care centers whose directors agreed to cooperate with the researchers for purposes of the study. The centers that participated were a representative sample of day nurseries for middle-class working families in a large southern city. A large proportion of the more expensive centers in the city were in this group because directors of these programs seemed most willing to cooperate with research studies.

The participating centers included those which were corporation-owned, church-sponsored, and privately owned and operated. One program was operated by a director with a background in early childhood education. The principal care giver in this infant program had been trained by the director in methods of caring for and interacting with infants and had been sent by the program to several workshops for day-care workers. The directors of five other centers in the study had some college work in early childhood education or child development. The care givers were mostly untrained for their child-care jobs, except for experience in rearing their own children. The centers, with few exceptions, seemed to provide routine custodial care to the infants.

The written descriptions of the care giver's and infant's behavior in each feeding observation were studied and a rating was given to the care giver for her sensitivity of response to the infant. For purposes of statistical analysis, some of the rating scales were combined. Scale positions 1 and 5 were given a weight of 1. These positions are at opposite ends of the continuum and represent the care giver's behavior that is least a result of awareness of the infant's affective state. Scale positions of 2 and 4, equally distant from the midpoint of the continuum, were given a weight of 2. Scale position 3, the midpoint on the scale, was given a weight of 3 and was the highest rating a care giver could receive. The care giver's rating for each feeding episode was converted to the correct statistical weight and the mean statistical weight was calculated. Five rating groups were determined: 3.0, 2.0, 1.7, 1.3, and 1.0. The mean statistical rating of the care giver's ratings was 1.71. (See table 7-1 for an illustration of the continuum of the care giver's behavior.) A rating of 1.71, and its counterpoint, 4.29, would fall two-thirds of the way between the optimal rating of 3 and the most insensitive ratings of 1 and 5.

Three care giver-to-child ratio counts were made at the centers, and the mean number of infants and children per care giver was computed for each infant subject. The range of ratios was 1:3.5 to 1:9.5 with a mean ratio of 1:6.3 (table 7-2). Most of the centers in this study were providing care that was not of the high standards of the university-based centers in other studies. Five or more infants were under the care of each adult in all but two of these seven centers. One of those two centers had a higher care giver-to-child ratio (1:3.7) only during feeding time when an extra aide was available. Only Center 1 provided care in which the care givers were rated as

Table 7-2
Mean Care Giver-to-Child Ratios and Care Giver's Sensitivity of Response Ratings for Care Givers Attending Fourteen Infants in Seven Day-Care Programs

Day-Care Center	Mean Care Giver-to-Child Ratio	Mean Care Giver's Sensitivity of Response Rating	Infant
1	1:3.5	3.0	F (female)
1	1:4.2	3.0	L (male)
2	1:3.7	1.0	B (female)
3	1:5.4	1.0	H (male)
3	1:5.5	1.3	J (male)
4	1:5.0	2.0	E (male)
4	1:6.5	1.0	C (female)
4	1:6.5	2.0	K (female)
4	1:6.7	1.7	I (male)
5	1:7.3	2.0	A (male)
6	1:7.3	2.0	D (female)
7	1:8.7	1.3	G (male)
7	1:9.0	1.0	N (female)
7	1:9.5	1.0	M (female)

accommodating to the infant's affective state, and in which the adult-to-child ratio was 1:4 or higher. This center was the only one in which the one-year-olds were allowed to feed themselves and in which infants were regularly held while being given their bottles, although young infants were sometimes held in Center 3. Two infants in this investigation attended Center 1. The other twelve infants received care rated as being given in a neutral manner; or in a reluctant perfunctory manner; or care that was controlling and dominating. Most of the feeding episodes observed were rushed—half were finished in three or four minutes. Mealtime was largely something to get over in a hurry, with as little mess and interaction as possible.

The investigator spent many hours in these centers, doing preliminary general observations, rating the feeding episodes, and administering Gesell Developmental Schedules. The care received by the infants during the feeding episodes was typical of the care observed being given to infants of all ages and at all times in these centers. It can be assumed that it was representative of the care these fourteen infants had been receiving during the six or more months they had been in the centers.

Descriptions of Feeding Episodes

Provence and Lipton (1962) observed infants cared for in residential institutions in mid-twentieth-century America. According to their descriptions of the feeding episodes, the youngest infants were fed on a regular schedule—every four hours. Older infants were fed according to the institution's routines rather than their own individual needs. When their food was ready, crying infants were usually the first ones to be fed; sleeping infants were awakened to be fed. Before the feeding, an infant was diapered and then returned to his crib. He would be placed on his side with a blanket rolled against his back to keep him in place. The bottle was supported by a pillow and the nipple placed in the infant's mouth. If he lost the nipple, he could not continue feeding until the attendant discovered his dilemma and reinserted the nipple. This depended on her watchfulness or on the baby crying loudly and long enough to attract her attention. Usually there was a delay before the nipple was returned (pp. 31–32).

In White's (1975) observations of infants in community group day-care programs, staff held infants for bottle feedings in only one of the centers in the study. The year-old subjects observed were typically fed on a set schedule and then were given bottles at the same time and expected to nap all at the same time. Some infants had their naptime delayed for the convenience of the care giver. The following observational record involving Infant C is illustrative.

At the conclusion of the feeding episode, the care giver picks up forty-four-week-old C, holds her over her shoulder, and rocks in the chair a moment, talking affectionately in baby talk. Then she stands up, walks into the crib room and puts C down. C lies on the floor and closes her eyes. The caretaker yanks her up by the arm and says firmly, "That's a no-no!" The care giver managed to keep C awake another thirty minutes until all seven infants had been fed, at which time each infant was put into a crib and handed a bottle. The care giver then went into an adjoining room and the babies were left to fall asleep alone. C went to sleep almost immediately after being put into her crib.

Other infants observed by White were not ready for sleep at naptime, as exemplified by sixty-week-old N.

N is sitting in her bed crying. Now she lies down and whimpers. The care giver brings N her bottle, hands it to her and says, "Go to sleep." N sits up and takes her bottle. She lies down and holds it but doesn't suck on it. She stands up and sucks on it. Then she lies down on her side and takes the bottle with both hands. N does not suck vigorously; she plays with it, putting the nipple into her mouth, removing it, looking at the bottle, and reinserting the nipple.

N plays with her bottle, mostly chewing on the nipple. Now she sits up and bites hard on the nipple. A caretaker calls to her from across the room, "Lie down, N." The care giver comes over and lays her down. Now one care giver goes for her lunch break, leaving only one care giver for the twenty infants in the forty-five minutes. Two other babies are crying. The care giver is straigtening equipment on the side counter. N is sitting in the corner of her crib. She chews and fingers the nipple. The care giver calls out loudly for another baby to lie down. N bends down from her sitting position and lays her head on the mattress, then pops right up again. N jargons loudly now from the corner of her crib where she is sitting. She has bitten off the top of the nipple. She picks up the piece and tries to fit it back on. Now she turns the bottle upside down and shakes it, pouring milk all over herself and the crib. She cries out, "Mommy!" There is no response from the care giver. N whimpers and stands up. She is standing in the center of the crib, fingering the nipple. Now she sits down. The care giver calls out to another baby, "Lie down!" N freezes and watches. The care giver doesn't observe her. Now N starts to cry. The care giver approaches her, asking, "What's the matter with you?" She discovers the hole in the nipple. "I know what's the matter with you," she exclaims. "You don't get another bottle." The care giver removes the bottle, puts N on the floor, and changes the sheet. Then she calls, "Com're, N." N walks over, the care giver picks her up by one arm, lays her down in the crib, saying, "Now you go to sleep," and spanks her leg. The care giver goes back to her chair and sits reading a book, with her back to the babies.

The older institutionalized infants observed by Provence and Lipton (1962) were fed in their cribs. Until they were about eighteen months old, they lay on their backs while being fed. After about eighteen months, the babies sat in a corner of their crib for their feeding. Attendants sat or stood close to the babies and held the bowl close to the infant's face. The food was spooned quickly and efficiently into the baby's mouth. During the feeding process, the infants watched the attendant's face attentively but remained inactive. The babies were not actively restrained, but attendants discouraged any movements by words, tone of voice, and facial expression. The infants made almost no attempts to touch the spoon, bowl, or attendant. During a feeding process, attendants often talked to each other, but seldom engaged in social interaction with the infants. They were generally pleasant in the their administrations to the infants before and after feeding, however. Infant-care staff seemed to believe that social interaction during feeding would prolong the feeding time by exciting the babies and thus make them uncooperative.

In group day-care programs, White (1975) observed several infants who were fed while lying on their backs in the caregiver's lap. On the day that the following observation was made, twenty babies, aged ten to twenty-two months, were being cared for by two adults. The subject, G, was fifty-four weeks old.

The care giver calls, "Okay, Mr. G, come here." With a big smile, G walks over to where she is standing by the diapering counter. She picks him up by lifting him under his arms, swings him up, and lays him on the counter, smiling briefly. His diapers are dry, so she sits in the chair, lays him down in her lap, and picks up the dish of food. G is reclining against her arm, almost lying down. His right arm is wedged against her body, and she holds his left arm against his side with her other arm, in which she holds the bowl. The bowl contains about a quarter of a cup each of strained vegetables with bacon, and of applesauce; each is kept more or less separate in the feeding bowl. The vegetables are fed first. A regular teaspoon is used for feeding. The food on the outside of his mouth is wiped away with the spoon between each bite. G swings his feet slightly. The care giver puts her hand on them and says, "Don't!" No other word is spoken to G during the feeding episode, which lasts about four minutes. When the last bite has been fed to G, the care giver exclaims, "All done!" She gives him a hug and puts him down on the floor. He smiles and walks off. She stands to put the empty dish on the tray and then gets another baby.

In another center, this observation was made of a forty-seven week old male in a room in which the care giver-to-child ratio was 1:5.

The care giver sits in a rocking chair and holds E on her lap in a reclining position. She holds his far arm, and the other one is squeezed next to her. The care giver gives him a bite, rhetorically asking, "Is it good?" and smiles at him. She cleans his mouth with the spoon after each bite. He is fed strained baby food and each food item is in a separate dish. E looks toward the dishes occasionally, but mostly gazes at the ceiling. He leans up once to look at the observer. The care giver again asks him, "Is it good?" He babbles, "Da!" There is not further comment from her. She is engaged in the work of scraping the last bite out of the bowl. She feeds him rapidly and is concerned with keeping his mouth clean and holding his wrist so he won't grab the spoon. The care giver moves her supporting arm so that he is reclining even more. She looks intently at the bowl of food and is engrossed with the process of getting food into his mouth. Now he is lying almost completely flat on his back. She wipes his mouth when he has been fed the last bite and then sits him up. She talks with him and smiles; making faces at him and clicks her tongue. Then she carries him to his crib and leaves him there while she tends to feeding the other babies.

Other twelve-month-old infants observed by White (1975) were fed in one center while standing or sitting in their cribs, in another center while sitting on top of a table or counter, and in two centers while sitting on the floor in front of the care giver. Two centers occasionally placed infants in an infant feeding table or jump-chair for a feeding.

In one center, a fourteen-month-old subject had just begun going to the dining room with older toddlers. The toddlers were expected to line up going to and from the dining room. There they sat in chairs at low tables and fed themselves with very little assistance, after previously having been fed while reclining on the care giver's lap. The meal was rushed in order to be over before the older children came to the lunch room. The care giver's comments to the toddlers consisted almost entirely of reprimands about being messy, or being slow. The following is illustrative:

Infant N, feeding episode 1. Care giver's rating: 4

N was sitting at a table with nine other toddlers, feeding herself. This was only the second week she had experienced self-feeding. For the care giver, the purpose of this feeding episode was to have the children eat as quickly and with as little mess as possible. N did seem to be allowed more freedom to play in her food and be messy than did the older toddlers. When N called the care giver she received no response. Later N banged her spoon and was given a slight verbal reprimand. The care giver held the cup to help N finish her milk, but it was more for the adult's purpose of finishing milk so fruit could be put into the cup. The dishes were cleared away at the end of each course more in an effort to get the meal finished than in consideration of the children's individual needs (White 1975, p. 94).

In only one center were the infants of about one year placed in high chairs and allowed to feed themselves. Feeding in this center was a pleasant time for both staff and infants. A typical feeding episode at this center is as follows for forty-eight week old Infant F. The adult-child ratio on this day was 3:9 (1:3).

Infant F, feeding episode 3. Care giver's rating: 3.

F was allowed to sleep until she awakened naturally. The meal did not begin until she had clean diapers. F was thus comfortable and alert before the meal began. She was allowed to feed herself and to experiment with the feel of the food. No fuss was made about any messiness. The care giver was nearby to assist with the feeding. The atmosphere in the room was warm and loving with the adults interacting pleasantly with the infants. No cross words were heard. When F seemed not to want to eat she was encouraged to do so in order that she would not get hungry later in the afternoon. She was given more of the food she seemed to prefer in an effort to get her to eat more. F was not forced to eat nor scolded for not eating. A plan was made by the adults for further feeding in the afternoon if F grew hungry. (p. 100).

Discussion of Care Provided to Infants in Centers

In White's study (1975) there was a trend, though not significant, in the direction of the fewer children cared for by each care giver, the higher the rating of the care giver's sensitivity of response. Of the seven community infant group day-care programs observed by White, Center 1 had an adult-to-child ratio, staff experience and adult-child interaction similar to the university-based centers of previous studies. Both infants enrolled in this program, Infants F and L, received a mean rating of care giver's sensitivity of response of 3.0. The care giver-to-child ratio was high: 1:3.5 and 1:4.2 calculated for the two subjects enrolled there. This was the only center in which the main care giver had received in-service training in child care. The infants in this center were held when they were given bottles. Beginning at about ten months, the infants were allowed to feed themselves, with the care givers help to the infants as they needed or wanted it. Infants in this center were allowed to follow their own eating and sleeping schedules. When the investigator arrived at the center for the feeding observations, she found the care givers and infants on the floor, singing, or looking at books and toys, or otherwise pleasantly interacting. Even the youngest infants participated and were laid on the floor on blankets, or held by a care giver. Mobiles and cradle gyms were on the cribs of the youngest infants, to provide visual stimulation. An awake infant was never observed to be just lying in a crib crying or otherwise unattended. The care givers initiated interaction with the infants, vocalized and played with them during diapering times and cuddled, patted, or rocked the infants. Rapport and cooperation between care givers was good.

One other center, Center 2, attended by Infant B, also had a high care giver-to-child ratio, calculated 1:3.7, but the rating of the care giver's sensitivity of response was 1.0. The recorded ratio was high because an extra care giver came in to help with the infants at feeding time. The care provided at this center was largely custodial and little interaction with the infants was initiated by the care givers during the times the investigator was observing. Infants spent most of the day in their cribs, which were stacked three high. The care givers had no training in child development. The main care giver worked at the center 9½ hours, five days a week. Her only break was when the infants were napping. At the University of North Carolina at Greensboro, a demonstration project, Group Care for Infants, (Keister 1970) the care givers had an eight-hour working day with a rest break of fifteen minutes each morning and afternoon and a forty-five minute lunch break.

In the study by White (1975), four infants, C, E, I, and K, attended a center in which the mean care giver-to-child ratios were 1:6.5, 1:5.0, 1:6.7,and 1:6.5, respectively. These ratios were higher than usual for the center. Widespread unemployment of one or both parents of infants had decreased enrollment so that only one-third of those normally served were in attendance. The mean caregiver's sensitivity of response ratings for these four infants were 1.0, 2.0, 1.7, and 2.0. The care giver was quite affectionate in her ministrations to the infants, but her response to them seemed to come from her own needs rather than in response to the infants' affective states. She was observed reprimanding an infant who was obviously not feeling well. This care giver often slapped the infants on their legs or arms if they did not behave as she thought they should. This care giver had never had training in child development, nor did she see a need for it. She commented to the investigator that she did not approve of parents who raised children without spanking them. Three of the mothers who participated in the study had infants attending this center; they seemed to lack understanding of children and parenting skills. These mothers made comments to the investigator which implied that the care giver knew more about child rearing than they did so they tried to do with their infants at home just as the care giver wanted them to do. The fourth mother whose infant attended this center seemed to be more concerned with her infant's affective needs and was warmer and more responsive to her child, C, when she came to the research room. For instance, this mother stated that she didn't want the care giver to know that she always held C to give her a bottle and, she said, "I don't know if it's all right to do that, but I just want to hold my baby."

Infants H and J came from a center with moderately low care giver-to-child ratios of 1:5.4 and 1:5.5. The care giver's mean sensitivity of response ratings were 1.0 and 1.3 respectively. The care at this center was largely custodial and little real affection was shown to any of the infants. The assistant care giver had received some training in child care and hoped someday to receive more, so she could "open me my own center." She quite obviously resented being given directions by the other care giver and there was a good deal of undercover tension between these two women. They performed the routine business of providing physical care for the infants with almost no vocalization or interaction between either care giver and infants or between the two care givers. The investigator spent approximately twelve hours in this center. Each day the infants were put on the floor to move around for about one hour in the morning and one hour in the afternoon. The infants spent the rest of their eight- to ten-hour-day in their cribs. These infants were usually fed while they stood in their cribs.

Infants A and D came from two smaller, more modest centers. For both infants, the care giver-to-child ratio was 1:7.3 but the mean care giver's sensitivity of response rating was 2.0. This rating reflects the more friendly and relaxed atmosphere which seemed to pervade these smaller centers. In each of these programs the infants were kept in separate rooms for sleeping and for some waking hours while the care givers were responsible for both the infants and older children. The rest of the time these year-old infants played in the same areas with the toddlers and preschoolers because, in both programs, there were only two or three infants and twenty or thirty older children. Feeding time for these infants were almost their only chance for a completely one-to-one relationship with an adult. This seemed to be true for most of the other day-care infants as well. This one-to-one relationship, for D, seemed to be more important than eating. The care giver, however, was hesitant about taking time to just play and interact with D for fear, as she said, of "spoiling her."

Infants G, M, and N came from an expensive program housed in a stylish new facility. The care giver-to-child ratio was the lowest of any of the programs: 1:8.7, 1:9.0, and 1:9.5. The care giver's sensitivity of response ratings were also among the lowest: 1.3, 1.7. and 1.0. G, described earlier, was a particularly happy and smiling infant and he evoked more interaction from his care givers than any of the other infants. During the six hours of observation in Center 7, the investigator never saw him cry. One time he was observed being scolded and his legs were slapped because he was not lying down at naptime. His response was to smile at the care giver, calmly take his bottle and lie down with it.

The other infants at this center, M and N, exhibited insecure behavior at the center, fussing and crying. Administration of research procedures on both of these infants were terminated because of a high degree of crying, or because great insecurity in the infants was indicated.

The investigator spent many hours in the centers during the feeding observations, the preliminary visits, and visits to contact parents or to test the infants. The length of time spent at each center for each observation ranged from ten minutes to 3½ hours. After one or two visits, or, in many cases, right away, the care givers were relaxed and chatted freely with the investigator or each other. The investigator felt confident that the rating of the care givers during feeding was tapping a representative example of the care givers' sensitivity of response to the infants in the entire program.

The observations made at the centers during feeding point up questions of concern to professionals interested in the welfare of infants. These questions are relevant to the quality of mass infant day care. What quality of care is being given to infants in community group-care programs and how can it be measured? How is the development of large numbers of infants in group care being affected? One of the original purposes of the investigator, when planning the study, had been to find a measure by which to rate the affective atmosphere of the center. Rating the care giver's sensitivity of response to the infants is one method of rating the care givers for their sensitivity to the infant's affective state. No other studies of infants in group day-care have been located that attempted to measure this aspect of care.

It can be assumed that the rating of the care giver's sensitivity of response during feeding can be applied, rather generally, to her sensitivity of response to the infant throughout his six months in the center. Brody and Axelrad (1970) found that the types of maternal behavior they identified in 118 of the 122 mothers in their study did remain internally consistent throughout the year of their study. Ainsworth and Bell (1970) too, found that maternal behavior with infants was consistent throughout the first year of life.

Implications for the Future

All indications are that, as we move toward and enter the 1990s, increasing numbers of mothers of infants will be working and needing child care. In 1960, 15.3 percent of all mothers of children under three were working. This percentage had increased to 29.4 percent in 1973 (Hayghe 1973). In 1979, 56.1 percent of women with children under six were in the labor force (Bureau of Labor Statistics 1980). Although this last statistic does not specify the percentage of mothers of children under and over three, it does clearly show that there is an accelerating increase in the need for care of very young children. Parents and professionals alike must be concerned with the effect on a child's development that the child-care arrangement may be having. The infants of the 1980s will be the teenagers of the 1990s, and the young adults of the year 2000.

Friedman and Rosenman (1974) have written with concern about the increasing incidence of coronary heart disease in the American population and have identified a complex of personality traits which they have called "Type A Behavior Pattern." They believe this pattern to be the major cause of coronary artery and heart disease. This pattern includes an excessive competitive drive, aggressiveness, impatience, and a chronic sense of time urgency. One may well wonder whether the foundations for these personality traits are laid in infant experience if an entire meal is silently urged upon a child in no more than a three- or four-minute feeding period, or when, at fourteen months of age children are forced to line up, go to a dining room, and rush through a meal to make room for the next group of children.

Brody and Axelrad (1970) found in their study that the close scrutiny of mothers showed many indications of pathology as well as of health. The total picture of the mothers and infants was far from the one frequently painted of smiling mothers and happy infants in an intact family home.

In the study by White (1975) of infants in group care, the picture of many of the care givers in the day-care programs was not the picture of the care-giving staff described by many of the model programs in previous studies. Keister (1970) described the staff of the Greensboro Demonstration Infant Project as showing their enjoyment of children through their ministrations and interactions with the babies. They were actively involved in arranging a good day for each baby, and showed obvious pleasure in the babies' new skills and learnings, and in their good health. Such behaviors were not seen in most care givers in White's study.

Brody and Axelrad (1970) reported finding many disturbed mothers and infants. The study by White (1975) found many care givers who were rated as caring for their infant charges in a reluctant, perfunctory manner or in a controlling, dominating manner. This compares unfavorably with care that accommodates smoothly to the infant's affective state.

One disturbed or noninvolved mother at home affects her own infant with who she is interacting, but one disturbed or noninvolved care giver, possibly untrained, underpaid, overworked, and insensitive to the affective state of the infants in her charge, affects as many as eight or ten or more infants, and perhaps their families as well. As long as there are widespread group day-care programs to serve the thousands of children of working mothers, there must be appropriate methods used to rate care givers and care givers-in-training for their competencies in promoting growth in affective as well as cognitive and physical aspects of development. One evaluative tool to use in training programs and in evaluation of workers might be Brody's General Scale of Maternal Response. Such a tool could be used for evaluation of students in training to become child-care workers, in field-based assessment of care givers and family day-care providers, or in in-service training programs. Educational programs must include measures of affective interaction of students with young children as well as objective measures of theory.

Erikson (1950) felt that the first step in developing a healthy personality was to develop basic trust. Basic trust, according to him, is developed primarily through the infant's feeding relationship with the mother. The infant's trust develops not only when his physiological hunger is satisfied by the mother or care giver, but also through the manner in which she or he holds and interacts with him. Many of the infants observed by White (1975) rarely or never were held while being given a bottle, at least during the eight to ten hours spent at the centers for the second half of their first year of life. Further research must be done to show how these early experiences will affect later ability to relate affectionately to others. Even more important, however, is the need to improve the education and educational requirements of care givers. Parents, too, must receive information about what is already known about the needs of infants and how to meet these needs. With this knowledge, parents might more selectively choose programs and care givers for their infants and young children.

The small body of research concerned with different child-care arrangements, such as group care, family day-care, or care in the infant's own home, indicates that it is the care giver who makes the biggest difference in the infant's experiences. Professionals must find practical ways to transfer to care givers, program administrators, parents, and students information about the kinds of care environments and experiences that are most appropriate for all aspects of an infant's development. In 1961 Brody observed that there was a great distance between what advanced professional workers believed to be good for children and what those who worked directly with children were aware of and were willing or able to do. Unfortunately, this is still true decades later when the need is even greater. It provides a continuing challenge for professionals and practitioners as they move their programs toward the 1990s.

References

Ainsworth, M.D.S., and Bell, S.M. Some contemporary patterns of mother-infant interaction in the feeding situation. In *Stimulation in early infancy,* ed. J.A. Ambrose. New York: Academic Press, 1969, pp. 133-170.

Ainsworth, M.D.S.; Blehar, M.C.; Waters, E.; and Wall, S. *Patterns of attachment: a psychological study of the strange situation.* Hillsdale, N.J.: Lawrence Erlbaum Associates, 1978.

Belsky, J., and Steinberg, L.D. The effects of day care: a critical review. *Child Development* 49:929-949, 1978.

Blehar, M.C. Anxious attachment and defensive reactions associated with day care. *Child Development* 45:683-692, 1974.

Brody, S. *Patterns of mothering.* New York: International Universities Press, 1956.

Brody, S., Preventive intervention in current problems of early childhood. In *Prevention of mental disorders in children,* ed. G. Caplan. New York: Basic Books, 1961.

Brody, S., and Axelrad, S. *Anxiety and ego formation in infancy.* New York: International Universities Press, 1970.

Brookhart, J., and Hock, E. The effects of experimental context and experiential background on infants' behavior toward their mothers and a stranger. *Child Development* 47:333-340, 1976.

Bureau of Labor Statistics, *Employment in perspective: working women.* Report #584, Fourth quarter 1979, January 1980.

Caldwell, B.M.; Wright, C.; Honig, A.S.; and Tannenbaum, J. Infant day care and attachment. *American Journal of Orthopsychiatry* 40: 397-412, 1970.

Erikson, E.H. *Childhood and society.* New York: Norton, 1950.

Ferran, D.C., and Ramey, C.T. Infant day care and attachment behaviors toward mothers and teachers. *Child Development* 48:112-116, 1977.

Friedman, M., and Rosenman, R.H., *Type A behavior and your heart.* Greenwich, Conn.: Fawcett Publications, 1974.

Grotberg, E. *The present status and future needs in day care research.* Washington, D.C.: Educational Resources Division, Capitol Publications, 1971.

Hayghe, H. Marital and family characteristics of the labor force. *Monthly Labor Review* 2:pp. 21-27, February 1973.

Hock, E. Working and nonworking mothers and their infants: a comparative study of maternal caregiving characteristics and infants' social behavior. *Merrill-Palmer Quarterly* 46:79-101, 1980.

Kagan, J.; Kearsley, R.B.; and Zelazo, P.R. The effects of infant day care on psychological development. *Evaluation Quarterly* 1:109-142, 1977.

Keister, M.E. *The good life for infants and toddlers.* Washington, D.C.: National Association for the Education of Young Children, 1970.

Maccoby, E.E., and Feldman, S.S. Mother-attachment and stranger reactions in the third year of life. *Monographs of the Society for Research in Child Development* 37 (1), serial no. 146, 1972.

Provence, S., and Lipton, R., *Infants in institutions.* New York: International Universities Press, 1962.

Ricciutti, H. Fear and development of social attachments in the first year of life. In *The origins of human behavior: fear.* ed. M. Lewis and L.A. Rosenblum. New York: Wiley, 1974.

Schaffer, H.R., and Emerson, P.E. The development of social attachments in infancy. *Monographs of the Society for Research in Child Development* 29 (3), serial no. 94, pp. 5–77, 1964.

U.S. Department of Health, Education, and Welfare. Day care regulations: proposed rules, *Federal Register* 44, June 15, 1979, p. 34768.

Vaughn, B.E.; Gove, F.L.; and Egeland, B. The relationship between out-of-home care and the quality of infant-mother attachment in an economically disadvantaged population. *Child Development* 51: 1203–1214, 1980.

Vaughn, B.E.; Taraldson, B.; Crichton, L.; and Egeland, B. Relationships between neonatal behavioral organization and infant behavior during the first year of life. *Infant Behavior and Development* 3:47–66, 1980.

White, S.A. The infant-mother attachment of infants in community group day care programs. Ph.D. dissertation. Florida State University, 1975.

8

Proposing Public Policy in Early Childhood Special Education

Rosemary F. Peterson and
Barbara J. Tardif

Early childhood special education is an expanding new field of knowledge, although many people with expertise are already working in this area that provides special educational services to exceptional young children—infants, toddlers, and preschoolers. Chronologically this includes children up to the age of six, although sometimes children up to the age of eight are included.

The emerging field of early childhood special education is based on the integration of some concepts from early childhood education and some from special education. Persons knowledgeable about these usually separate fields of expertise are beginning to pool their resources. Although early childhood special education practitioners have for years been working with exceptional young children, it now seems that this newly integrated field is beginning to define itself.

A recent impetus for the growth of this field is the implementation of Public Law 94-142, the federal special education law of 1975. In California, the special education law, SB 1870, was introduced in 1980 and is based upon the federal law. It provides that exceptional children, age three to four years, nine months (in addition to older children) requiring intensive special education services, will be provided such services. Services for children under three were, and continue to be, permissive in California.

Public Law 94-142, the federal special education law, has had an impact upon various aspects of early childhood special education. Some states have initiated laws to mandate services for handicapped preschoolers, although at this time, most states have laws that permit but do not mandate services. However, many states are beginning to develop training and standards for those persons working with young exceptional children and some states already have instituted teaching credentials for this area. Universities and colleges are initiating teacher training programs in early childhood special education as well. More school district and private programs for young exceptional children are appearing. Public policy issues in early childhood special education are being decided at both state and national levels.

This paper does not necessarily represent the official position of the Commission for Teacher Preparation and Licensing in California.

129

This chapter, dealing with the development of public policy in early childhood special education in California, is divided into three sections. The first gives an overview of early childhood education and of special education, with the intent of integrating this information as it relates to the development of early childhood special education. The second concerns the formation of public policy in California and the process that an advisory committee for a state agency went through to arrive at its decision. This Advisory Committee for Young Children with Special Needs to the Commission for Teacher Preparation and Licensing made proposals for public policy on teacher training standards. The final section discusses the implications of this public policy for the future.

Review of the Literature

A brief review of the fields of special education and of early childhood education will provide a perspective from which to consider the growth of the integrated field of early childhood special education. Since the field of early childhood education is just beginning to develop into a cohesive field of its own, the following focuses on the separate fields of special education and early childhood education with a consideration of their historical integration (Montessori) and of current research.

In reviewing the literature we have selected research in early childhood and special education that seems to provide conceptual antecedents for the field of early childhood special education. More research specific to this integrated field can undoubtedly be expected in the future. This present review will help to establish an historic perspective of why and how the committee which determined early childhood special education policy in California arrived at its recommendations.

Special Education

Historically, two pioneers in the field of special education were the French physician-educators Jean-Marc Gaspard Itard (1775–1838) and Edouard Seguin (1812–1880). Itard (1962) spent five years on his classic study of "The Wild Child" where he first used the clinical method to observe, study, and educate an exceptional child. Although Itard focused on the sensory training of the child, he used many behavioral techniques in use today. These included matching, successive approximation, fading, generalized imitation, escape-avoidance conditioning, and the breaking down of complex tasks into their component subskills (Ball 1971). Itard also voiced the sentiment that is a basic tenet of stimulus-response (S-R) psychology when he stated, "Believing that if I had not been understood by my pupil, it was my fault rather than his" (1962, pp. 68-69). While applying and elaborating Itard's techniques, Seguin introduced motor training as a significant component of educating the retarded (Lane 1980). He formulated the three-period lesson to associate language with perceptions, effectively applied reinforcement principles (Ball 1971, p. 77), and is best known for his didactic apparatus (educational materials manipulated by the child, for example, stacking blocks and nesting cubes or kegs).

In the early twentieth century, psychology began to emerge as a dominant force in special education. In the United States, E.L. Thorndike (1874-1949) and John B. Watson (1878-1958) were developing theories which would form "the dominant stream of psychological thought about learning for the next half century" (Rohwer, Ammon, and Cramer 1974, p. 15). Both focused on overt, measurable responses and on the conditions under which particular behavior occurred. This was complementary to the mental measurement procedures being developed by Alfred Binet and others to determine mental deficiency.

It is from these antecedents that current practices in special education have been refined and developed (Kirk 1951; Mussen 1970; Skinner 1968). Testing is of the utmost importance in order to diagnose individual deficits. The prescriptive instruction that follows testing is designed to correct or compensate for these deficits and depends on a careful task analysis (Gagne 1970) to provide the appropriate instruction. Behavioral objectives are written in specific, measurable terms. The proliferation of both diagnostic and instructional techniques has led to more and more specialization with emphasis on the handicapping condition(s) or deficit(s) rather than the child. Bijou (1973, cited in Kaufman 1980) suggests that special education is dominated by two theories of exceptionality: defect and deficit.

Early Childhood Education

The field of early childhood education has developed from far different antecedents. The "garden of children" which Frederic Froebel (1782-1852) set up in Germany in 1837 had, as an underlying assumption, the principle that childhood was a unique period in which the world was viewed from a perspective qualitatively different from that of the adult. The child needed to be free to unfold according to a natural plan (as a flower in a well-tended garden). The total child was the focus, with play regarded as the means to stimulate learning. The first kindergarten in the United States was founded in 1855, and as the philosophy spread, it was supported by John Dewey who established a kindergarten in his laboratory school at the University of Chicago. Until recently, the main focus of most nursery schools and kindergartens has been to develop the child's social skill through play. During

World War II, child care for working mothers became an important objective of preschool programs, and currently, with the increasing number of working mothers, this aspect has again become one of the major focuses of early education. Nonetheless, play continues to be of utmost importance for the preschool child. "Braun and Edwards (1972) consider play the crux of preschool pedagogy" (Kaufman 1980).

At present, much in early childhood education is based on the cognitive theory of Piaget. The child must be free to interact with the environment in order to construct his knowledge of the world. How the child organizes reality is qualitatively different from the way the adult does it and changes according to the stage of cognitive development the child has reached. As the child develops, his cognitive structures are reorganized and integrated into the next stage. Play is seen as a necessary element of the child's cognitive, as well as social, development.

As the work of Jean Piaget (1896–1980) began to influence American psychology (Flavell 1963; Piaget and Inhelder 1969) new interest was shown concerning the effect of the preschool years on later intellectual achievement. Bloom's study (1964) had a major effect on how educators perceived the early years when he stated that 50 percent of a child's intellectual development takes place before the age of four, 80 percent before the age of eight. In the same year (1964), the Economic Opportunity Act gave Head Start a mandate for a nationally sponsored program for preschool development focusing on early intervention. In 1967, the National Laboratory in Early Childhood Education was established as a program of the Elementary and Secondary Act of 1964 (Title IV legislation). Research to obtain knowledge about child development and developing early childhood research-based programs are the goals of the centers and programs operating under this organization (Weber 1970).

Early Childhood Special Education

Montessori. One major early childhood philosophy which could be a valuable resource for early childhood special education has not yet been tapped by public education. Maria Montessori's interest in education began in the 1890s when, as a physician, she visited "idiot" children in Rome's insane asylums. She studied the work of Seguin and soon was directing and teaching school for children considered "hopelessly deficient" (Montessori 1964, p. 32). "I followed Seguin's book and also derived much help from the remarkable experiments of Itard [with the Wild Boy]. Guided by the work of these two men, I manufactured a great variety of didactic materials. My ten years of work may. . . . be considered as a summing up of 40 years work done by Itard and Seguin" (pp. 36, 47).

Montessori's great success with her method aroused interest, but it ran counter to the teacher-directed programs that had evolved from Froebel's work and that were prevalent during the first part of the century. When asked the difference between her system and Froebel's, as Froebel also felt children should "work in freedom," Montessori replied, "Ah, but whose freedom? Froebel's, not the child's. He came to the child with his philosophy about the child. I go to the child to get mine." (*The Times* (London), January 28, 1914, cited in Kramer 1976, p. 203).

William Heard Kilpatrick, a disciple of John Dewey and the best-known teacher of education of his generation, criticized Montessori's system for not providing more situations for social cooperation and imitative play (Kramer 1976, pp. 227–229). As Montessori had applied her methods to normal children, she became classified (and criticized) as an early childhood educator and so did not come to the forefront in the field of special education. Her methods and materials, however, have been utilized: task analysis, which allows for isolation of difficulty, sequential teaching of subskills, control of error in the materials rather than in the teacher (programmed learning), education of the senses, lessons in practical life, muscular education, the use of a great variety and quantity of manipulative materials, such as sandpaper letters, blocks, graded sequences of stimuli, and the like, always moving from the concrete to the abstract. Perhaps as the field of early childhood special education develops, it will acknowledge Montessori as a rich resource.

Current Research. Ideally, the early childhood teacher facilitates the child's development by providing an environment responsive to the child's needs and experiences relevant to the child's stage of development (Felton and Peterson, 1976). But what of the child who does not develop in rhythm with the timetable most children follow? The research of Piaget and other developmental psychologists was concerned with "normal" children. Some handicapping conditions have been found to slow the progress through the stages although the invariant sequence remains unchanged. As summarized by Cowan (1978, pp. 331–370), research in this area (Boland 1973; Broadley 1973; Furth 1966; Gottesman 1971, 1973; Inhelder 1943, 1966; Woodward 1959, 1961) strongly supports this position. One of the authors of this paper (Peterson) has found that in over a hundred different projects, teachers of children with a variety of handicapping conditions have discovered that the timing of developmental progress shows great variation but the sequence of stages does not.

Other research focuses on the handicapped child in his family environment. Young children with special needs have powerful influences on family life (Carver and Carver 1972; Ehlers 1966; Farber 1959). The entire family must be included in the education of young handicapped children. More recently, culture and socialization practices have been found to have profound influences on how children learn and interact with teachers, parents, and peers (Ramirez and Castaneda 1974). Implications for the young handicapped child's education from this and similar research must be studied when considering public policy and the planning of programs.

The state of Indiana's "Rationale for the Provision of Early Intervention" (1979) drew upon Lillie's conclusion (1975) that the optimum period for interaction of maturation and learning is the preschool period. The need for specific intervention to make the most of this interaction is greater for the handicapped preschool child. Therefore, the teacher of young handicapped children, while emphasizing the child's total development, must be sensitive to the effective practices researched and developed in the field of special education in order to provide specific intervention when needed. Model projects serving young handicapped children were provided funds by the Handicapped Children's Early Education Act of 1972 and are providing much needed information to the field. Research by Kephart (1960) and from the field of language development (Berko and Palmer 1972; Bloom and Lahey 1978; Kirk and Kirk 1971; Wiig and Semel 1976), the many projects supported by the Bureau of Education for the Handicapped (BEH), and the evaluation of educational programs (see Sapir and Wilson 1978) are adding to our knowledge.

The development of public policy in the field of early childhood special education will, of necessity, draw on philosophies, research, and practices from the fields of early childhood and special education, but will also require more than the blending of these two fields. Continuing new research and critical analyses of practices and programs will lead to the development of a new field which integrates the concepts of a holistic view of the child, a qualitative unique period of human development, the inseparable nature of the child, his family, and his culture, and the necessity for carefully planned specific intervention as needed. Such research offers new insights particular to early childhood special education.

The review of the literature points to the need for integrating knowledge gained from an historic perspective of both early childhood education and special education. Concepts from Froebel to Piaget focused on the whole child and his development while those contributing to the body of knowledge of special education, such as Seguin and Kephart, focused on the particular needs of the handicapped child and how to remediate these problems through precision teaching and working with the particular disability. With the recent move to integrate aspects of the two fields, it is necessary to see where the two areas fit together and how this new knowledge can then be used to help exceptional young children. The conceptual frameworks from early childhood education and from special education must not be seen as separate and conflicting areas. Rather, certain elements from each can be viewed as complementary and appropriate. Future research and practices should lead to a more integrated perspective for the developing field of early childhood special education.

Now that we have reviewed the literature we have an historic backdrop against which to view the process through which the Advisory Committee for Young Children with Special Needs developed public policy for early childhood special education.

Public Policy

The Process of Developing Public Policy

The necessity of proposing public policy in the field of early childhood special education came to the attention of the (California) Commission for Teacher Preparation and Licensing (CTPL) from professionals and interested individuals in the field who expressed concern that appropriate teacher training and standards were needed in this area. The commission formed an Advisory Committee for Young Children with Special Needs to provide leadership in determining public policy and the training needs of early childhood special education teachers before most of the school programs were established.

Public Policy in Education

Public policy whether at federal, state, or local levels, consists of major decisions that affect large numbers of persons and programs in different areas. Policy at the state level is determined by the legislature and approved by the governor.

By authority delegated by the California state legislature, the Commission for Teacher Preparation and Licensing formulates public policy in the area of teacher credentialing. This ensures better training for educators, having a positive effect on programs and, more important, on children's learning. These educational policy decisions have a direct effect on programs in the public sector and an indirect effect on the private sector.

Policy decisions should be viewed as being on a continuum from standardization on one end to flexibility on the other. A certain amount of statewide standardization in teacher training programs is necessary to ensure the same high quality from program to program, but flexibility provides for variety and individual difference among the programs. A balance is needed to ensure both quality and creativity.

Public policy decisions in the field of education need to be made carefully, intelligently, and with planning and foresight. These decisions should be based upon sound theoretical principles and successful practices. Research that supports, contradicts, or modifies the theoretical foundation and practices must be analyzed and carefully considered in developing a recommended model. First, the philosophical base needs to be established and agreed upon; the model programs can then be derived from this base. How the policy will be implemented in the field needs to be carefully developed, taking into account the qualifications of existing personnel, the needs of all affected groups, community needs, governmental regulations, financial factors, and most important of all, the needs of the children and their parents.

Public policy is not always determined so carefully. Practical considerations are of course important, but expedience is not a legitimate basis for determining policy. All too frequently, policy is determined by political pressure from one or another special interest group. After policy has been set, the why and how are worked out in committee, sometimes not very successfully. The political power of special interest groups must not be allowed to dominate, but the needs of various groups who have legitimate interests in the policy must be considered. Cost considerations also need careful study.

Public Policy for Young Children with Special Needs

The CTPL Advisory Committee for Young Children with Special Needs developed a public policy proposal for those working with exceptional young children. The committee was organized because of concern at the lack of specific standards especially designed for persons working with exceptional infants, toddlers, and preschoolers. Membership on the advisory committee was drawn from people with various backgrounds and levels of training who shared a common commitment to young children with special needs.

Review of Current Practices

The committee began by hearing presentations from people in the field and by visiting various kinds of early childhood programs, including special education programs and mainstreaming programs, to determine the needs of children, staff, and programs. This information was to be used to determine criteria for staff qualifications.

Philosophical Basis

The committee formed definite attitudes regarding the training of early childhood special education teachers based upon the needs of the children, the teacher, and the program. These were drawn from the backgrounds and experience of the committee members and were firmly supported by those currently in this particular field of special education. There was strong agreement that the strengths of the children rather than their disabilities must be emphasized. All children have many things in common; these similarities among children, including exceptional children, are more prevalent than differences. The emphasis should be on what the children *can* do, rather than on what they *cannot* do. This was stressed time and again by those in the field at presentations and on-site visits when they were asked, "What is the most important training for people in your field?" The overwhelming answer was "an understanding of normal child development." It is important to look at the whole child first, and then remediate all aspects, rather than focus on one aspect at a time.

The committee also found teacher attitudes to be very important. Teachers need to view young exceptional children as active learners, not passive ones. Teacher competence should be based upon the needs of the particular group under consideration and therefore, teachers need to be able to demonstrate skills in a variety of settings, including school programs, hospital programs, home-based programs, and others.

Finally, the committee felt that the program should focus on the child and his or her family, and strongly support the child's culture and community. Community members and parents should be involved and included in the school program and act as resource people for it. Because the committee was concerned with children under the age of six, continuity between the home and the community and the educational setting, be it hospital-based, school-based, or home-based, was considered essential.

Theoretical Positions

On the basis of the committee's philosophy, three underlying theoretical positions emerged: a developmental-interactionist perspective; a learning/remediation perspective; and a psychosocial perspective.

The Developmental-Interactionist Perspective. The developmental-interactionist perspective focuses on the whole child with an emphasis on normal child development. In this theory, most often associated with the work of

Jean Piaget, it is postulated that all children go through the same stages, but not necessarily at the same rate. As the stages are hierarchical, mastery of the processes at one level are necessary for their integration into the more advanced processes of the next higher stage. Thus, an understanding of how the child is processing information is essential in order to plan appropriate tasks, curriculum, and activities to facilitate the child's development. The implications of this theory for the work of the committee were that handicapped children go through the same stages as other children, but they may be developmentally delayed, sometimes severly.

The Learning/Remediation Perspective. The learning/remediation perspective indicates that, just as the teacher must be able to assess the child's level of development and how information is being processed, he or she must also understand the task or skill that is the focus of remediation. The child must be taught in a logical sequence requiring the teacher to have the ability to analyze a task into all its prerequisite skills and components (Gagne 1970). Only then can the teacher match the requirements of the task to the developmental level of the child. This process involves careful assessment of the task and the child in order to determine what skills the child needs to learn.

The Psychosocial Perspective. The psychosocial perspective, with stages that closely parallel the cognitive stages of the developmental-interactionist theory, emphasizes the role of the family and the larger community and culture of which the child is a member. In each stage the child must resolve a conflict of opposing forces, such as trust versus mistrust, and autonomy versus shame and doubt, in a way compatible with his own personality development and yet acceptable to his family and culture (Erikson 1963). The committee saw it as important to consider the child, his or her family, and his or her culture; the child was not living in a vacuum. Also, parents must be seen as the primary educators of young children, including those children with special needs.

Professional Training

The teacher of early childhood special education must have competence in all three theoretically based areas. In addition, practical and regulatory considerations must be included in the teacher training program. Translating skills and knowledge into effective practice is vital; experience in working with young exceptional children is imperative. Each of the general competence areas suggested by the committee thus has the following components: knowledge and understanding; application; evaluation and continuing assessment of the programs' effectiveness.

The general competency areas suggested by the committee are:

1. *Child Development.* Understands normal development, prenatal through the first eight years, including motor, language, cognitive, perceptual, psychosocial sequences, affective needs, and individual differences. Knows and understands the current research relating to the young child; the relation and influence of the family, society, and culture; the role of play as a critical developmental task and applies normalizing principles.

2. *Child Development—Atypical.* Understands the causes and consequences of developmental variations in relation to the child, family, and society; the multifaceted needs of the child and his family and the implications of handicapping conditions in relation to learning and maturational growth sequences.

3. *Assessment.* Understands and interprets the available instruments and techniques as the basis for designing individualized intervention programs, carrying them out and continually monitoring their effectiveness; considerations of health and related needs; the family needs; and the limitations and problems of current instrumentation for children of various ethnic and cultural backgrounds. Uses community resources and understands community responses to the young child and the family.

4. *Program Planning and Implementation.* Includes description and evaluation of several theoretical approaches for designing programs for exceptional infants, toddlers, and preschoolers, as well as the ability to design programs; devises appropriate early childhood developmental activities, as opportunities for problem solving and responsible learning are provided; demonstrates skills in teaching strategies and developmental activities which capitalize on the strengths of the child, and skill in performing task analysis. Provides effective mainstreaming opportunities and prepares children to enter public school kindergarten.

5. *Evaluation of Program Effectiveness.* Analyzes and evaluates all program elements in terms of effectiveness for meeting the needs of the child and his family, while interpreting the child's developmental progress; uses the principles and practices of program evaluation for young handicapped children and evaluates the effectiveness of the program with parents.

6. *Parent/Family Counseling (Cultural).* Understands the variety of ways in which parents can participate in and support the educational program, while attending to the social, cultural, and linguistically relevant patterns and parenting styles of families. Understands the attachment process between young children and their families, while knowing how to utilize individualized planning, counseling techniques, and communication skills with them.

7. *Legal and Administrative.* Knows the history and philosophy of special
   education, emphasizing early childhood education; knows current federal and state laws and regulations, and current issues and future implications regarding early childhood special education; knows one's professional rights and responsibilities; knows the variety of program and
   service delivery alternatives; knows the Individual Educational Plan
   (IEP) process, confidentiality requirements, parents' rights, and due
   process procedures; knows the variety of agencies and support systems
   for young handicapped children and their families.
8. *Professional Behavior.* Demonstrates behavior, occupational standards, and personal qualities appropriate to functioning effectively in
   one's professional role, including displaying effective qualities which
   support instructional interactions with children and adults. Develops
   and coordinates a multidisciplinary team, using the expertise of each
   team member.

Again, it needs to be stressed that each competency area has three
essential components: knowledge and understanding; application; and
assessment and evaluation. Therefore, in order to assure the candidate's
competence, coursework, fieldwork, supervised placement, and continual,
inservice professional development must be integral parts of training.

There are implications for other states besides California that are developing their own early childhood special education standards, as well as
implications for other policy areas. First, it is important to establish an
underlying model or body of principles upon which to determine competencies and practices—in this case, teacher training standards. These theoretical principles, training competencies and standards, and successful practices
must be constantly reviewed in the light of new research, and those hypotheses which are not supported should be modified.

Public Policy: Implications for the Future

This chapter has dealt with the issue of public policy in early childhood special education, specifically the problem of how the Advisory Committee for
Young Children with Special Needs developed a proposal for a teaching credential in early childhood special education.

Development of Public Policy

An aspect of this topic that may be applicable to other areas is in the development of public policy itself. The advisory committee went through a spe-

cific process in arriving at its credential proposal. This proposal was determined by careful study of the problem and was based on a common philosophy rather than one determined by expediency or by special interest groups. The committee members worked for almost a year before deciding. During this first year, the committee visited many programs in the state and heard from many students and workers in the field. Uninfluenced by existing laws or other requirements governing special education, it considered what young handicapped children and their families would need first, and what would be the best training for those persons serving them. The committee was willing to propose a credential structure that would require changes in the law rather than continue with certain traditions that might be inappropriate.

Members of the committee encourage other groups developing public policy to engage in the same type of deductive process, moving from a set of values and beliefs about the needs of young handicapped children to the needs and training of the staff who would serve them. It seems more important to deduce this than to base public policy on immediate pressures and historical precedents.

This "generalist" credential proposal also has implications for other states which are developing a similar credential. A teacher holding a generalist credential must be able to work with children with varying handicaps, not just one type. This idea was based on the Committee's understanding of children and their needs, as well as on the implications of the California special education law, SB 1870.

California SB 1870, based on PL 94–142, discourages categories which tend to segregate and label children. The committee members agreed, thinking it important to look at the whole child first, then at his disability. Furthermore, it is not viewed as desirable or even feasible to classify young infants and toddlers. In addition, handicapped children often have more than one disability.

Another interesting aspect of this proposed credential that may interest other states is that entering the training program does not require a basic teaching credential. Eliminating the basic teaching credential requirement would mean changing the California credential law, but the Advisory Committee members did not view the basic elementary or secondary teaching credential as appropriate or necessary preparation for working with young handicapped infants, toddlers, and preschoolers. Student teaching experience at the elementary or high school level, for instance, did not seem applicable for later work with infants, toddlers, or preschoolers.

Another reason for eliminating the basic teaching credential requirement was to enable people from other fields, including psychologists, occupational therapists, physical therapists, and nurses, already working with young handicapped children in private programs, to continue working in publicly funded programs. Most of these professionals do not have the basic teaching credentials prerequisite to entering California's special education credential programs at this time. With the proposed change, they would be able to enter the early childhood special education credential program, which would increase the expertise and skills of people working with young exceptional children, and would not restrict the credential to educators. Other states developing such a credential might be interested in exploring a similar proposal.

Benefits of Early Childhood Special Education

Early intervention programs are beneficial for several reasons. Research indicates that such programs are valuable since they help the children involved and are also cost-effective. Various research studies may be cited to support this (Lazar and Darlington 1979; Weikart and Schweinhart 1980).

As indicated earlier, Bloom (1964) points out that by the time a child is four years old, he has already developed 50 percent of his total intellectual capacity; by the time he is eight years old, he has reached 80 percent of his intellectual development. The best time to intervene in reducing or preventing a child's mental, physical, emotional, or mental handicaps seems to be the time from birth through the preschool years. It is even more imperative to provide special intervention for handicapped preschoolers in order to make the most of this important period.

Research indicates that preschool programs for handicapped children are also cost-effective. Different studies point out that early childhood intervention programs can reduce the need for special education programs. Skeels (1966) reported on a longitudinal study of retarded orphans, which compared children who received environmental stimulation with a group who received no stimulation. Skeels found significant differences in occupational and income levels between the two groups as adults. At the time of the follow-up study, all of the experimental group subjects were self-supporting and none were wards of institutions. In the control group, most remained dependent on government assistance. Skeels's study demonstrates that early intervention is cost-effective in addition to helping young children who indicate high risk for exhibiting developmental difficulties.

Weikart and Schweinhart (1980) report a study on the effectiveness of preschool education for children at risk who were from low-income families and who were diagnosed as borderline retarded. The study indicated that preschool education prevented school failure for those children as compared to a matched sample who did not attend preschool. The experimental group was found to maintain higher school achievement and need fewer educational services. The resulting economic benefits were figured to be a 248 percent return on the original preschool investment.

Lazar and Darlington (1979) point out in the summary of a consortium report of longitudinal preschool studies (which included Weikart's study) that fewer experimental children were kept back a grade during their later schooling. They also emphasized the same factors that Weikart indicated in his separate report. Lazar and Darlington concluded that the consortium preschool intervention programs had significant long-lasting effects on low-income children.

To summarize, these early intervention studies indicate that preschool education is cost-effective and helps prevent retardation in young children. These studies also indicate that the preschool period is very important for intellectual development. This should be an indication to government officials to fund programs at this age level, rather than waiting to fund for remediation purposes. Remediation is usually less effective than prevention.

Funding and Other Related Issues

Funding, or the lack of it, in the field of early childhood special education will have far-reaching implications in the future. California special education services have been mandated for preschoolers, age three to four years, nine months, who have intensive special needs. Children younger than three may receive special services, but this remains an option for the school districts. However, no specific funding for such preschool programs has been provided in the California special education bill, SB 1870. Funding could become a serious problem for programs for young handicapped children in the future.

Due to SB 1870's mandate that preschool handicapped children be served, it is likely that more and more preschool programs for the handicapped will be initiated in the near future. This legislation permitted special education infant programs to occur in 1981-1982.

Countrywide, the trend also seems to be moving in the direction of mandatory special education services for handicapped preschool children; over two-thirds of the states allow, through legislation, special preschool education programs. About half of the states offer some type of preschool education for their handicapped children; most of these state provisions, however, are for children three years old and above, and more are permissive than mandatory.

The expansion of preschool programs for exceptional young children also indicates there will be a growing need for more qualified personnel to staff these programs. Publicly funded programs will therefore require credentialed personnel and training programs. There already is a shortage of qualified special education teachers in California and elsewhere. Training programs at the university level will need to be started, and these trained teachers will need credentials.

Conclusion

It is clear that early childhood special education has definite implications for the future in terms of funding, staffing, and training. In particular, the development of this public policy has implications for other groups and states formulating similar policies; states in the process of developing policy might gain useful insights from the California proposal.

Early childhood special education is a growing instructional area and valid field of study; for this field to continue to grow in all aspects, attitudes toward preschool education must change. Too many people continue to view preschool education, including early childhood special education, as "baby-sitting" or simply child care; the field should rather be viewed as educational. Early childhood special education helps young exceptional children learn and develop a variety of skills. At the same time, educators in this field must perceive parents of exceptional children as primary educators, and help them participate in the learning process.

References

Ball, T.S. *Itard, Seguin and Kephart: sensory education—a learning interpretation.* Columbus, Ohio: Merrill, 1971.

Berko, F., and Palmer, M. *Communication training in childhood brain damage.* Springfield, Ill.: Thomas, 1972.

Bijou, S. Behavior modification in teaching the retarded child. In *Behavior modification in education,* ed. Thoresen, C.E. Chicago: University of Chicago Press, 1973.

Bloom, B.S. *Stability and change in human characteristics.* New York: Wiley, 1964.

Bloom, L., and Lahey, M. *Language development and language disorders.* New York: Wiley, 1978.

Boland, S. Conservation tasks with retarded and nonretarded children. *Exceptional Children* 40:209–211, 1973.

Braun, S., and Edwards, E. *History and theory of early childhood education.* Worthington, Ohio: Jones, 1972.

Broadly, D.L. *The use of Piaget's developmental psychology in a study of trainable mental retardation.* Honors thesis. University of California at Berkeley, 1973.

Carver, J.W., and Carver, W.E. *The family of the retarded child.* Syracuse: Syracuse University Press, 1972.

Cowan, P.A. *Piaget with feeling.* New York: Holt, Rinehart and Winston, 1978.

Ehlers, W.H. *Mothers of retarded children: how they feel, where they find help.* Springfield, Ill.: Thomas, 1966.

Erikson, E.H. *Childhood and society.* 2nd ed. New York: Norton, 1963.

Farber, B. Effect of a severely mentally retarded child on family integration. *Monographs of the Society for Research in Child Development* 24 (2): 1959.

Felton, V., and Peterson, R. *Piaget: a handbook for parents and teachers of children in the age of discovery, preschool—third grade.* Moraga, Calif.: Mulberry Tree Books, 1976.

Flavell, J.H. *The developmental psychology of Jean Piaget.* Princeton, N.J.: Van Nostrand, 1963.

Furth, H. *Thinking without language: psychological implications of deafness.* New York: Free Press, 1966.

Gagne, R.M. *The conditions of learning.* New York: Holt, Rinehart and Winston, 1970.

Gottesman, M. A comparative study of Piaget's developmental schema of sighted children with that of a group of blind children. *Child Development* 42:573-580, 1971.

Gottesman, M. Conservation development in blind children. *Child Development* 44:824-827, 1973.

Indiana State Ad Hoc Committee on Early Childhood Intervention. *Rationale for the provision of early intervention programs for handicapped children,* 1979, pp. 11-18.

Inhelder, B. *The diagnosis of reasoning in the mentally retarded child.* New York: John Day, 1968. (Originally published 1943).

Inhelder, B. Cognitive development and its contribution to the diagnosis of some phenomena of mental deficiency. *Merrill-Palmer Quarterly* 12: 311-319, 1966.

Itard, J.M.G. *The wild boy of Aveyron.* Translated by G. Humphrey and M. Humphrey. New York: Appleton-Century-Crofts, 1962.

Kaufman, B.A. Early childhood education and special education: a study in conflict. *The Volta Review,* 1980, pp. 15-24.

Kephart, N.C. *The slow learner in the classroom.* Columbus, Ohio: Merrill, 1960.

Kirk, S. *Education of exceptional children.* New York: Houghton Mifflin, 1951.

Kirk, S., and Kirk, W. *Psycholinguistic learning disabilities: diagnosis and remediation.* Urbana: University of Illinois Press, 1971.

Kramer, R. *Maria Montessori, a biography.* New York: G.P. Putnam's Sons, 1976.

Lane, H. Itard and Seguin, forerunners of Montessori. *The American Montessori Society Bulletin,* 1930, p. 18.

Lazar, I., and Darlington R., *Summary report: lasting effects after preschool.* U.S. Department of Health and Human Services, Office of Human Development Services, Administration for Children, Youth and Families, DHEW Publ. No. (OHDS) 8030179, 1979.

Lillie, D.L. *Early childhood education: an individualized approach to developmental instruction.* Chicago: Science Research Associates, 1975.

Montessori, M. *The Montessori method.* Translated by A. George. New York: Schocken Books, 1964. (Originally published 1912).

Mussen, P.H., ed. *Carmichael's manual of child psychology.* New York: Wiley, 1970.

Piaget, J., and Inhelder, B. *The psychology of the child.* New York: Basic Books, 1969.

Ramirez, M. III, and Castaneda, A. *Cultural democracy, bicognitive development, and education.* New York: Academic Press, 1974.

Rohwer, M.D. Jr.; Ammon, P.R.; and Cramer, P. *Understanding intellectual development.* Hinsdale, Ill.: Dryden Press, 1974.

Sapir, S.G., and Wilson, B. *A professional's guide to working with the learning disabled child.* New York: Brunner/Mazel, 1978.

Skeels, H.M., Adult status of children with contrasting early life experiences: a follow-up study. *Monographs of the Society for Research in Child Development* 31 (3), serial no. 105, 1966.

Skinner, B.F. *Technology of teaching.* New York: Appleton-Century-Crofts, 1968.

Weber, E. *Early childhood education: perspectives on changes.* Worthington, Ohio: Jones, 1970.

Weikart, D.P., and Schweinhart, L.J., Effects of the Perry Preschool Program on youths through age 15. Paper presented at the Conference of the Handicapped Children's Early Education Program, Washington, D.C., December 1–3, 1980; summarizes a monograph by Schweinhart and Weikart (1980).

Wiig, E., and Semel, E. *Language disabilities in children and adolescents.* Columbus, Ohio: Merrill, 1976.

Woodward, M. The behavior of idiots interpreted by Piaget's theory of sensorimotor development. *British Journal of Educational Psychology* 29: 60–71, 1959.

Woodward, M. Concepts of number in the mentally subnormal: studies by Piaget's method. *Journal of Child Psychology and Psychiatry* 2: 249–259, 1961.

9

Sex-Role Development in Transition

Jeanne Kohl

Consider the following situations:

> While feeding their dolls, four-year-olds Maria and Cindy looked at Mark strangely as he came into the kitchen area and selected a pan to place on the stove. Right away, Maria got up, telling him emphatically, "You can't play here, Mark—boys can't cook!"

> Asked what she wants to do when she grows up, six-year-old Joanna responds, "I want to be an astronaut." Her teacher, very excited about receiving such a nontraditional response, asks Joanna why, to which she replies, "So I can go up to the moon and clean it up."

> Asked what they would want to be when they grew up if they were of the opposite sex, some kindergarten children answered:

> "Well, I guess if I was a girl, then I'd have to grow up and be nothing." (boy)

> "Oh, if I were a boy, I would grow wings and fly across the city." (girl) (Lever 1977)

> "Boys are rotton, made of cotton; girls are dandy, made of candy." (common schoolyard chant)

> Asked if her three-year-old son, Brian, plays with dolls, his mother said, "Oh, no. My husband would never allow that—we don't want him to become a sissy!"

> Introducing some new blocks to her kindergarten class, Ms. Bennett asked Roberto to demonstrate. When she dismissed the children for their free play time, she suggested that the boys might like to work with the new blocks.

Children have definite ideas about what they and adults should or should not and can or cannot be and do, and the overriding variable appears to be that of sex—whether one is female or male. Not only in preschool, but at home, in play with peers, and in school, children base their behavior on what they *believe* is appropriate for them as being male or female.

Of particular interest here is whether their beliefs accord with the realities of the times in which they presently live and will live as adults. Do adult

147

men cook? Will Mark and other of today's male preschoolers cook when they are young men and adults in the 1990s? Can Joanna become an astronaut and, if so, can she do work other than sweep the moon's surface? Will today's kindergarten girls work as adults or will they "be nothing?" Will Brian become a sissy if he plays with dolls, or, if he does play with dolls, will he be better able to learn to become a father if he so chooses? Are there early childhood teachers who, unlike Ms. Bennett, encourage their female students to play with blocks and perhaps strengthen their spatial-relationship skills and consequently their performance and interest in mathematics?

This chapter will explore how young girls and boys in the eighties are being differentially treated and prepared for the nineties. Specifically, current trends in employment and family structure will be presented, followed by differences in early childhood sex-role socialization practices which have present and potential impact on children's aspirations and behavior—all of which will have consequence in what children will be doing in the nineties. Finally, suggestions will be made with regard to providing a more equitable treatment of and provisions for a wider range of options for both girls and boys.

The Needs of the Nineties

Although it is difficult, if not impossible, to predict the future, reasonable projections can be made. A picture can be drawn of societal conditions and needs for the nineties, given the current state of the economy, the conservative trend in governmental policies and expenditures, the rapidly-changing technology, demographic changes (for example, population shifts to the South and West, marriage-divorce and childbirth rates), and societal recognition of the rights of women and minorities as brought about by the civil rights and women's movements.

Labor Force

Compared to 1979 when the civilian labor force totaled 103 million persons, including 43 million women, there will be an estimated 119 million employed persons in the 1990s, of whom slightly over 52 million or 45 percent will be women.[1] By 1980, women's representation in the labor force had increased to over 43 million, 42 percent of the total labor force, up from 2.5 million a century before. In 1990, 57 percent of all women sixteen years and older, will be working or seeking employment, while 72.4 percent of all prime working-age women (25–54 years of age) will be working. Even now, the U.S. Department of Labor projects that nine out of every ten girls in school today will work at some time in their lives. Jobs in the professions and technical fields will increase 19 percent by 1990, whereas those in management and administration will increase by 21 percent. Persons with preparation in science and math will obtain positions most easily.

Superficially the job outlook appears good; however, based on present conditions, one's gender and ethnicity may matter very much. With affirmative action and other equity-based and nondiscrimination programs and regulations being targeted for recission by the present administration and many congressional leaders as well as by many vociferous citizen groups, female, minority, and disabled persons may find the going rough. Even now, with these programs having been in operation for a number of years, over one-half of the women working are in just 20 traditionally female jobs out of 441 listed in the Census of Occupational Classification System; women earn on the average only 59 percent of what men earn, minority women having the lowest income; women high school graduates earn less than men who have only completed eighth grade and women college graduates earn less than men who have only completed high school. Much of the earning discrepancy between the sexes can be attributed to women being concentrated in traditionally lower-paying jobs, for example, over one-third are in clerical positions. These facts are especially disturbing given the legislation which has been enacted over the past decade in order to open educational and employment opportunities to women and minorities.

More and more often, women are working out of economic necessity. Nearly two-thirds of working women are single, widowed, divorced, or separated, or have husbands whose earnings are less than $10,000 a year. Seventy-five percent of minority women workers are either the sole support of their families or through their earnings bring the family income to over $7,000 per year and thus help keep the family afloat.

Women are working today, and more will be employed in the 1990s. Given today's rising standard of living as well as inflation and more single-parent families headed by women, it is a myth that women are home-makers and that young girls will marry Prince Charming and will never need to work. It is even unrealistic for young girls to grow up counting on getting a job after their children are grown. The most significant statistic to shed light on this relates to the increase in the percentage of women aged 25–34 years who are working: from 45 percent in 1970 to 64 percent in 1979, over 70 percent of whom are married with children under the age of eighteen. Fifty-five percent of all mothers with children under eighteen were working in 1979, with 45 percent of all mothers of preschool children working. This percentage and others are expected to increase by 13.7 percent by the 1990s (Smith 1979).

Family Status

More and more women are becoming divorced.[2] The divorce rate in 1979 was triple that of 1959; 1.18 million divorces were granted in 1979. This represents 5.4 new divorces per 1,000 population. For every two new marriages there is one new divorce.

Child Care

Given the increasing number of divorces and labor force participation by mothers of young children, adequate child care can reasonably be seen as a growing problem. In a survey conducted by the National Commission on Working Women, child care was listed as a serious problem by one-third of employed women. At present, the administration evidently does not consider the resolution of this problem a priority. Furthermore, if the proposed Human Life Amendment were to be adopted, the birth rate would probably increase, thus exacerbating the child-care problem. (The amendment would make illegal all abortions and many forms of contraception.)

The number of preschool-aged children is expected to increase from 17.1 million in 1977 to 23.3 million in 1990 (Women 1980). Also, child-care needs will increase for women preparing to enter the labor force. The numbers of women aged 35 or older in college in 1980 increased dramatically to 11 million. As a large proportion of these can be expected to have children, an anticipated consequence, one that will very much affect women and minorities, according to an affirmative action study in progress by the California Postsecondary Education Commission, is that neighbors and family members traditionally available to help out with child care are now themselves working or attending college. Thus, increased needs for alternate arrangements for child care are being created.

Consequences for Males

It is widely recognized that women have been the ones to suffer most from job discrimination. Although this is manifested in lower wages and status as well as economic and emotional dependence on men, as well as lower self-esteem, males have been victimized by discrimination as well. Many men would prefer traditionally female jobs, such as nursing, clerical work, and early childhood teaching, but have not taken up this work because of overt discrimination, perceived bias, or unwillingness to suffer the consequences. In addition, men are known to have a higher incidence of heart disease and briefer life span than women, as well as a higher rate of suicide (Waldron 1976).

Changing Roles

Changes in male and female roles are occurring and can be expected to continue into the ninetees. As more married women enter the labor force, couples are trying alternate lifestyles and nontraditional child-care arrangements. For those whose jobs permit, sharing of child care by both parents is seen as a positive force in children's upbringing, since fathers become more involved in housekeeping responsibilities and nurturant activities, and express their emotions more freely, and mothers assume more of the responsibility of income-providing, and car and yard maintenance. Single parents are having to learn and handle both traditionally male and female roles. Many women are becoming more instrumentally-oriented, independent, and capable, both economically and emotionally; many men are becoming more expressive-oriented, integrally involved with the families, capable in the home setting. However, wives still have the major responsibility for household tasks, even when working. In a study of 1,400 families, the average combined time spent by husbands, teenage and younger children in housekeeping tasks never exceeded three hours a day whereas the average time for wives was always more than four hours a day (Ganger and Walker 1979). Also, it has been projected that the number of single heads of households will increase from 26 million in 1975 to 40 million in 1990, of which 6.6 million will be women with children and 4.7 million of these will be working.

Today's Children

What are the children learning? What are their expectations for the future? Are there differences for girls and boys? Is it safe to assume that they will be equally prepared to face the challenges of the nineties? In the next section we will explore the reality of what young children are learning, doing, and thinking—at home and at school.

Girls and Boys: Differential Sex-Role Development

Today's young children will be youths and young adults in the nineties; what they are learning now will be carried over into their adult roles. This section wil provide an overview of children's sex identities, roles, and aspirations, followed by a discussion of *how* these are learned including differential expectations for and treatment of girls and boys. The focus will be on early childhood years, although what is relevant to older children will also be discussed.

Sex Identity

By the time children are three years old, they know their sex identity as being male or female (Kagan 1969), although some researchers believe that by the age of two, children have acquired beliefs about differences in males and females and recognize themselves as being of one or the other sex (Kuhn, Nash, and Brucken 1978). By the age of three or four, they understand what is expected of them with regard to their behavior, preferences, and psychological characteristics (Kohlberg 1966). Social, rather than biological, criteria—often in the form of stereotypes—(except for an occasional recognition that "men can't have babies") are used to make this distinction, such as dress and hair style, name, toy use, and the like (Emmerich et al. 1977). The use of sex-role stereotypes has been found to decrease with age (Kohlberg 1966; Masters and Wilkenson 1976).

Once children have a cognitive understanding of sex identity and sex roles, they are able to express preferences, including those involved with an ideal sex identity, toys and play activities, and occupational and educational aspirations, many of which are manifested in behavior.

Roles

Sex roles are manifested in young children in various ways, including play and aspirations.

Play. Young children spend a good part of their waking hours in play; in a sense, play is the "work" of children. Through play, they learn about their world—a world that expands daily. Toys and activities provide the instrumental framework for this learning, much of which involves the learning of sex roles. Research findings indicate that boys have a stronger and less variable preference for same-sex identified toys and activities than girls have (DiLeo, Moely, and Sulzer 1979; Fagot and Littman 1975; Flerx, Fidler, and Rogers 1976; Nadelman 1974; Schau et al. 1980); that young girls are more likely than boys to play in a greater variety of places, but more often indoors (Lott 1978); and that as children become older, their preference increases for same-sex toys (DiLeo, Moely, and Sulzer 1979; Flerx, Fidler, and Rogers 1976). Type of play and size of group can also make a difference, as was found by Booth (1972). In late preschool years, girls are not as frequently exposed to team activities in which initiative, competition, and cooperation can be learned, as well as group process and procedures.

Occupational Aspirations. A very important and perhaps widely unrecognized consequence of toy play is that of its contribution in setting educational, occupational, and lifestyle aspirations. Sociologists refer to this as a form of "anticipatory socialization," that is, the learning of future roles through role-play. Traditionally, young girls have confined their play to toys involving nurturing and domesticity which prepare them for the roles of mother and housekeeper. They play with dolls, toy irons, toy cleaning and kitchen equipment. They also play "dress up," thereby learning to look beautiful for males. Boys, on the other hand, have traditionally played with toys involving adult work roles and physical manipulation. They play with trucks, fire engines, blocks, and balls. Although there are male dolls, most are of the superhero genre, at least those which are the most popular and approved of by parents. In an interesting study of bedrooms of 100 children aged one to six, the toys typically found in girls' rooms were dolls with related paraphernalia as well as domestic toys; the rooms characteristically had floral furnishings. Boys' rooms typically contained vehicles, toy animals, and sports equipment, with the rooms decorated in animal motifs. While thirty-six of the boys' rooms contained riding toys, such as, wagons, buses, and the like, *none* of the girls' rooms had such toys (Rheingold and Cook 1975). Furthermore, boys receive severer negative sanctions for playing with "girls' toys" than do girls who play with "boys' toys" (Fein et al. 1975; Fling and Manosevitz 1972).

Also, recent research indicates that toy and play preference can influence cognitive development and ultimately career choice. The most striking example is with block play—a favorite of preschool boys and usually passed over by girls. Serbin, in several studies (for example, Serbin and Connor 1979), has found that block play facilitates visual-spatial relationship abilities. Although differences in visual-spatial skills normally do not begin to appear until the age of six, with boys typically having higher scores, girls have been able to obtain high performance scores in this skill after having participated in block play extensively in the preschool years. In fact, girls seem to benefit more than do boys. The very imporatant implication for aspirations is that a strong correlation has been demonstrated between proficiency in visual-spatial skills and math ability. Increasingly, ability in math is a requisite for many occupations, including those in the sciences, engineering, and other technical fields, all of which are projected to be important for the nineties. Yet, although girls tend to do better than boys in math in elementary schools, their scores decrease vis a vis boys' at the secondary school level (Maccoby and Jacklin 1974). Thus, math becomes stereotyped as a male domain, although increasingly more by males than by females, and females have been found to be less confident in math (Fennema and Sherman 1978; Ernest 1976; Fox 1974).

Through play as well as other influences, young children begin to form conceptions of appropriate adult occupational roles for females and males as well as aspirations for their own future roles. Research indicates that sex differences in children's occupational interests and aspirations are persistent at a very early age (Beuf 1974; Harris 1974), although children are less rigid in use of stereotypes as they get older (Kreinberg 1980; O'Bryant, Durrett, and Pennebak 1978). Even so, stereotypes can be very deeply ingrained. In one study in which 128 five- and six-year-olds were shown four films depicting all possible combinations of male and female nurses and physicians, children irrespective of sex or age tended to relabel the counterstereotyped occupational portrayals (for example, female doctor) into stereotyped ones (for example, female nurse or male doctor). A stronger tendency toward relabeling male nurses than toward relabeling female physicians was noted (Cordua, McGraw, and Drabman 1979). Girls tend to be more restricted than are boys in their perceptions of the number of appropriate occupations for females and in their own aspirations (Hartley 1959; Kreinberg 1980; Looft 1971; Tremaine and Schau 1979; and Vondracek and Kirchner 1974), although in one study with black, Hispanic, and Angle fourth, fifth, and sixth graders, black girls were found to hold the most stereotyped views (Frost and Diamond 1979). Even so, and especially with in increase in age, girls are more easily able to break free of stereotypes and aspire to nontraditional occupations (Frost 1979; O'Bryant, Durrett, and Pennebak 1978; Tremaine and Schau 1979) which can have important implications for educational programs aimed at broadening career interests and opportunities. Even though boys tend to be more rigid in adhering to stereotypes, they are more likely than girls to express a wider range of jobs suitable for males as well as ones of interest to them (Kreinberg 1980; Tremaine and Schau 1979). However, boys are also more likely than girls to have higher expectations for their own careers than are realistic considering their abilities, and this often results in emotional problems (Frazier and Sadker 1973; Pleck and Brannon 1978; Waldron 1976).

Just as young children's stereotypical views affect their conception of occupational roles, the same is true for their educational aspirations and achievement.

Educational Achievement and Aspirations. While girls remain more likely to think of and express desire in becoming a parent than do boys, they think less of college attendance and of adequate career preparation. Even though females receive better grades than do males while in school, they are less likely to believe they are capable of doing college work (Gross 1968). Girls tend to do better in math in the elementary years, but their interest and scores in math and science tend to decline in secondary school; this significantly affects their decision to enroll (or not to enroll) in the college-preparatory math classes increasingly necessary for high-paying and status career positions (*Time,* 1977; Maccoby and Jacklin 1974; Sells 1978). Sells found that of the entering students at the University of California at Berkeley, only 8 percent of females compared to 57 percent of males had sufficient math prerequisites to enable them to major in science, engineering, or other math-based courses. Women represent only approximately 8 percent of the science and engineering Ph.D.'s in the country. Yet in a study of students in grades 2–12, boys and girls alike (30 percent of all) said math was their favorite subject with 24 percent liking it second best (Ernest 1976).

Thus, early sex-stereotyping of educational as well as career fields can greatly influence children's behavior and their aspirations. But how are these notions formed? The next section will focus on sex-role development—the learning of sex identity, roles, and aspirations.

Sex-Role Development

Although most social scientists agree that there is probably an interactive influence, controversy still exists regarding the origin of sex differences—whether they arise from innate biological differences or are acquired as a result of learning social and cultural roles, norms, and values. Three prominent perspectives will be briefly discussed—the biological, environmental, and cognitive.

There are some obvious physical sex differences, for example, greater size and strength, higher metabolic rates and slower rates for physiological maturation, and higher rates of injury, disease, and developmental problems for males (Maccoby and Jacklin 1974). Less obvious but generally agreed upon differences (or potentials) which are *perhaps* due to biological conditions are those of higher verbal ability in girls and spatial ability and aggressiveness in boys, although the research findings are mixed (Block 1976; Maccoby and Jacklin 1974; Lewis and Weinraub 1979). Even more difficult to determine as being based on biological differences are findings that girls are more passive, dependent, suggestible, less achievement-oriented, and have lower self-esteem than boys (Block 1976; Maccoby and Jacklin 1974; Lewis and Weinraub 1979). Aggression and dominance differences have been found to be widespread—even cross-culturally, although not universally, and thus most likely not based on biological differences alone (Mead 1939). Jacklin hypothesizes that the greater aggression for boys may be attributable to a "toughness" hierarchy which develops from the larger-sized play groups formed by boys than by girls, who tend to play in groups of two or three.

Opposition to the view that sex differences are primarily biologically based derives from an assumption that socialization, or environmental factors, are the most critical. Environmental approaches stress the importance of learned differences and the transmitting of sex roles, the emphasis being on the differential behavioral reinforcement patterns shown by others—

parents, teachers, peers, as well as the media. While biological influences may predispose males and females to behave differently, socialization is viewed as reinforcing or limiting persons in their options. As sex roles vary by culture and within a society, individuals are viewed as being able to vary the boundaries between masculinity and femininity and the societally acquired personality characteristics.

A third and increasingly used perspective is that of a cognitive explanation, in which the children actively construct their sex roles through cognition. It is this approach which combines both biological and environmental factors (Lewis and Weinraub 1979). Kohlberg (1966) is most prominent in developing this theory. According to Kohlberg, children's social cognitions, which include gender identity and an awareness of sex-role stereotypes, play a critical role in developing sex-typed behavior. Three steps are involved: children becoming aware of their own gender (or sex) labels; children exhibiting differential behaviors, attitudes, and preferences common to their sex; and children finding rewarding opportunities to behave in sex-appropriate ways.

A possible link between sex-role socialization and cognitive theories relates to age of onset. Cognitive development is viewed as beginning not before the age of three, whereas sex-role socialization is thought to begin at birth. Perhaps the link is that socialization prepares the way for, and continues through reinforcement to influence, cognitive development of sex identity and sex-role acquisition. The age of onset of sex-role acquisition is a controversial one, with many researchers and theoreticians believing that children have formed their sex identities before the age of three and, in fact, understand the sex-appropriateness of toys, activities and other behaviors by then. Also, children who are exposed to either appropriate or inappropriate sex-typed labeling of neutral activities have been found to be influenced in their activity preferences and performances (Montemayor 1974; Stein et al. 1971; and Thompson 1975).

Regardless of the approach, there is much evidence to support the notion that a substantial portion of sex identity, sex roles, and aspirations is acquired through learning and cognition, based on culture, environment, and interaction with significant others. Of interest now is *how* this occurs, and *who* and *what* influence children in their sex-role development.

Agents of Sex-Role Development

Agents of sex-role development include the family, the media, and the school.

Family. Traditionally, the family has been viewed as being the primary agent of overall socialization. However, recent research results have been mixed with regard to girls and boys being treated differentially by their parents (Block, 1976; Langlois and Downs 1980; Maccoby and Jacklin 1974).

Many of the studies that find a difference in parental treatment of boys and girls indicate that boys, rather than girls, are taught stereotyped behaviors earlier and more harshly, and that parents tolerate daughters playing with sex-inappropriate toys (and behaving in boyish ways) more than they tolerate similar behavior from sons (Fein et al. 1975; Fling and Manosevitz 1972; Langlois and Downs 1980; Maccoby and Jacklin 1974). Masculinity for boys is viewed as more important to be learned and preserved than is femininity for girls, which may be because male role attributes are seen by society as more positive than those of females. In fact, males are still favored over females in parental preference for newborns, and parents of only children are more likely to want a second child if the first is a girl (Hoffman 1977).

Also, adolescents perceive different forms of play as sex-appropriate (Fagot and Litzman 1975) and parents of six-year-olds have very different views of the behavior of "typical boys" and "typical girls" (Lambert, Yackley, and Hein 1971) as do parents of three- to five-year-olds (Muller and Goldberg 1980).

Although Langlois and Downs (1980) found little empirical evidence for the view that rewards are given for sex-appropriate behavior, they did find the sex of the parent and the age of the child to be relevant variables. In a study of forty-eight three- and five-year-olds they found that mothers rewarded both boys and girls more than did peers and that fathers gave more rewards to females and three-year-olds and more punishment to boys and five-year-olds. However, research findings vary with regard to sex of parent and its influence on sex roles. Huston-Stein and Higgins-Trenk (1978) found that girls are more likely to engage in traditionally feminine behavior when their fathers encourage them to do so, yet Tauber (1979) found that it is the mother who is more important in determining sex-typed behavior with both girls and boys. Other interesting findings of this study were that the sex of the siblings is most important, at least in toy preference, and that children are more likely to play with toys that are nontraditional for their sex when in single-parent families. This was also found by Hunt and Hunt (1977) who noted that girls in particular benefit from father-absence in terms of being freed from sex-typing. Elrod and Crase (1980) found that fathers tend to interact more frequently with sons and that mothers interact more frequently with both sons and daughters than fathers do. Meyer (1980) found in a study of six- to twelve-year-old working-class girls that the older the girl the more her sex-typed role prescriptions and attitudes corresponded with her mother's sex-role attitudes and with the mother's goals for her daughter's future. In keeping with the notion of parental influence as related to learning of sex roles and aspirations, boys

and girls tend to be assigned household responsibilities based on a traditional division of adult responsibilities (Duncan, Schuman, and Duncan
1973). This may be changing with the increase in single-parent families as
well as with the trend toward parent-shared responsibilities.

Boys are more likely to experience anxiety over sex identity and sex
roles and to refrain from doing anything "feminine" (Hartley 1959; Maccoby and Jacklin 1974).

While it is not clear at this time whether infant sex differences are a
result or a cause of sex-differentiated parental behavior, it is apparent that
parental influences begin early. Parents do act in certain ways based on
their own attitudes, values, cognitions, and perceptions.

In a study of parents of new-born infants, mothers and fathers were
asked to describe their newborns within twenty-four hours of birth using an
eighteen-item bipolar scale with the health and size of sampled babies being
controlled. Stereotypes were prevalent; girls were described as softer, pret-
tier, more inattentive, awkward, and delicate. Boys were described as
firmer, larger-featured, fussier, more coordinated, alert, stronger, and
hardier (Rubin, Provenzano, and Luria 1974). In fact, toddler girls may
receive more verbal stimulation from adults (Gunnar and Donahue 1980),
whereas boys receive more physical stimulation (Moss 1967).

Findings from the scant research involving social class and ethnic differences indicate that socialization practices in working- and lower-class
families are more rigid and reliant on stereotypes than they are in middle-
class families (Rubin 1976; Scanzoni and Scanzoni 1976).

Media. Television is an increasingly influential agent of sex-role development. It has been estimated that children under five watch 25.5 hours of
television a week and that by the time children finish high school, they will
have watched fifteen thousand hours (Action for Children's Television
1978). Children learn about adult roles as well as sex-appropriate and inappropriate behavior by viewing TV programs and commercials (Sternglanz
and Serbin 1974). Children who view highly stereotyped programs tend to
adopt sex stereotypes in their behavior and attitudes (Davidson, Yasuma,
and Tower 1979; Frueh and McGhee 1975).

Picture books are also a significant influence in sex-role development,
as many studies demonstrate. It is through books that children are reinforced by pictures as well as words with regard to female and male roles for
both children and adults. A classic in this field is the study conducted by
Weitzman et al. (1972) in which award-winning picture books were analyzed
for treatment of sex roles. For the most part females were invisible in terms
of their representation in titles, central roles, pictures, and stories. Eleven
pictures of males were found for every picture of a female. Stereotypes were
prevalent, including passive and doll-like females who were mainly in ser-

vice roles, and males who were active, adventuresome, independent, and self-confident. Most women were shown as mothers and wives only. In another study, sex-role stereotypes in children's stories were found to have an immediate effect on the achievement behavior of children (McArthur and Eisen 1976). Books can also be used to *reduce* the use of stereotypes, however, as was found in a study in which sex-role beliefs decreased after four- and five-year-olds were exposed to egalitarian models in picture books (Flerx, Fidler, and Rogers 1976).

School. As children grow older, school takes on an increasingly important role in influencing sex-role development. Teachers, peers, the curriculum, textbooks and other curricular materials, guidance-testing practices and materials, and tracking systems all contribute to providing a different education for girls than for boys. Although Title IX of the 1972 Education Amendments of the 1965 Civil Rights Act has made possible significant advances toward sex-equitable educational programs and educators' awareness of their advantages, differential treatment still exists. Our focus here is on early childhood years.

It has been consistently found that most of the common school practices reinforce traditional sex-role stereotypes (Frazier and Sadker 1973; Guttentag and Bray 1976; Simmons and Whitfield 1979). The most influential agent is likely to be the teacher, whose expectations and treatment of girls and boys closely parallel those of parents (Cherry 1977; Maccoby and Jacklin 1974). As do parents, teachers tend to respond more negatively to boys engaging in sex-inappropriate behavior but also tend to give more attention to boys, both positive and negative (Maccoby and Jacklin 1974; Alfren, Aries, and Oliver 1979). In particular, teachers respond to boys and girls for different types of behavior, for example, to disruptive and aggressive behavior of boys and neatness of girls (Serbin, O'Leary, Kent, and Tolnick 1973). As do parents, teachers and counselors (in the secondary school grades) advise students, especially boys, to aspire to sex-stereotyped careers (Frazier and Sadker 1973; Pleck and Brannon 1978). Stereotyping and discrimination can occur even with feminist teachers; a study found them to be more attentive to preschool girls who wore dresses (Joffee 1971).

The structure and environment of the school have also been found to be germane to sex-role development, particularly in play and toy preference. Preschool children are more likely to engage in mixed-sex groupings for play in open schools as compared to traditional schools (Bianchi and Bakeman 1978). Also, when activities are highly structured, both girls and boys tend to spend more time in organized activities. This has important implications in that girls, when given a chance, tend to spend more time in highly structured activities and boys more time in less-structured activities (Carpenter and Huston-Stein 1980).

Serbin (1980) found that preschool classrooms as well as play groups for three-year-olds are less segregated than those for five-year-olds and that this has changed little in the past ten years. She also has found different consequences of sex-differentiated treatment for boys and girls. Boys and girls learn different social skills, for example, leadership roles and interactional skills. Boys participate in male-dominated activities and learn large-motor-related skills of climbing, three-dimensional perceptions, riding, and building, whereas girls participate in activities and learn skills relating to fine-motor development, drawing, book "reading," doll-playing (nurturing), and housekeeping. Also, there are significant cognitive consequences, such as boys learning visual-spatial skills and girls verbal skills. Also, in an experimental setting, girls were found to spend more time interacting with the adult experimenter and boys were found to be more exploratory and more influenced by the number of toys available (Vliestra 1980).

Within their preschool environment, children are influenced by behaviors and preferences of their peers, for example, by being excluded from certain activities because of sex discrimination. But influences are also positive—when shown films of same-sex peers playing with non-sex-typed toys, children's sex-typed toy choices were found to decrease. This was found at all ages tested (preschool–grade 1), but more strongly with girls and the younger children (DiLeo, Moely, and Sulzer 1979; Wolf 1975).

Summary

The influences on sex-role development are many and diverse, not all of which have been covered here. However, it can be readily seen that even in today's world, young children are still exposed to traditional and in many cases outmoded concepts, expectations, and treatment that all serve to influence the formation of their own identities, roles, and aspirations. The last section will cover suggestions for changes to meet the needs of the nineties.

Meeting the Needs of the Nineties

Regardless of all of the pressures to conform to traditional sex roles, many children are able to break free of restraining stereotypes and influences and become well-rounded, independent, and self-confident in their childhood and their adult years. This can only be seen as increasingly important, given the projections for the 1990s. The needs of the nineties will *not* be met if girls of today learn to believe they will always have their economic needs met by a man; they need to learn self-sufficiency and assertiveness skills.

The needs of the nineties will *not* be met if boys of today learn to believe they will always have their housekeeping needs and children's needs met by a woman; they need to learn domestic and child-rearing skills. This is not to suggest that roles should be reversed; rather that children of today will be better prepared to become adults of tomorrow if they develop a wide range of interests and abilities instead of being limited in their options. Today's child—girl or boy—may be tomorrow's single parent, supporting a family; today's child may be a single adult without children and needing to take care of her- or himself; as an adult unemployed worker, today's child will be best prepared if able to pursue different lines of work. Girls as well as boys need to acquire all the education available to them depending on their interests and aptitude, not on their sex. In particular, mathematics and science instruction is critical for entrance into the expanding technological fields. Children need to be encouraged and supported, rather than restrained and channeled toward what is considered sex-appropriate.

But how can this be done? Structural changes in society are critical; here we will focus on one—necessary changes in preschool education. These must occur at both the personal and institutional levels and involve changes in the physical environment, curriculum, and teacher behavior.

Physical Environment. Children's play preferences and behavior can be affected by the physical environment—the more open the structure (social and physical), the less stereotypical and conforming is the child. As girls have been found to interact with and conform to expectations of adults more than boys do, it is important to be aware of this and encourage girls to interact more with their environment, be more adventurous and risk-taking. Girls also can benefit from participating in physical activities and in group activities, rather than playing almost exclusively in twos and threes. Physical activity can be stressed and encouraged. Boys need to be encouraged in small-group play as well as quiet activity. The physical environment provides an important incentive as it can create a mood conducive to certain activities. Seating, working, eating, and play areas should be integrated. There should never be an area reserved only for boys or for girls; this is particularly important with block and housekeeping areas. The bulletin boards and displays should portray females and males, adults and children, in a wide range of roles without any use of stereotyping. Not only should "sex-fair" criteria be used, but also "sex-affirmative" ones such that limiting, confining, and damaging stereotypes are countered, for example, showing people in nontraditional or integrated roles and activities.

Curriculum. The curriculum needs to be nonsexist, or based on a commitment to sex equity. Of course, most preschools could not afford to discard materials, even if they are somewhat stereotypical; however, staff can be trained to use them in a sex-affirmative way, for instance, by discussing with the children the outdated, often ridiculous, stereotypes. All new purchases of toys, books, records, and equipment should be scrutinized for their suitability. A growing number of nonsexist toys and books is available for purchase[4] which can provide important models for children; there are also photo sets, films, and other audio-visual items, as well as reference books on nonsexist parenting and teaching. Units of instruction on contributions of women to society, nontraditional jobs, homemaking, and families, to name a few, can be taught separately or incorporated into the existing curriculum.

Teachers. Teachers perhaps have the most important contribution to make. It is they who set the tone, provide role models, encouragement, and support, as well as intervene and redirect when necessary. According to Shargel and Kane (1974), teacher and parent interventions and examples are the only way to challenge stereotypes as new ideas are introduced which combat society's sexist and racist messages that children have been learning. These authors advocate four forms of adult intervention: supporting and encouraging of children who themselves challenge stereotypes and traditional male and female roles; exploring sex role stereotyping with children and their rights to engage in nontraditional behavior; encouraging children to question outdated, stereotyped attitudes and to experiment with new activities; and providing nontraditional, nonstereotypical role models—themselves, other adults and children (Shargel and Kane 1974, p. 13).

Teachers can also analyze their own beliefs, attitudes, expectations, and behaviors with regard to bias and discrimination and should be extremely careful in their messages to and interactions with children. They can encourage children in ways which will combat stereotypical behavior, such as having female teachers in the block area and male teachers in the housekeeping area; by complimenting children who engage in non-sex-typed activities and who use non-sex-typed toys; and by having children demonstrate the use of toys, materials, and equipment that are not sex-typed for their sex (Serbin 1980). Teachers can also encourage boys and girls to play together. They can treat both boys and girls warmly and affectionately, encouraging both to be independent, active, and to express their emotions (girls in particular need to know it is all right to be assertive and express anger; boys need to express fear and sadness and to know that by doing so or by participating in certain activities, they are *not* sissies). Teachers should also intervene when children discriminate against one another.

Teaching staff can receive in-service training so that they become aware of their own attitudes and behavior, and can develop strategies to use in overcoming bias and in promoting equity. Teachers will then be able to help parents in these endeavors.[5]

Children need to learn that they can develop to their fullest potential and need not be limited because of their sex, although they may encounter difficulties along the way. Children can learn how to cope with stress, bias, and to pursue options if they are sufficiently assertive and have self-confidence.

Besides the matters which we have already discussed, to be prepared for the 1990s children need to learn about parenting as a shared responsibility; that a wide range of jobs can be obtained whether they are female or male, if they develop the appropriate skills; that there are benefits to being able to express all emotions, and that boys need not hold in their feelings; females and males interacting in play and work enriches the experience, and that boys and girls can be friends with one another; and about developing their fullest potential—physically, as well as emotionally, socially and intellectually—which has not been typically the case for girls.

Fulfilling the needs of the nineties will be a real challenge for us, especially considering society as it is today. However, it is a challenge that we can face and can meet if we are willing.

Notes

1. Data come from the U.S. Department of Labor, *Job Options for Women in the 80's,* Pamphlet 18, 1980, and U.S. Department of Labor, *20 Facts on Women Workers,* Dec. 1980.

2. Data are from a 1981 report from the National Center for Health Statistics.

3. The following definitions will be used throughout this chapter. Except where indicated otherwise, these are drawn from Jenkins and Macdonald, 1979. *Sex:* the biological condition of being female or male; *Gender:* the psychological differentiation describing femininity and masculinity; *Sex Identity:* one's understanding of being male or female: I am a boy; I am a girl; *Sex (or Gender) Roles:* behavioral and personality characteristics associated with being feminine or masculine; for example, a female being feminine by being emotional and "playing the role" of a housewife or nurse; a male being masculine by being independent and "playing the role" of provider or doctor; *Gender Identity:* one's internalization of the sex roles associated with being female or male. Sex identity is a girl's or woman's self-concept of being feminine and of being biologically female; a boy's or man's self-concept of being masculine and of being biologically male; *Sex-Role Stereotypes:* overgeneralizations concerning expectations about "sex-appropriate" activities, abilities, attributes, and preferences; *Sex-Typing:* process by which adults help children acquire an understanding of their masculine and feminine sex roles (Robinson and Flake 1978); *Sex-Role*

Socialization: process by which persons come to understand and accept masculine and feminine sex roles.

4. For a detailed list, see Jenkins and Macdonald 1979; Non-Sexist Child Development Project 1980; Shargel and Kane 1974; Sprung 1975.

5. For more information on nonsexist parenting, see Carmichael 1977; Daley 1979; Dunn and Dunn 1977; Greenberg 1978; Levine 1976; Lyon 1978; Pogrebin 1980.

References

Action for Children's Television, 1978.

Alfren, S.H.; Aries, E.J.; and Oliver, R.R. Sex differences in the interaction of adults and preschool children. *Psychological Reports* 33: 115-118, 1979.

Beuf, A. Doctor, lawyer, household drudge. *Journal of Communication* 24:142-145, 1974.

Bianchi, B.P., and Bakeman, R. Sex-typed affiliation preferences observed in preschools—traditional and open school differences. *Child Development* 49:910-912, 1974.

Block, J. Issues, problems, and pitfalls in assessing sex differences: a critical review of the psychology of sex differences. *Merrill-Palmer Quarterly* 22:283-309, 1976.

Booth, A. Sex and social participation. *American Sociological Review,* April 1972, pp. 183-93.

Bracken, J. and Wigutoff, S. *Books for todays' children.* Old Westbury, N.Y.: Feminist Press, 1979.

Carmichael, C. *Non-sexist childraising.* Boston: Beacon Press, 1977.

Carpenter, J.C., and Huston-Stein, A. Activity structure and sex typed behavior in preschool children. *Child Development* 51:862-872, 1980.

Cherry, L. The preschool teacher-child dyad sex differences in verbal interaction. *Child Development* 46:532-536, 1977.

Cohen, N.L., and Tomlinson-Keasey, C. The effect of peers and mothers on toddlers' play. *Child Development* 51:921-924, 1980.

Cordua, G.; McGraw, K.; and Drabman, R. Doctor or nurse: children's perceptions of sex-typed occupations. *Child Development* 50:590-593, 1979.

Daley, E. *Father feelings.* New York: Simon and Schuster, Pocket Books, 1979.

Davidson, E.; Yasuma, A.; and Tower, A. The effects of TV cartoons on sex-role stereotyping in young girls. *Child Development* 50:597-600, 1979.

DiLeo, J.C.; Moely, B.E.; and Sulzer, J.L. Frequency and modifiability of children's preferences for sex-typed toys, games, and occupations. *Child Study Journal* 9:141–159, 1979.

Duncan, P.; Schuman, H.; and Duncan, B. *Social change in a metropolitan community*. New York: Russell Sage, 1973.

Dunn, R., and Dunn, K. *How to raise independent and professionally successful daughters*. Englewood Cliffs, N.J.: Prentice-Hall, 1977.

Eisenberg-Berg, N.; Boothby, R.; and Matson, T. Correlates of preschool girls' feminine and masculine toy preference. *Developmental Psychology* 15:354–55, 1979.

Elrod, M., and Crase, S. Sex differences in self-esteem and parental behavior. *Psychological Report* 46:719–727, 1980.

Emmerich, W.; Goldman, K.S.; Kirsh, B.; and Sharabany, C. Evidence for a transitional phase in the development of gender constancy. *Child Development* 48:930–936, 1977.

Ernest, J. Mathematics and sex. *American Mathematical Monthly* 6, April 1976.

Fagot, B.J., and Littman, I. Stability of sex role and play interests from preschool to elementary school. *Journal of Psychology* 89:285–292, 1975.

Fein, G.; Johnson, D.; Josson, N.; Stork, L.; and Wasserman, L. Sex-stereotypes and preferences in the toy choices of 20-month boys and girls. *Developmental Psychology* 11:527–528, 1975.

Fennema, E.H., and Sherman, J.A. Sex-related differences in mathematics achievement related factors: a further study. *Journal of Research in Mathematics and Education* 9:189–203, 1978.

Flerx, V.; Fidler, D.; and Rogers, R. Sex-role stereotyping: developmental aspects and early intervention. *Child Development* 7:101–109, 1976.

Fling, S., and Manosevitz, M. Sex typing in nursery school children's play interests. *Developmental Psychology* 7:146–152, 1972.

Fox, L.H. Facilitating the development of mathematical talent in young women. Ph.D. dissertation. John Hopkins University, 1974.

Frazier, N., and Sadker, M. *Sexism in school and society*. New York: Harper and Row, 1973.

Frost, F., and Diamond, E. Ethnic and sex differences in occupational stereotyping by elementary school children. *Journal of Vocational Behavior* 15:43–54, 1979.

Frueh, T., and McGhee, P. Traditional sex role development and amount of time spent watching television. *Developmental Psychology* 11:109, 1975.

Ganger, W.H., and Walker, K. The dollar value of household work. Ithaca, N.Y.: Cornell 1979.

Garrett, C.S.; Ein, P.L.; and Tremaine, L. The development of gender stereotyping of adult occupations in elementary children. *Child Development* 48:507–512, 1977.

Greenberg, S. *Right from the start*. Boston: Houghton Mifflin, 1978.

Gross, Patricia. College women: a research description. *Journal of National Association of Women's Deans and Counselors* 1:12–21, 1968.

Gunner, M.R., and Donahue, M. Sex differences in social responsiveness between six months and twelve months. *Child Development* 51: 262–265, 1980.

Guttentag, M., and Bray, H. *Undoing sex stereotypes*. New York: McGraw-Hill, 1976.

Harris, S.R. Sex-typing in girls' career choices: a challenge to counselors. *Vocational Guidance Quarterly* 23:128–133, 1974.

Hartley, R.E. Sex role pressures and the socialization of the male child. *Psychological Reports* 5:457–468, 1959.

Helson, R. Childhood interests related to creativity in women. *Journal of Consulting Psychology* 29, 1965.

Hoffman, L.W. Changes in family roles, socialization, and sex differences. *American Psychologist* 32:644–657, 1977.

Hunt, J.G., and Hunt, L.L. Race, daughter, and father-loss: does absence make the girl grow stronger. *Social Problems* 25:91, 1977.

Huston-Stein, A., and Higgins-Trenk, A. Development of females from childhood through adulthood: careers and feminine role orientations. In *Life-span: development and behavior,* ed. P. Baltes. New York: Academic Press, 1978.

Jacklin, C.N. Sex differences and their relationship to sex equity in learning and teaching. Paper prepared for National Institute of Education, September 1977.

Jenkins Kohl, J.; and Macdonald, P. *Growing up equal: activities and resources for parents and teachers of young children,* Englewood Cliffs, N.J.: Prentice-Hall, 1979.

Joffee, C. Sex role socialization, and the nursery school: as the twig is bent. *Journal of Marriage and the Family,* August 1971, pp. 467–475.

Kagan, J. On the meaning of behavior: illustrations from the infant. *Child Development* 40:1121–1134, 1969.

Kohlberg, L. A cognitive-developmental analysis of children's sex-role concepts and attitudes. In *The Development of Sex Differences,* ed. E. Maccoby. Stanford: Stanford University Press, 1966.

Kreinberg, N. EQUALS: a program to promote sex-fair mathematics instruction and counseling. *EQUAL PLAY* 1, nos. 2 and 3, 1980.

Kuhn, D.; Nash, S.; and Brucken, L. Sex role concepts of two- and three-year-olds. *Child Development* 49:445–451, 1978.

Lambert, W.E.; Yackley, A.; and Hein, R.N. Child training values of English Canadian and French Canadian parents. *Canadian Journal of Behavioral Science* 3:217–236, 1971.

Langlois, J.H., and Downs, A.C. Mothers, fathers, and peers as socialization agents of sex-typed play behavior in young children. *Child Development* 51:1237–1247, 1980.

Lever, J. Ms. gazette. *MS,* February 1977.

Levine, J. *Who will raise the children: new options for fathers and mothers.* Philadelphia: Lippincott, 1976.

Lewis, M., and Weinraub, M. Origins of early sex-role development. *Sex Roles* 2:135–153, 1979.

Looft, W.R. Vocational aspirations of second grade girls. *Psychological Report* 28:241–242, 1971.

Lott, B. Behavior concordance with sex role identity related to play areas, creativity, and parental sex typing of children. *Journal of Personality and Social Psychology* 36:1087–1100, 1978.

Lyon, H. *Tenderness is strength: from machismo to manhood.* New York: Harper & Row, 1978.

Maccoby, E., and Jacklin, C.N. *The psychology of sex differences.* Stanford, Calif.: Stanford University Press, 1974.

Masters, J.C., and Wilkenson, A. Consensual and discriminative stereotyping of sex-typical judgments by parents and children. *Child Development* 47:208–217, 1976.

McArthur, L., and Eisen, S.V. Achievement of male and female storybook characters as determinant of achievement behaviors by boys and girls. *Journal of Personality and Social Psychology* 33:467–473, 1976.

Mead, M. *Sex and temperament in three primitive societies.* New York: Morrow, 1939.

Meyer, B. The development of girls' sex-role attitudes. *Child Development* 51:508–514, 1980.

Minton, C.; Kagan, J.; and Levine, J. Maternal control and obedience in the two-year-old. *Child Development* 42:1873–1894, 1971.

Montemayor, R. Children's performance in a game and their attention to it as a function of sex-typed labels. *Child Development* 45:156–166, 1974.

Moss, H. Sex, age and state as determinants of mother-infant interaction. *Merrill-Palmer Quarterly* 13:19–36, 1967.

Muller, R., and Goldberg, S. Why William doesn't want a doll: preschooler's expectations of adult behavior towards girls and boys. *Merrill-Palmer Quarterly* 26:259–269, 1980.

Nadelman, L. Sex identity in American children: memory, knowledge, and preference tests. *Developmental Psychology* 10:413–417, 1974.

Non-sexist Child Development Project. A bibliography of materials for equal early education. New York: Women's Action Alliance, 1980.

O'Bryant, S.L.; Durrett, M.E.; and Pennebak, J.W. Developmental and sex differences in occupational preference. *Journal of Psychology* 39: 466–472, 1978.

Pleck, J., and Brannon, R. Male roles and the male experience. *Journal of Social Issues* 34:1, 1978.

Pogrebin, L.C. *Growing up free.* New York: McGraw-Hill, 1980.

Rheingold, H.L., and Cook, K.V. Contents of boys' and girls' rooms as an index of parents' behavior. *Child Development* 46:459–463, 1975.

Robinson, B.E., and Flake, H. Beyond sex-role stereotyping. *Day Care and Early Education* 6:16–18, 1978.

Rubin, J.; Provenzano, F.J.; and Luria, Z. The eye of the beholder: parents' views on sex of newborns. *American Journal of Psychiatry* 44: 512–519, 1974.

Rubin, L. *Worlds of pain: life in the working class family.* New York: Basic Books, 1976, pp. 125–126.

Scanzoni, L., and Scanzoni, J. *Men, women and change: a sociology of marriage and family.* New York: McGraw-Hill, 1976.

Schau, C.G.; Kahn, L.; Diepold, J.; and Cherry, F. The relationships of parental expectations and preschool children's verbal sex typing to their sex typed play behavior. *Child Development* 51:266–277, 1980.

Sells, L. Mathematics—a critical filter. *The Science Teacher,* February, 1978, pp. 28–29.

Serbin, L.A. Remarks presented at Congress on Equal Early Childhood Education, Grailville, Ohio, June 1980.

Serbin, L.A.; O'Leary, D.; Kent, R.; and Tolnick, J. A comparison of teacher responses to the preacademic and problem behavior of boys and girls. *Child Development* 44:736–804, December 1973.

Serbin, L.A., and Connor, J.M. Sex typing of children's play preferences and patterns of cognition performance. *Journal of Genetic Psychology* 134:315–316, 1979.

Shargel, S., and Kane, I. We can change it. *Change for Children,* 1974.

Simmons, B., and Whitfield, E. Are boys victims of sex-role stereotyping? *Childhood Education* 56:75–79, 1979.

Smith, R. *The silent revolution: women at work.* Washington, D.C.: The Urban Institute, 1979.

Sprung, B. *Non-sexist education for young children.* New York: Citation Press, 1975.

Stein, A.H.; Pohly, S.; Pohly, R.; and Mueller, E. The influence of masculine, feminine, and neutral tasks on children's achievement behavior, expectancies of success, and attainment value. *Child Development* 42: 195–207, 1971.

Sternglanz, S.H., and Serbin, L.A. Sex role stereotyping in children's TV programs. *Developmental Psychology* 10:710–715, 1974.

Tanner, J.M. Physical growth. In *Carmichael's Manual of Child Psychology,* ed. P.H. Mussen. New York: Wiley, 1970.

Tauber, M. Parental socialization techniques and sex differences in children's play. *Child Development* 50:225–234, 1979.

Thompson, S.K. Gender labels and early sex role development. *Child Development* 6:339–347, 1975.

Time, Math mystique: fear of figuring. March 14, 1977.

Tobias, S. *Overcoming math anxiety.* New York: Norton, 1978.

Tremaine, L., and Schau, G. Sex role aspects in the development of children's vocational knowledge. *Journal of Vocational Behavior* 14:317–328, 1979.

Vliestra, A.G. Effects of adult-directed activity, number of toys, and sex of child on social and exploratory behavior in young children. *Merrill-Palmer Quarterly* 26:231–238, 1980.

Vondracek, S.E., and Kirchner, E.P. Vocational development in early hood: an examination of young children's expression of vocational aspirations. *Journal of Vocational Behavior* 5:251–260, 1974.

Waldron, I. Why do women live longer than men? *Journal of Human Stress* 2:1–13, 1976.

Weitzman, L.J.; Eifler, D.; Hokada.; and Ross, C. Sex role socialization in picture books for preschool age children. *American Journal of Sociology* May 1972.

Wolf, T. Response consequences to televised modeled sex-inappropriate play behavior. *Journal of Genetic Psychology* 127:35–44, 1975.

Women, Project on the Status and Education of. Campus child care: a challenge for the 80's. May 1980.

10 The Structure and Content of Early Representational Play: The Case of Building Blocks

Stuart Reifel

In early childhood education, there have been many trends over the decades. In both intervention programs and noncompensatory programs, we have seen experimentation with ideas such as didactic teaching methods (for example, Bereiter and Engelmann 1966), Piagetian curricula (for example, Kamii and DeVries 1977; Lavatelli 1970), British infant education models (for example, Weber 1971), and literally dozens of other educational approaches. All of these perspectives have contributed something to our ways of working with young children. Each has had a period of ascendency, when its new techniques or materials have been tried with interest by concerned educators. When a technique or material is sensed to be of merit, it remains as a more or less permanent fixture in our classrooms. One material that has endured in early childhood education at least since the time of Froebel (1895) is building blocks.

In this chapter we will take a look at building blocks as young children make use of them for symbolic representation. A review of the literature will show that blocks historically have been viewed as a representational material for young children. That view of blocks has not been well documented by research. The results of several current studies will be presented (Reifel, 1981a, 1981b; Reifel and Greenfield 1982), showing how representational block constructions become more differentiated with children's increasing age. Evidence will be presented showing that, with increasing age, children represent different conceptions of a referent (that is, the content of representation), and they demonstrate more complex combinations of blocks (that is, structures) in their depictions of specific referents. These findings suggest a number of implications for teachers regarding the use and interpretation of block use in the classroom. This information can be used to argue for the inclusion of play activity as an important part of learning in early childhood.

The illustrations for this chapter were prepared by the staff of the Media Laboratory, College of Education, University of Texas at Austin. Their cooperation and fine work are appreciated.

171

Before discussing the research findings, it is pertinent to make a number of comments regarding block play as an issue of interest for us now and into the 1990s. In one sense, play in the early childhood curriculum is an old topic, dating back to the thinking of Froebel and Comenius. Ideas about the value of block play continued through the centuries and received a good deal of attention, especially during the Progressive Era in education (see Winson 1973); blocks are still important in today's classrooms. There is a need to know more about this material that is a part of many early childhood programs.

Over the past ten years or so, play in general has become a more common focus of research. We have become much more aware of the significance of young children's playful gesture (Barten 1979; Fein 1975), language (Garvey 1977), and other forms of play. Studies in this vein have begun to show the role that various types of play have in the child's understanding of the world and in the child's impact on the world. We are now establishing the groundwork for research that will demonstrate the meaning that young children's play has in their development. For those of us who firmly believe in the thoughtful use of play experiences in early childhood education, this research will be valuable evidence to support our rationales and practices. It is clear that more research on many types of play will be forthcoming over the next decades.

One major thrust in research on young children's play has focused on the symbolic representational attributes of play (for example, Fein 1979a, 1979b). These studies of play have shown how young children indicate their knowledge of the world through their play activities. Educators and psychologists are coming to understand more about symbolic representation and its development. A recent book, *Symbolic Functioning in Childhood* (Smith and Franklin 1979), dealt entirely with theoretical and empirical knowledge of children's representation. Other current work has focused on language (for example, Bates, 1979), pretending and gesture (for example, Fein 1975, 1979a, 1979b), drawing (for example, Goodnow 1978; Smith 1972), and general artistic development (for example, Wolf and Gardner 1979). The importance of understanding the role of symbolic representation and its development was powerfully stated by Gardner (1979), who argues for inquiry into symbol systems. He states that symbolic development should be described in its various forms, and that each of those forms may take a different developmental route. Any number of symbol systems may make a different contribution to adult symbolic functioning. The cognitive aspects of symbol use in early childhood are an important place to look at symbolization. It is clear from this work that there is growing interest in the symbolic aspects of play, interest that will be built on into the 1990s. We have at this time only a glimpse of the complexity and importance of representation in early childhood. What we do know is presented in the following section of this chapter.

Definitions and the Literature on Block Play

Symbolic representation, sometimes simply referred to as representation, includes any of the methods humans use to express the activities of their minds. Among Webster's definitions of *represent* are "to bring clearly before the mind," "to serve as a sign or symbol," "depict," and "to present by means of something standing in the place of." A person with a given mental state (thoughts and feelings) selects some method for depicting that mental state, perhaps with the intent of making the mental state more clear either to himself or to others.

Examples of representations are diverse. Picasso represented a perception (that is, his mental state) of the Spanish Civil War with his canvas "Guernica." Piaget represented his thinking (that is, his mental state) with his book *The Origins of Intelligence*. One represents recognition of a friend (that is, a mental state) either with a wave of the hand or with another form of salutation. A child might represent his experience of visiting a farm by constructing a play farm with building blocks.

These diverse examples give a sample of the range of possible symbolic representations. People represent any number of mental states, both complex and seemingly simple. Piaget's written representation on thought in infancy is qualitatively different than a gestural representation of salutation with a wave of the hand, yet both are representations of something that has transpired in the minds of their creators. Likewise, "Guernica" is a representation of Picasso's powerfully emotional view of war, and the child's block play farm represents those aspects of his experience that he, for any number of reasons, has selected to reconstruct. Theories, data, social customs, emotions, lived experiences and so on, all provide content, or meanings, that can be represented. Some represented content, such as scientific theory, may seem to be objective, while other representations, such as paintings, music, or poetry, may seem to reflect personal or emotional perspectives. Representation, however, includes the full range of human expression. In all cases, a form of expression has been created to represent, or to stand for, something else that has been on the mind of its creator.

Children's representation by drawing, painting, modeling, and block play is standard educational activity in early childhood programs (for example, Brophy, Good, and Nedler 1975; Fein and Clarke-Stewart 1973; Fowler 1980; Hess and Croft 1975; Read and Patterson 1980; Sears and Dowley 1963). Plastic materials are made available to young children so that they can express any of the ideas or feelings that occupy their minds. It is presumed that children learn from their representation of what they know and feel (Biber, Shapiro, and Wickens 1971).

Representational use of building blocks has been central to many early childhood programs (for example, Pratt 1948; Mitchell 1963; Hirsch 1974).

Children use blocks to re-create their experiences on trips to farms and harbors, to construct their impressions of houses, roads, and landscapes, and to reconstruct neighborhoods in miniature. Block play, along with other forms of representation such as painting and modeling, form the central activities that occupy children in these programs. Yet, we know little about the nature of such representations.

What we do know about block play is documented either by recognition of blocks standing for something else or of the structural complexity of nonrepresentational block configurations. The following two sections present that literature.

The Child Representing with Blocks

Several studies document instances of children labeling or naming their block constructions, giving them representational meaning (Bailey 1933; Gesell and Ilg 1946; Hartley, Frank, and Goldenson 1952; Hartley and Goldenson 1963; Robinson 1958). Some authors simply list the names children give block constructions, either in classrooms (Hartley, Frank, and Goldenson 1952) or in experimental sessions (Bailey 1933; Robinson 1958). A child's designation of a construction as a house or as a road is documented as such.

Analytic literature adds additional interpretation to children's representational block constructions. Erikson (1951, 1963) describes many cases of children who create (that is, represent) scenes with blocks and other toys. Erikson has interpreted the forms of these representations as reflecting sex-role morphology and cultural roles; boys represent phallic towers and social setting from the work-world, while girls represent internal space and home scenes.

These interpretations of block constructions recognize a manifest meaning for block constructions (such as, house, tower, building), but also interpret the structure in terms of underlying psychological motivations (such as need for power, fear, control, release, and so on).

In all of these studies, an observer has documented the child's labels for block constructions, then has gone on to address nonrepresentational attributes of play. It seems possible to conclude that children do use blocks representationally, although we have little descriptive data on the form, content, or development of representation.

The Child Representing a Referential Object

Schuster (1973) attempted to control the object of representation by having two age groups of children (ages 5–7 and 9–11) construct a tower, a house, and another structure of their own choice. In the structured construction situation, when children built houses and towers, the author found no age or sex differences in the structures. All children demonstrated a "reality based building style," reflecting what from an adult's view seem to be the actual characteristics of houses and towers. Given our interest in the use of blocks to represent a referent, this study provides some insight into the child's representation of a specified object (house, tower).

From his observations, Piaget (1962) documents children's "brick" (that is, block) representations of houses and other objects. He describes a child who re-created a house, a stable, a woodshed, a garden, paths, and avenues, all out of building blocks. The child used this block setting as a stage for doll play. Piaget asserts that the child attempted to make these block constructions "exact and true to life." (p. 137). He relates such behavior to the semiotic function and discusses how representations reflect the child's differentiation of the signifier (the block construction) and the signified (the house, woodshed, path, and the rest).

After documenting the development of formal aspects of classroom block play, Guanella (1934) suggested four sources for children's classroom representation: home environment, city environment, country environment, and school environment. She does not develop this hypothesis or analyze data in terms of these sources.

In *Young Geographers* (Mitchell 1963) and *I Learn From Children* (Pratt 1948), the authors demonstrated representational uses of blocks with cases of children's classroom experiences. Blocks and other constructional materials were used by children to re-create experiences on field trips. Photographs demonstrate groups of children reconstructing in their classroom a harbor and a section of the city they had visited (Mitchell 1963). The relationship of representational constructions to previous objective experience is clear from those photos.

There is little validated evidence regarding the representational use of blocks or of its development. Children appear to use blocks representationally. We know little about how representation develops or about what it can be associated with, such as cognitive or affective development. No studies have compared the relative appropriateness of blocks (as opposed to other representational media) for representing various objects or concepts. Neither has there been a study of development of this hypothesized relationship. Also, no studies have documented the interpretation of block representation; it is not clear when or in what manner block representations become accessible, "public" symbols, understandable to adults or to other children.

Structural Complexity of Block Constructions

In two studies young children have been asked to duplicate constructed patterns (that is, three-block arches or combinations of such arches). Vereeken

(1961) found that younger children could not duplicate a pattern. Slightly older children could duplicate parts of the pattern and, by age seven, children could replicate the entire structure with all its parts in detail. Vereeken relates this increasing skill to the child's emerging comprehension of spatial relationships.

In a similar study, Hubner and Greenfield (no date) and Greenfield (1978) documented the development of children's ability to reproduce the complex structure of interconnected set of arches, that is, pairs of arches connected with other arches made of three blocks. Older children had progressively greater success with this task, a fact that those authors attribute to the more mature cognitive structures of the older children (Piaget 1971).

Several naturalistic studies of block construction have documented the ways older children use more complex block structures in the classroom (Guanella 1934; Johnson 1974). Johnson (1974) observed an age-related sequence to block use. Younger children will first combine blocks into rows or towers. Later, they will use a block to bridge two others, thereby forming an arch. After that, they will construct enclosures, flat on the floor. At this stage, all the previous skills will be used in the creation of patterns. When the child has mastered these skills, block constructions will begin to be used for representational purposes.

Guanella (1934) found evidence of more diverse constructional complexity in the early childhood classroom. The first use of blocks by the young child is nonorganized; blocks are carried or used to fill containers. Next there is a linear use of blocks, when children form rows or piles. The third stage in block use is an "areal" stage, when areas or surfaces are formed. There are two substages for the areal use of blocks. First, the child will construct a surface of blocks, forming what might be called a floor or a wall. second, the child will construct an enclosure, forming an area surrounded by blocks. The child may construct using these forms in a series. The final stage is the tridimensional use of blocks, which also has substages. The child's tridimensional use of blocks generally begins with the formation of solid, three-dimensional piles of blocks. Later the child will use blocks to enclose space, forming what might be seen as buildings with many stories. Guanella demonstrates that children's constructions in the classroom clearly do become more complex as children become older.

In all of these studies of block structure, there has been virtually no recognition of the child's possible representational intent as these various structural forms are used. All structural forms are treated as if they had no meaning for the child, with the exception of Johnson's comments that block constructions do eventually have representational meaning for children. We know that children use blocks to represent their knowledge of any number of things that they have experienced. What we have not known is the manner in which they make use of structural complexity as they represent at different ages.

Research Questions

In the next section of this chapter, findings will be presented that pertain to several aspects of representational block construction. First, looking at the content of representational block constructions, in what way is the content of a given referent included in the block representations of children at different ages? One would expect that children of different ages would have a different conception of or memory for the referent (Piaget 1962; Werner and Kaplan 1963), so their representations of the story would be uniquely different. Second, looking at the structure of block constructions, in what way do children's representations reflect the use of structural complexity? One would expect the use of more complex structures by older children, as suggested by the literature reported above.

Some Current Research on Representational Play

The research reported here is part of a larger study on the development of symbolic representation (Reifel 1981a, 1981b). Additional findings on block instruction and detail on methodology can be found in Reifel (1981b) and Riefel and Greenfield (1982).

Forty children from a laboratory school contributed data to this study. There were twenty four-year-olds and twenty seven-year-olds in the sample, with an equal number of boys and girls in each age group. The children were randomly selected from the population of four- and seven-year-olds in the school. There was some ethnic and socioeconomic mix in the sample, but all the children came from homes where English is the spoken language.

Each child was taken to an experimental room in the school, where a table was arranged with a box containing a set of table-top blocks. The child played with the blocks for a short time to become familiar with them and with the situation. Virtually every child appeared pleased to work with the blocks as soon as he or she sat at the table. After returning the blocks to the box, the child was asked to listen closely to the story of *Little Red Cap* (Grimm 1972), a version of *Little Red Riding Hood*. This provided the child with a referent that could be represented. When the story was finished, the child was directed, "Use the blocks to show me the story of *Little Red Cap*. You can use the blocks any way you like to show me the story we just read." The children began to construct with the blocks. A videotape camera was focused on the table and operated all the time each child built. When the child paused or indicated being finished, the researcher asked the child to describe in detail what the blocks showed. That description was also videotaped. After the child was escorted back to the classroom, a complete set of photos was taken of the block constructions.

Content of Block Representations

In what way is the referent represented in the block construction of children at different ages? Given the story of *Little Red Cap* as a referent for this study, we might expect that children would represent content from the story, such as Little Red Cap's house, the path, the trees, the flowers, Grandmother's house, and possibly the five characters from the story (Little Red Cap, her mother, the wolf, the grandmother, and the huntsman who saved them). Younger children who view the referent differently are expected to represent other things as well.

From the end-of-session child descriptions of construction, two adults transcribed child labels of what was represented with the blocks, agreeing on 283, or 97 percent of labels. Ninety-two (54 percent of the 170 seven-year-olds' representations) referred to the following story parts: characters (Little Red Cap, her mother, the wolf, her grandmother, and the hunter), Little Red Cap's house, Grandmother's house, the path, the woods, the flowers, and Grandmother's bed. Only 31 (27 percent of the 113 four-year-olds' representations) referred to those story parts. The higher percentage of story parts represented by seven-year-olds suggests that they were including more of the referent in their block constructions.

To test whether older children included proportionally more of the referent in their block constructions and whether younger children included proportionally less of the referent in their representations, each child was assigned a score equal to the proportion of story content to the total number of labels. This proportion gives a sense of how salient story content is in the total block representation, which is to say what part the referent has in the child's block representation. For example, a child who used blocks to represent Little Red Cap, the wolf, the woods, a path, Little Red Cap's house, and Grandmother's house was assigned a proportional equal to six out of six, or 100 percent story-related labels; a child who represented Grandmother's house, a path, flowers, a rainbow, and signs along the path was assigned a proportion equal to three out of five, or 60 percent, because only three of the representations refer to items in the story.

The mean proportions for younger children ($M = 23.9$) and for older children ($M = 56.0$) proved to be significantly different ($t = 5.07$, $p < .001$, $df = 38$, two-tailed test). The block representations of four-year-olds are composed of proportionally fewer elements from the referent and of more material that seems extraneous to the referent.

A comparison of the four-year-olds' representations with the seven-year-olds' representations will demonstrate what this analysis means. In figure 10-1, a four-year-old includes a flagpole, a bridge, a road, and a place to sit, in addition to the grandmother's house, woods, flowers, and path, from the story. Half of her total representation is not mentioned in

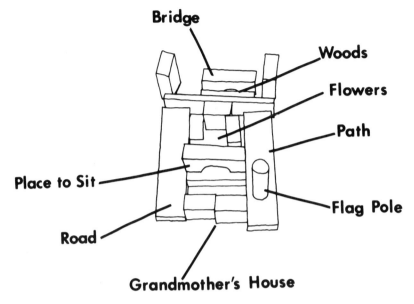

Figure 10-1. Four-year-old Girl's Representation

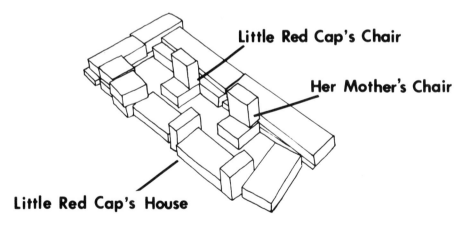

Figure 10-2. Four-year-old Boy's Representation

the story at all. Figure 10–2 shows a four-year-old boy's version of Little Red Cap's house, with two chairs inside. The chairs are not from the story. Other four-year-olds included representations of cars, camper-vans, furniture, airplanes, refrigerators, radios, and other things not part of the story. These things are frequently combined with representations of the grandmother's house or with characters from the story.

In contrast are the elaborate representations of the story by the seven-year-olds. For example, a boy shows the grandmother's house (with steps) and Little Red Cap approaching Grandmother's bed, on which lies the wolf with Grandmother in his stomach (figure 10-3). A girl has shown, in figure 10-4, the houses, path, and trees, and has removed the roof from Grandmother's house to show the bed and the two characters. And in figure 10-5, a girl also shows the houses, path, and Little Red Cap, this time with the flowers in the background. Each of these representations draws its content directly from the story, almost creating a setting for the story. In none of these cases are there flagpoles, cars, or other extraneous content.

The content of representations gets its meaning from the person's view of the referent. Referents clearly play an important role in the creation of representations, especially for older children. Based on the data from this study, it seems that a given referent (the story) plays an increasingly greater role in representation as children grow older. This raises several questions about the nature of the relationship of the referent to the person and to the symbolic vehicle (the blocks).

It seems likely that some of the age differences for represented content reported in this study can be attributed to the better memory for stories of seven-year-olds. One can, with some confidence, state that younger children are not as capable on many variables that are associated with memory, so they do not keep the referent in their minds as older children do. We also know that older children in this study are likely to rehearse the story in their

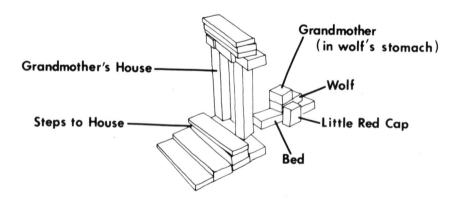

Figure 10-3. Seven-year-old Boy's Representation

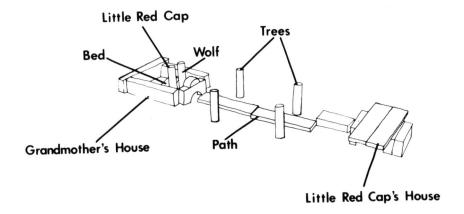

Figure 10–4. Seven-year-old Girl's Representation

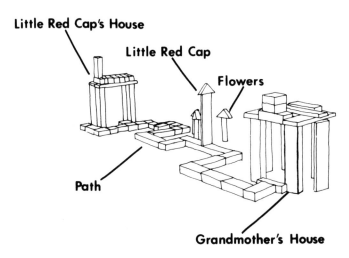

Figure 10–5. Seven-year-old Girl's Representation

minds while they construct with blocks. This ability is not available to the younger children, possibly allowing their representations to diverge from the content of the story.

It might be interesting to explore and document the "sources" for children's representational use of blocks, other than the referential objects we know have been presented. Where did the younger children get their ideas for ladders, cars, airplanes, and all the other nonstory material that they represented? It would be fascinating to be able to track down all of the sources for representation (that is, referents) that contributed to the block representations of some of the four-year-olds in this study.

Another possibility is that children of different ages conceive of referents in totally different manner. Older children may conceive of the story of *Little Red Cap* as a story about a little girl; they appear to represent it as such. Younger children may conceive of the story as "something I don't like" or as "something that's fun," or they may not actually conceive of the story, as such, at all. What goes into their minds as "referent" may not be what we would think of as the referent.

Structure of Block Representations

Blocks can be combined in any number of ways by children as they represent. Earlier research has shown that children's nonrepresentation block constructions become more complex as children grow older (Greenfield, 1978; Guanella, 1934; Hubner and Greenfield no date; Johnson 1974). Can this progression be seen in representational block construction as well?

What could this structural complexity look like in block play? Figure 10–1 shows a grandmother's house that is a simple row of two blocks. Many younger children construct houses that are piles or rows of blocks, blocks simply placed on top of or beside one another. Figure 10–2 shows a slightly more complex form for a house; the child has formed an enclosure by creating four walls. The child has formed a structure that shows one aspect of interior and exterior space, all on a horizontal plane. This same structuring of space is shown in the house in figure 10–3, where the child has used the arch-shape to stand for the basic form of the house. This structure is vertical, while the one in figure 10–2 is horizontal.

A whole new level of structural complexity is achieved when the child combines the enclosures seen in figures 10–2 and 10–3. The child forms both vertical and horizontal enclosures at one time, roofing the walls of the house. This can be seen in figure 10–4, where the child has made houses that are horizontal enclosures with roofs arching over the top. This is more complex than either of the earlier structures. Another level of complexity is shown by the child who creates arches, then arches the arches (figure 10–5).

An analysis reveals that older children are signficantly more likely to construct block houses at the higher levels of complexity described above (Reifel and Greenfield 1981). Fully 57 percent of the four-year-olds' houses were simple piles, while 80 percent of the seven-year-olds' houses were at least one arch. Only two four-year-olds constructed houses that were boxes. The only arched arch houses were built by seven-year-olds.

Clearly, the more complex constructions can be associated with the older children, who can be assumed to have more complex cognitive structures. It is interesting that older children apear to make selective use of their abilities with regard to the use of structural complexity; they use it only when it seems called for and apply it to the most appropriate cases. They do not waste time attempting to make complex characters, but they do try to show the complex part—whole relations of houses. Younger children, on the other hand, do not appear to be as able to produce complex structures. Their representations, as a result, are more global and less distinguishable to an observer (Reifel 1981b). Younger children are far more likely to use one block to stand for one referent, making it much more difficult to tell exactly what their representations are intended to mean (figure 10-1).

Not all older children, however, do make use of more complex structures; one seven-year-old made houses that are tiny piles of blocks. This suggests either that not all children gain the ability to build complex structures at the same rate or that even though the child may have the ability, he may not always demonstrate it.

The ability to construct more complex structures is important, because it is with these more complex structures that a child can show knowledge of detail and parts of the whole. If a child cannot construct a box shape, it is difficult to show walls, roof, and other house parts. These are signs of knowledge that cannot be demonstrated well with language, drawing, or other forms of communication.

Implications for Teaching

The findings from this study have implications for teaching in early childhood education. These implications will be stated in the form of principles that pertain to what a teacher can understand of children's behavior in the classroom and to how a teacher can provide educational experiences for young children through block use. A list of nine principles for teachers follows.

1. Representational block play is only a part of the child's development with blocks. Children need to have experiences feeling blocks, stacking blocks, carrying them, and so on before they can make use of them representationally (Guanella 1934; Johnson 1974).

2. It may be necessary for children to transform materials physiognomically (that is, simply pretend with blocks) before they can use blocks to represent content (such as a story or a field trip). It might be necessary to allow children time (possibly several years) to use the blocks to mean what they choose, before expecting them to represent an experience (Johnson 1974).

3. Younger children's constructions will transform, even while they are working on them. A new idea coming into the mind or an accidental disarrangement of blocks may change not only the form of the block construction, but also the meaning that a young child gives to block construction.

4. The block constructions of children have both content and form. These are ideas represented by children's block constructions, ideas that represent what is on the child's mind. The form of the blocks may or may not reveal those ideas, especially for younger children. Find a way to (discreetly) ask the child what the blocks show.

5. The block constructions of children of different ages will reflect content differently, syncretically for younger children and discretely for older children. Do not be surprised when a younger child includes any number of seemingly unrelated concepts in block play; that is typical for the age. Older children are more likely to focus their play on a discrete theme, but even then they will include some content that appears to be tangential.

6. The block constructions of children of different ages (and sexes with young children) are formally different. One cannot expect the same structural articulation from younger and older children. Chances are that teachers will not be able to distinguish the meaning of the block structures of younger children, based only on observation of those structures, although they will have a better chance of doing so for boys (Reifel 1981a, 1981b). Do not expect what children are not yet developmentally able to do.

7. To use blocks representationally, the child must have exposure to a referential object. Some children document their experience spontaneously with blocks. Others need encouragement and ideas before they will represent with blocks. Provide children with experiences that will serve as referential objects, such as field trips, literature, or films. Children need to experience before they can represent an experience.

8. Again, ask questions as the child constructs. The well-timed question can stimulate additional representation by reminding the child about relationships they have experienced and about details they might include. Construction can continue and elaborate in that way. By getting answers to questions, a teacher can evaluate the most salient aspects of the child's referential experience, then build on it.

9. What was most important for the child, as reflected in the representation? Might another experience provide important information that has been overlooked by the child in representation?

If teachers make use of these principles, they can encourage the use of blocks and learn to interpret children's meanings and materials use (Tyler 1977). Blocks can become a medium for understanding individiual children's learning and development, as well as a clue for planning and implementing classroom experiences that will be instructive to the children. By observing children's representation and knowing what they are thinking about, further experiences can be planned that build on that thinking.

Implications for Public Policy

Block play, per se, is not a critical topic for public debate. It is important to remember, however, that decision makers at all levels of our government are always in the position to require that we meet their specifications with regard to what goes on in our classrooms. All of us have had to deal on some level with Title XX specifications for the classroom or with state Department of Education guidelines for our curricula. An argument can be made that research findings, such as the ones regarding block play reported here, can be used by educators to convince policy makers that block play is a cognitive activity for young children, an activity that deserves serious attention in our planning, practice, and evaluation.

Government agents are not always attuned to the significance of some activities for young children. They do not understand the function of sand play, art, cooking, or block play in the development of young children. This research on block play demonstrates the extent to which young children's construction with blocks reveals what they know about a referent (in this case a story). Their play shows what they have learned about the story, in a medium that allows them to show details that language or drawing might not permit as easily at these ages. Simply put, blocks are a material that allow us to see and evaluate young children's knowledge. This is important, because we can now attempt to evaluate what children know based on observation of children's play in the block corner. Block play is one way for documenting what children are learning in the early childhood program. We must begin to inform state agencies and federal bureaucrats that block play is important in this way.

When policymakers design their regulations and evaluation standards, they must be made aware of the place of play in the early childhood classroom. It is not enough that they recognize the presence or absence of blocks in the classroom as an indicator of good programming. They also must be made aware of how blocks can be used by children in our programs to demonstrate knowledge. Are teachers recording children's descriptions of their constructions? Are teachers asking questions of children in an attempt to expand their knowledge of different referents? Are teachers aware of the structural complexity of children's constructions? Are they asking questions about the parts of what children show, indicating relationships in the world around us? All of these questions could serve as guides for the evaluation of practice in early childhood programs.

These questions draw attention to classroom activity that is both fun for the child and reflective of cognitive development. Children seem to take naturally to their play with blocks, so if we can make use of that natural interest for our educational purposes it will be to the child's benefit. We can, quite literally, turn our work into play.

Needs of the Nineties

Looking to the future of early childhood education research and practice, there are two avenues that can be followed with regard to children's representational skills. One avenue relates to policy questions (standards, regulations, and evaluation). The other relates to our understanding of representational skills.

In the policy domain, we must gather evidence and be ready to argue that classroom activities that we know to be healthy for young children are also significant for our understanding of child growth. I think the data reported here provides some evidence that block play is a cognitive activity for children. (It is also an activity that is social, affective, motoric, and fun.) When policymakers come to understand this point, they may become more receptive to our claims about the importance of the activities we provide for children.

In terms of research on early representation, we must begin to take a close look at all the forms of representation that children can use (Gardner 1979). Children can tell us a great deal about what they are thinking and feeling through their use of representational media. We need to describe in great detail the developmental stages in children's representational abilities so we can learn to interpret their classroom behavior. It may be that some representational media are more appropriate for some purposes. It may be that some children have better skills with some media. It is possible that the use of certain materials facilitates learning at later ages. All of these conjectures are potential research topics for the coming decades.

References

Bailey, M.W. A scale of block constructions for young children. *Child Development* 4:121–139, 1933.

Barten, S.S. Development of gesture. In *Symbolic functioning in childhood*. ed. N.R. Smith and M.B. Franklin. Hillsdale, N.J.: Lawrence Erlbaum Associates, 1979.

Bates, E. *The emergence of symbols*. New York: Academic Press, 1979.

Bereiter, C., and Engelmann, S. *Teaching disadvantaged children in the preschool*. Englewood Cliffs, N.J.: Prentice-Hall, 1966.

Biber, B.; Shapiro, E.; and Wickens, D. *Promoting cognitive growth*. Washington, D.C.: National Association for the Education of Young Children, 1971.

Brophy, J.E.; Good, T.L.; and Nedler, S.E. *Teaching in the preschool*. New York: Harper and Row, 1975.

Erikson, E.H. Sex differences in the play configurations of preadolescents. *Journal of Orthopsychiatry* 21:667-692, 1951.

Erikson, E.H. *Childhood and society*. 2nd ed. New York: Norton, 1963.

Fein, G.G. A transformational analysis of pretending. *Developmental Psychology* 11:291-296, 1975.

Fein, G.G. Pretend play: new perspectives. *Young Children,* 34(5):61-66, 1979a.

Fein, G.G. Play and the acquisition of symbols. In *Current topics in early childhood education,* vol. 2, ed. L.G. Katz. Norwood, N.J.: Ablex, 1979b.

Fein, G.G., and Clarke-Stewart, K.A. *Day care in context*. New York: Wiley, 1973.

Fowler, W. *Infant and child care*. Boston: Allyn and Bacon, 1980.

Froebel, F. *Pedagogies of the kindergarten*. translated by J. Jarvis. New York: Appleton, 1895.

Gardner, H. Developmental psychology after Piaget: an approach in terms of symbolization. *Human Development* 22:73-88, 1979.

Garvey, C. *Play*. Cambridge: Harvard University Press, 1977.

Gesell, A., and Ilg, F. *The child from five to ten*. New York: Harper, 1946.

Goodnow, J.J. Visible thinking: cognitive aspects of change in drawings. *Child Development* 49:637-641, 1978.

Greenfield, P.M. Structural parallels between language and action in development. In *Action, gesture, and language: the emergence of language,* ed. A. Lock. London: Academic Press, 1978.

Grimm, The Brothers. *The complete Grimm's fairy tales*. New York: Pantheon Books, 1972.

Guanella, F. Block building activities of young children. *Archives of Psychology,* no. 174, 1934.

Hartley, R.E.; Frank, L.K.; and Goldenson, R.M. *Understanding children's play*. New York: Columbia University Press, 1952.

Hartley, R.E., and Goldenson, R.M. *The complete book of children's play*. New York: Crowell, 1963.

Hess, R.D., and Croft, D.J. *Teachers of young children.* 2nd ed. Boston: Houghton Mifflin, 1975.

Hirsch, E.S., ed. *The block book.* Washington, D.C.: National Association for the Education of Young Children, 1974.

Hubner, J., and Greenfield, P.M. Building tree structures at three levels of hierarchical complexity: a developmental study. Manuscript. University of California at Los Angeles, no date.

Johnson, H. The art of block building. In *The block book,* ed. E.S. Hirsch. Washington, D.C.: National Association for the Education of Young Children, 1974.

Kamii, C., and DeVris, R. Piaget for early education. In *The preschool in action,* 2nd ed. ed. M.C. Day and R.K. Parker. Boston: Allyn and Bacon, 1977.

Lavatelli, C. *Piaget's theory applied to an early childhood curriculum.* Boston: American Science and Engineering, 1970.

Mitchell, L.S. *Young geographers.* New York: Basic Books, 1963.

Piaget, J. *Play, dreams and imitation in childhood.* New York: Norton, 1962.

Piaget, J. *Structuralism.* New York: Harper and Row, 1971.

Pratt, C. *I learn from children.* New York: Simon and Schuster, 1948.

Read, K., and Patterson, J. *The nursery school and kindergarten.* 7th ed. New York: Holt, Reinhart and Winston, 1980.

Reifel, S. An exploration of block play as symbolic representation. Ed.D. dissertation. University of California at Los Angeles, 1981a.

Reifel, S. The development of symbolic representation: the case of building blocks. Paper presented at the annual meeting of the American Educational Research Association, Los Angeles, April, 1981b. (ERIC Document Reproduction Service No. ED 200 333).

Reifel, S., and Greenfield, P.M. Structural development in a symbolic medium: The representational use of block constructions. In *Action and thought: from sensorimotor schemes to symbolic operations.* ed. G. Forman. New York: Academic Press, 1982.

Robinson, E.L. The form and the imaginative content of children's block buildings. PhD. dissertation. University of Minnesota, 1958.

Schuster, R.J. Sex differences and within sex variation in children's block constructions. PhD. dissertation. New York University, 1973.

Sears, P.S., and Dowley, E.M. Research on teaching in the nursery school. In *Handbook of research on teaching,* ed. N.L. Gage. Chicago: Rand McNally, 1963.

Smith, N.R. Developmental origins of graphic symbolization in the paintings of children three to five. Ph.D. dissertation. Harvard University, 1972.

Smith, N.R., and Franklin, M.B., eds. *Symbolic functioning in childhood.* Hillsdale, N.J.: Lawrence Erlbaum Associates, 1979.

Tyler, L. Materials in persons. *Theory Into Practice* 16:231–237, 1977.

Vereeken, P. *Spatial development: constructive praxia from birth to the age of seven.* Cyroningen: Walters, 1961.

Weber, L. *The English infant school: a model for informal education.* New York: Agathon Press, 1971.

Werner, H., and Kaplan, B. *Symbol formation.* New York: Wiley, 1963.

Winsor, C., ed. *Experimental school revisited.* New York: Agathon Press, 1973.

Wolf, D., and Gardner, H. Style and sequence in early symbolic play. In *Symbolic functioning in childhood.* ed. N.R Smith, and M.B. Franklin. Hillsdale, N.J.: Lawrence Erlbaum Associates, 1979.

11 Transformational Knowledge: Perceptual Models as a Cooperative Content Base for the Early Education of Children

Doris Fromberg

In the year 2000, most of the young children in schools today are likely to be working adults. What they will face, having survived a time when rapid changes become commonplace, "small futures" (de Lone 1979) are to be expected, computers will be able to "learn from experience" (Stockton 1980), can be described by the imaginings of the science-fiction writer. Faced with this prospect, society needs to meet the challenge of finding human uses for human beings (Wiener 1954).

The stand-up teacher-entertainer, the Victorian pigeonholes of knowledge, and the learning of basic skills-without-substance are eclipsed by the need for participant learners in decentralized instruction, cooperative patterns of communicating and creating, and a concept of content that is transformational and in which skills are applied to learning.

This chapter focuses on a transformational view of knowledge, through a perceptual models, content base for curriculum in early education. The relations of transformational theory and early education practice is discussed. Examples of concrete activities are related to the visual representations of perceptual models. Based upon a transformational theory of knowledge, the implications for curriculum research are discussed.

Perceptual Models as a Form of Transformational Knowledge

Knowledge that is tranformational involves the potential for a seemingly finite set of elements, when combined, to generate a seemingly infinite set of

Parts of the "exemplar" were prepared pursuant to a grant by the Teacher Corps, United States Office of Education, to Hofstra University. Points of view or opinions do not necessarily represent official United States Department of Education position or policy. I gratefully acknowledge the cooperation and enthusiasm of the teachers and children of the Park Avenue Early Childhood Center, Westbury, New York, and the Teacher Corps staff and interns. Ms. Delores Hunter, Principal, and Dr. Rose Greenspan, Prekindergarten Director, deserve special thanks for their support of project curriculum activities.

representations. For example, the alphabet can generate words. The syntax of a language generates varied sentence forms. The DNA molecules generate diverse human characteristics. A limited set of mythological structures generates a vast variety of myths across different cultures. A number of universal symbols generate an infinite assortment of personal representations in dreams.

In a similar way, perceptual models, a set of topological patterns, can serve as a unique syntax of experience in early childhood education. Perceptual models consist of such interacting elements as the experience of synergy, double bind, dialectial processes, indirect progress, and cyclical change. They are perceived through varied tranformational experiences in varied forms. Perceptual models are the images experienced when one finds answers to problems, makes new connections, and assimilates new understandings. A perceptual model is a personal experience that human beings may share implicitly. For example, synergy, the whole being more than the sum of its parts, is experienced in melody as well as in mob violence; double bind is experienced whenever appearance and reality deny each other in "love through clenched teeth" or conservation of quantity.

An early childhood perceptual models curriculum can provide an alternative unifying framework that generates a variety of implementation forms. In this context, different children, engaged in different activities at different time, can have equivalent experiences. (Fromberg, 1977, p. 84)

This potential equivalence of experience through different activities is particularly relevant in the early years of children's development. In particular, young children construct their cognitive development most readily when they can perceive connections and patterns through physical, aesthetic, and social means. The early childhood teacher who plans for the repetition of perceptual models embedded in varied forms of activities, smooths the way for young children to become more flexible in their use of experience.

The perceptual model of cyclical change is embedded in varied forms of activities described in the exemplar that follows. Recognition of perceptual models as a classification system that is integrative, builds from a network of concrete activities. The concrete instance can more readily reveal the underlying structure, especially when a transformational potential is present.

An Exemplar: The Perceptual Model of Cyclical Change

Weather. If one were to point to a possible safe topic in a universal culture dealt with in schools, one might turn toward the weather. I propose that the culture-free, competition-free equalizer of what-is-happening-out-of-doors ought to become a more controversial subject—or at least be considered more seriously. There is sufficient reason to reassess the school's preoccupation with weather if only to break out of a morning ritual of "Today is Monday. It is cloudy and raining. We will have indoor lunch. . . ." There is a time when educators must look at those things that are taken for granted and accepted because that is the way it has always been done, because it is folklore of the school.

People have always been interested in the weather because they depend upon its functioning, sometimes even for survival. Weather can create a degree of powerlessness in human life. Not only does the weather dictate those activities that are possible or comfortable; the economic cycle of our food supply is also affected. Even the Old Testament deals with major meteorological upheavals such as drought, lightning, floods, and hailstorms. The very course of ancient history was attributed to the drought/flood conditions of the Red Sea in Moses' time.

When seen in these contexts, the impact of the weather on food supplies, transportation routes, and the possibility of settlement, there is delineated a study of the social aspects of the weather. Usually, weather has been viewed as a science study in schools—a study of the rain cycle, the related study of seasons, and of growing things. However, weather conditions represent social as well as scientific issues. Weather represents Cyclical Change, a perceptual model.

It is worthwhile to look at weather as a part of, rather than the focus for, the study of cyclical change. Looking at cyclical change as a basis for connecting activities can provide a broader range of options and activities for teachers and children. As the Cyclical Change Map (figure 11-1) indicates, there is a natural flow of imagery that connects across subject disciplines.

For example, meteorology, the study of weather, is connected with other subject area concerns radiating from life cycles, migrations, and evolution to ecology, outdoor education, and the food cycle. Even dinosaur study, and the young child's preoccupation with mythic monsters as part of his or her emerging conscience development, becomes related in this network of study possibilities. And since helping children to make connections among ideas is one of the purposes of education, the perceptual model of cyclical change is a relevant planning framework.

Holidays. A parallel situation exists in the acknowledgement of holidays. Since holidays are dictated by the calendar, one must be alert in order to avoid being seduced into a kind of ritual pagan calendar worship. Rather, the cyclical changes inherent in the study of the "social" in social studies, such as human efforts or struggles and successful revolutions worth celebrating, become the focus of holiday study.

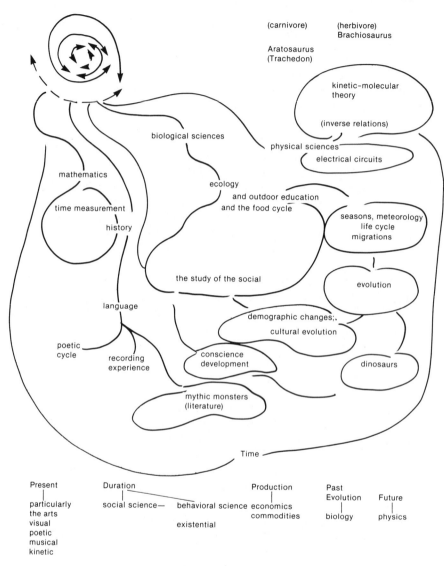

Figure 11-1. Perceptual Model: Cyclical Change Map

A graduate intern (Ellen Ray) has engaged in creative dramatics activities that provided a truly *social* study of various holidays such as: Martin Luther King's birthday (Rosa Parks); St. Patrick's Day, (the potato famine); and Thanksgiving (the peaceful strivings of the Iroquois nation). A social scientist (Donna Barnes) has worked out some concrete activities around the Thanksgiving theme which reflect the role of colonial women.

Superficially, holidays differ from outdoor education or the weather. On the deeper level, they represent cyclical changes of passing-through struggles in human lives.

Young children begin to experience cyclical change directly through their eating and sleeping schedules, and through seasonal changes. Since change is a constant factor in life, activities themselves may build *toward* an understanding of cyclical change even if only part of a cycle of change is reflected in the activity.

Time. Time is an important element in cyclical change. Time is also a constraint for teachers working with young children who are still learning to sort out distinctions and sequences of events through concrete experiences. Analogy as well as concrete activity can help children deal with the distant in time.

The time line has been used in kindergartens and the primary years. In prekindergarten, teachers have hung children's baby pictures beside September pictures. After a few weeks, the chart was stored until May when another set of recent photographs was added. Children have noticed changes in hair length and, in some cases, sleeve length. A prekindergarten variant of the time line is a photographic sequence of events during trips as well as a sequence of pictures representing a variety of the other group projects, including parties. Tape recordings are other kinds of records that can contribute to a sense of temporal order.

Immediate duration of time occurs when children wait patiently for pudding to cook and cookies to bake, a film to end, or a story to begin. When seven-year-olds survey the rate of heart beats for ten seconds before and after running for two minutes, or the number of birds at a bird feeder during a ten-minute period, they deepen their sense of time on a personal level. Many events that are recorded with such graphic surveys or with experience charts measure changes and time. Children can use clocks with second hands, mechanical timers, metronomes, and such nonstandard measures of time as water wheels. Sometimes, children are quite ingenious about suggesting ways to record changes. In addition, they can keep records through communal or individual "books of changes" at their own levels of representation.

Growth. Human beings of all ages wonder what will happen when they grow older. For young children, visiting a family with an infant, and talking to elderly people are important supplements in an age of nuclear families. The presence of senior citizen volunteers and babies in a school support this growth. There is an extended body of books for young children that deal with growth, generations, reproduction, birth, and death.

The notions of death and extinction are important human concerns.

Considering the limits of children's grasp of time, it is a constant wonder to notice children of five, six, and seven years of age wrapped up in dinosaur lore. It is hard to say whether dinosaurs have more appeal because of their lengthy varied labels that have prestige in the child culture, or because of their appeal as libidinal monsters. Children are able to see actual-size replicas or fossilized remains in local museums as well as in special films and pictures. When the children compare the different varieties of dinosaurs, they can learn about the different limb structures and running capacities that distinguished the vegetarian from the carnivore. This frequently leads to classifications of other animal forms and their varied tails, paws, ears, sizes, teeth, skin textures, mobility, and patterns of adaptation.

Some children bring to share with others fossils that their families acquired on vacation trips. Plaster-of-paris hand- or footprints and printing activities with sponges and vegetables, and later with words, build toward the fossil concept. Early childhood exposure lays a base for later ties to geologic changes.

In spring, it is possible to find frog's eggs or tadpoles in ponds and raise them on crumbs and fish food in an aquarium. Children take great pleasure in watching them develop into peeper frogs. Children have raised many significant questions when exposed to these dramatic events. They have even developed their own booklets. Alternative activities have included raising mealworms from a local pet shop or incubating chicken eggs with equipment available from the local 4-H club. Rabbits, guinea pigs, and hamsters serve similar purposes. However, with rare exceptions, a fish aquarium along with any animals kept around young children for more than a month or two fade into the background. Perhaps interchanging animals from time to time with other groups could keep children's interests high and budgets solvent.

Plant growth is another responsible activity that helps children see changes occur. They can even create part of their own food chain by sprouting mung beans or alfalfa, which takes a matter of days, or watching the variety of growths from carrot tops, avocado pits, sweet potatoes, green peas, bulbs, flower seeds, and vegetable seeds. Children can vary growth conditions such as amounts of water, light, and heat. They can measure what happens using rulers and nonstandard lengths of string or oaktag. In order to create longer-range associations in time, pumpkin seeds, dried and saved in the autumn, can be planted in the spring.

Temperature. Change in density itself is a perceptual model basic to the kinetic-molecular theory of matter. An understanding of engine cycles requires prior understanding, that is, heat speeds the movement of molecules that expand away from each other, whereas cooling slows the movement of molecules while compressing them. Children's many random exposures to temperature changes are obvious. Focused observations and contrasts help children to order their random experiences.

When children have observed the thermometer's activity across different conditions, it is possible for them to pretend to be the liquid inside of the thermometer. How is the compressing of mercury in cold like a child curling up in bed on a winter night? Personal analogy helps children to experience concepts.

Measurement with a thermometer comes in handy on many occasions. Before children can read the thermometer, the teacher might mark a large one by color designations for three or four distinctions such as red for hot, yellow for medium, and blue for cold.

Children enjoy melting ice cubes in their mouths or in their hands in the prekindergarten. It is interesting for them to hypothesize and then observe what happens to the ice cubes on a radiator or in a pot on the radiator. It is also interesting to see what happens to the water that they find when they remove a pan from the radiator and place it outdoors. Similar cycles are represented by creating a rain cycle in a terrarium or when laundering doll clothes, by simply inverting a jar over garments drying on a radiator.

Second graders similarly see the cycle of liquid to solid to gas in a candlemaking activity as well as in cooking activities. Even a carrot that is eaten, grated, juiced, and the remaining end planted, can serve young children as an examplar of change. While this planned variation is useful, it is rare excitement to turn an unexpected snowfall into a spontaneous aesthetic experience that can be appreciated in different ways when it is an indoor visual activity and when it is an outdoor tactile immersion.

Woven through each day are such fleeting moments that hold the potential for deeper meanings when one takes the time to appreciate them with children. Children can dance the snow falling and the wind shifting, the surprises of growing things, and their own changing feelings and explorations with their bodies in space. All can appreciate the mobiles that children build which require precise balance yet change appearance in a breeze.

Analogies. Notice that one cyclical change leads to another and here we are, talking about the weather again: Imagine that the weather today were . . . (the opposite of current conditions). What would you (. . . the children in Puerto Rico . . . in Jamaica . . .) be doing? What do those clouds look like? . . . remind you of? What else? How is a rainy day like a jail? What animal is like a rainy day? Why is a laugh like a rainy day? What kind of weather is like a song? . . . a dance? . . . like you? What makes you feel like a sunshine sky? . . . thunder and lightning?

Imagine you are a spider trying to spin a web on a rainy stormy day—like today. Try to feel what the spider feels. As the spider, what does the storm do to you? How do you feel about it? What other things do you do? Feel? (adapted from Gordon and Poze 1968, 1972)

You can walk or dance or write about some of these analogies, as seems relevant. Children have talked about, danced, and dramatized plant growth: Imagine that you are a seed in the ground. Try to feel what the seed might feel if it could feel. What might happen? What do you know that is like a seed? Children who have been exposed to eggs hatching have made connections between the seed and the eggs. Children who have been exposed to the changes in the mealworm have connected its transformation to other life forms—when they were ready to do so. In these instances, looking and thinking need plenty of time before we can expect to hear words.

Surveys. One can develop surveys based upon the cyclical changes that children observe. Were there more rainy days or more days without rain this week? . . . month? In which month are there fewer . . . the largest number of . . . people having birthdays? Should we classify this as mathematics, social science, science, or language study? Consider that the perceptual model of cyclical change is represented in particular concrete activities that children can experience. These experiences cut·across separate subjects (disciplines). The activities are within the teaching range of practicing teachers, and can serve to integrate children's learning in ways that can be personalized, in which children can feel successful, and in which teachers feel comfortable.

Kindergarten children have measured the length and girth of classroom pets such as hamsters and guinea pigs, using bright yarn as a nonstandard measure. Children have had a chance to see size changes over time when the lengths of yarn have been added to a chart and they have learned to make comparisons with their own growth.

Cyclical change is a perceptual model that cuts across many fields. When you refer to the perceptual model map of cyclical change, you can see that many studies are tied together. The entry point of cyclical change may be found in the interdisciplinary study of birds, trees, mealworms, or microclimates. Opportunities for the observation of terrarium conditions abound and the noting of seasonal uniqueness and fluctuations in the weather takes place for all of us.

The presence of cyclical change in many concrete activities provides further support for the theoretical contentions toward which we now turn.

A Theoretical Reflection

Because perceptual models are the isomorphic images that bind new learnings, metaphors or common properties assist the process of making connections. Young children's thinking frequently combines ideas in new and flexible ways, a characteristic that can serve to maintain creativity throughout life. Although a lost fact or concept may be found, lost flexibility may be beyond salvage. The teacher of young children has the responsibility of helping children maintain this flexibility of thought in a world marked by explosive change.

Activities that involve the use of tools, broadly defined, form the medium through which perceptual models are acquired. The teacher continually introduces perceptual models that are embedded in different activities. Thus, the interplay of varied methods of inquiry on concrete data is a way to go beyond the cultural limitations of knowledge. Interdisciplinary study is furthered through perceptual models which serve to unify the diverse ways that children can use to extend their knowledge.

Roots in Transformational Theory. The perceptual model is part of the human potential for pattern recognition. Thus, the perceptual model itself has greater generality than its representations, just as the finite structures of language relationships or genetic molecules or myths can generate infinite possibilities. Perceptual models are paralleled by transformational theories in linguistics (Chomsky 1971), computer technology (Minsky 1967), genetic research (Pfeiffer 1962), game theory (Moore and Anderson 1968), anthropology (Lévi-Strauss 1969a; 1969b), topology (Steiner 1970), psychology (Jung 1970), and communications theory (McLuhan 1963). The interdisciplinary confluence between visual art, music, and mathematics presented by Hofstadter (1980) is a compatible theory.

The various positions cited point out that some patterns and transformational processes appear with amazing frequency under disparate cultural circumstances. On the face of it, a pattern of underlying transformations appears to suffuse each example offered on a distinctly theoretical level. The distillate of these transformational theories can assist teachers in creating a more unified approach to curriculum decision making. Perceptual models are a useful lever to help children's knowledge expand beyond separate subjects.

*Perceptual Models Contrasted with the Structure
of Disciplines*

Approach. The structure of disciplines movement of the past few decades has marked an attempt by educators to elicit from subject matter specialists a definition of the uniqueness of their respective areas of knowledge. A complete definition for each discipline would describe its idealized "domain" or parameters, its unique methods of inquiry, its language, and its distinctive "key" concepts (Bruner 1961; Phenix 1964). Bruner's "spiral curriculum" proposes that continuity develops through using the unique methods of inquiry of each discipline and that sequence develops through a person's exposure to central concepts which recur and are studied in appropriately expanded, increasingly abstract forms.

The perceptual models framework and the structure of disciplines view of knowledge both are compatible with Dewey's vision that the teacher helps children move toward humanity's "fund of knowledge" (1933, p. 137) in ways that are consistent with children's total capacities. Each has a different approach to identifying humanity's "fund." Both models conceive of learning as an experience that involves active learners, emphasizing the importance of children using inquiry through concrete activities appropriate to their capacities and consistent with a constructionist view of knowledge (Piaget and Inhelder 1964).

Phenix (1964) presents a masterful analysis of the generally accepted view of organized knowledge as separate subjects. He distills and presents the essential structures of separate domains of knowing that can be useful from the structure of disciplines view. This analysis demonstrates the richness of organized knowledge that can provide a wealth of opportunities for children to learn.

However, a separate subjects view of knowledge is limiting to the 1990s learner because human experience is a continuous rather than a separated phenomenon. Both Phenix's (1964) and Bruner's (1961) attempts to define Dewey's projected "fund of knowledge" in terms of key concepts and separate ways of knowing create problems for the teacher. It may be unrealistic to expect the generalist to grasp the key concepts and means of inquiry of ordered disciplines and then translate these frameworks single-handedly into a variety of consistent activities confined to each discipline's parameters.

In addition, advocates of a separate subjects curriculum would present children with a preconceived view of knowledge. Although they would not spoon-feed it, they propose that the school provide children with a precut pie. Children are expected to act upon, process, and order events within the scope of existing disciplines. Imagine that each discipline exists as a piece of pie. One may detect occasional effluents dripping into adjacent pieces but the cuts have, after all, already been made, and the relative sizes are culturally determined.

These conceptions of knowledge stand *outside* children—and this is the core of the problem. While reality may exist "out there," knowledge is an *inside* experience—the child's construction, a product of the child's responsiveness. Children's responsiveness is the medium by which a change in perception defines new learning. Teachers cannot simply "give" experience to young children. The basic contrasting process of learning is a personal struggle, the process of becoming. Children must be active in the construction of their own meanings for which they can assume ownership.

The perceptual models framework varies from the separate disciplines view. Teachers need to deal with the complexity and blending of knowledge so that they can see "mathematics as conceptual music and music as sensuous mathematics" (Polanyi 1963, p. 38). Teachers who use the perceptual models framework are open to viewing and experiencing a specific datum or activity from either mathematical and/or musical and/or social and/or any other possible perspective. I propose that the place to look for a selection framework is not first in the separate areas of knowledge but in their integration, the connective dynamics between them. Teachers need to encourage plasticity rather than containment. The manner in which the teacher functions becomes part of the substance that is communicated.

In using a perceptual models approach, teachers begin with concrete activities that consist of *any* methods of inquiry rather than *the* method of inquiry of any one discipline. In this way, children avoid seeing a tree as only a poem or only an experience in natural science. Young children naturally engage in cutting across many ways of knowing. Different methods of inquiry would be singularly, relatively, and respectively weighted for different children at different times. The perceptual models framework helps children define, organize, and live out their own definitions of reality.

One must keep in mind that a perceptual model may be a helpful generator for planning, but it is only a source of energy requiring application to substantive activities. The teacher provides choices and materials. Each activity reflects the particular match that the teacher has made between the substance and the child's future directions of thought, and the depth of their involvement with preceding experiences. Each such interaction between teacher, child, and activity is a unique fingerprint in time, since real learning is a change in an individual's own experience of connectedness.

On Theory and Practice in Curriculum Development

In actual practice, as one looks around, it is evident that curriculum theory has not led to changes in curriculum practice. In the early childhood field in particular, practice has been derived largely from the folklore of the field. Even Sarason's (1971) view, deploring the lack of content and the ascendancy of socioemotional concerns in the early years of schooling, as well as the isolation of content from affective considerations in the secondary schools, can be reconsidered. I content that the fact-stating and memory-based conception of content that has suffused school programs needs an infusion of substance that moves beyond an appeal to linear rote processes but extends toward nonlinear as well as linear connection-making processes. Such connection-making is created by opportunities for *active* manipulation of materials and ideas.

There is a parallel gap between expressed curriculum theory and actual practices in the in-service education of teachers. This gap is created by the low priority accorded to actual concrete, substantive activity in in-service teacher education. Substance in in-service teacher education is an issue often addressed in a parenthetical style, as the kernel purpose surrounded, supported, idealized, and de-emphasized by concerns such as legislation, governance, roles, communication systems, and incentives. Rather, the what, how, and whys of substantive functioning are central to an endeavor that is to have an impact on children's lives.

A focus on the substance of education is needed, and it is needed for teachers in the same systematic ways that may affect children. Educators have accepted on a verbal level that young children learn best through the inductive mode which reflects the child's developmental capacity. When we consider how adults learn, we have been seduced by the cognitive developmental model that assumes the possibility of behavioral practice that is derived from the deductive application of theory. However, the face validity of field observation reveals that the deductive mode, represented by the format of university credit-bearing courses and journal articles, has minimal influence on the practice of experienced teachers. Extended research in teacher education supports this contention. (Joyce and Showers no date)

A counterintuitive outlook becomes fruitful when looking at the in-service education process of changing the ways in which teachers work with children as a central purpose. Rather than conceptualizing a direct deductive line from theory to practice, it is relevant to consider a "new theory of theory" (Charles Swensen: personal communication, 1977) in which theory begins with the practitioner's base-line practices. (See the exemplar, which began with the weather.) When we deal with children we propose the dictum: start where the child is and then move to his or her next step. This principle works as effectively with adults as with children.

From the position where initial movement originates with perceived needs for education stated by the in-service teacher, there is growing potential for an interaction between theory and practice. Possible learnings of new ways to act grow from changes in perception.

To begin with, the experienced in-service teacher's view of the world is to recognize the power of intrinsic motives as a level for effecting change. When a teacher, through collaborative planning, has the opportunity to perceive a contrast between personal expectations and first-hand experience, the discrepancy created by "cognitive dissonance" (Festinger 1957) is a profoundly effective way for perception to change. Education occurs for teachers no less than for children "when the individual learns to question the assumptions that lie behind existing classifications of information" (Theobald 1972, p. 171). This notion of education involves the development of intrinsic motives that are needed in order for the critical awareness, necessary for change, to occur.

Also underlying the potential for change is one's sense of competence and effective power. Freire (1970, 1973) has documented the progress of adults whose learning expectations change when they change their own perceptions of their potential for competence. Such progress is supported by horizontal dialogue among participants who together establish and pursue "generative themes." The process of using the generative themes of critical education integrates many dimensions for knowing through the use of tools drawn from many ways of knowing. In this sense, the early childhood perceptual models curriculum approach can develop a foundation for critical education.

Implications for Educational Policy

Processes that serve changing and new orderings in the world need support. In these rapidly changing times, and for a long time past, accumulated knowledge has been uncontainable in any finite form. In addition, there are ways of knowing and perceiving that are beyond the conceptual boundaries of existing scholars.

Activities that involve the use of tools, broadly defined, form the medium through which perceptual models are acquired. Perceptual models create a sense of connectedness, blending "interdisciplinary" interrelations. The relations themselves become the basic elements for planning. In this sense, perceptual models are a unique syntax of experience.

Beyond today, teachers, need to be able to assist children's education next year and twenty-five years from now. Socialization, the roles of men and women, of minority groups, of poor people, of citizens, and of workers are evolving into new forms. Technology creates new literacies as varied as those in mathematics, radio astronomy, film, and the other arts. Perceptual models serve as a way to help young children develop the resources that they will need in order to deal with change.

Teachers need better ways to decide what is worth their personal investment of time and energy with children. There is a need to change the process and politics by which decisions for activities are made and implemented by children, teachers, administrators, and communities.

Implicit as well as explicit theoretical stances influence what is taught and what is assessed. A consistent process is needed that begins with the development of curriculum theory, continues with implementation within

the teacher education field, becomes supported through the institutionalization of related educational practice, and meets the challenge of a contextually valid assessment system.

If a contextually valid assessment system is to reflect theoretical roots,
then in the early education context we need to consider collaborative
involvement among participants. Therefore, if one perceives that learners
are active in constructing their own realities and that teachers alone do not
"cause" learning to occur, then statistical correlations between teacher actions and children's performance are not sufficient alone to shed light on
the educative process. .

Elliott contends that, "the assumption of teacher causality implies a
division of labor between researchers who produce causal knowledge and
teachers who apply it in practice." (1979, p. 4) In a similar vein, Sanders
(1981) is concerned about research by an "elite" in relation to whom practicing teachers are "dependents." (p. 10) Much of this sort of one-way con-
sumerism in research lends itself to assessing more denotative, information-
oriented learnings rather than to studying transformational knowledge.

The acquisition of transformational knowledge is evident in the way
humans make connections through the particular application of knowledge,
within the context of each fresh fingerprint in time. Therefore, inasmuch as
both teacher and learner have been presented as active builders of their own
cognitive structures, curriculum development research needs the validation
of participants. Ideally, as in the form of in-service teacher education in
which teachers participate in identifying the substance of study, teachers
ought to participate in identifying the need for data collection that would
provide particular information about classroom events.

Elliott proposes adopting the process of "triangulation" through
dialogue that includes researchers, teachers, and children (1979, p. 21). The
dialogue "enables teachers to use it as a tool for developing awareness and
understanding of what they do in classrooms" (pp. 16–17). In this manner,
the sharing of, and consensus about, findings constitutes a form of in-
service teacher education. Such dialogue provides the data collectors with a
necessary form of validation for their findings.

The capacity of a teacher to alter some behaviors following possible dissonance between expressed values and reflected actions is quite another
matter in which the institutional context may be a consideration. In any
event, institutional structures and role definitions may require conscious
rearrangements in order to improve the capacity of educators to create the
moments of "cognitive dissonance" through which motives for change may
surface.

Therefore, looking toward the 1990s, a transformational view of educating young children leads to consideration of teacher education and
classroom research that is a process constructed by active participants. I

propose that this integrative "fingerprint" approach is a "human use for human beings" (Wiener 1954).

References

Bruner, Jerome S. *The process of education*. Cambridge: Harvard University Press, 1961.

Chomsky, Noam. *Language and mind*. New York: Harcourt Brace Jovanovich, 1971.

deLone, Richard H., and the Carnegie Council. *Small futures: children, inequality and the limits of liberal reform*. New York: Harcourt Brace Jovanovich, 1979.

Dewey, John. *How we think*. Boston: D.C. Heath, 1933.

Elliott, John. The implications of classroom research for the professional development of teachers. England: Cambridge Institute of Education, 1979, Mimeographed.

Festinger, Leon. *A theory of cognitive dissonance*. New York: Harper and Row, 1957.

Freire, Paolo. *Pedagogy of the oppressed*. New York: The Seabury press, 1970a.

Freire, Paolo. The adult literacy process as cultural action for freedom. *Harvard Educational Review* 40:205–225, 1970b.

Freire, Paolo. Cultural action and conscientization. *Harvard Educational Review* 40:452–477, 1970c.

Freire, Paolo. *Education for critical consciousness*. New York: The Seabury Press, 1973.

Fromberg, Doris P. *Early childhood education: a perceptual models curriculum*. New York: Wiley, 1977.

Gordon, William J.J., and Poze, Tony. *Making it strange*. New York: Harper and Row, 1968.

Gordon, William J.J., and Poze, Tony. *Teaching is listening*. Cambridge, Mass.: Porpoise Books, 1972.

Hofstadter, Douglas R. *Gödel, Escher, Bach: an eternal golden braid*. New York: Vintage Books, 1980.

Joyce, Bruce, and Showers, Beverly. "Training ourselves to teach: The messages of research." Mimeographed, n.d..

Jung, Carl Gustav. *Analytical psychology*. New York: Vintage Books, 1970.

Levi-Strauss, Claude. *The elementary structures of kinship*. Translated by James Harle Bell, John Richard von Sturmer, Rodney Needham, Editor. Boston: Beacon Press, 1969a.

Lévi-Strauss, Claude. *The raw and the cooked.* Translated by John and Doreen Weightman. New York: Harper Torchbooks, 1969b.

McLuhan, Marshall. We need a new picture of knowledge. In *New Insights and the Curriculum,* ed. Alexander Frazier. Washington, D.C.: Association for Supervision and Curriculum Development, 1963, pp. 57–70.

Minsky, Marvin. *Computation: finite and infinite machines.* Englewood Cliffs, N.J.: Prentice-Hall, 1967.

Moore, Omar K. and Anderson, Alan Ross. The responsive environments project. In *Early Education,* ed. Robert D. Hess and Roberta Meyer Bear. Chicago: Aldine, 1968, pp. 171–189.

Pfeiffer, John. *The thinking machine.* Philadelphia: Lippincott, 1962.

Phenix, Philip H. *Realms of meaning.* New York: McGraw-Hill, 1964.

Piaget, Jean, and Inhelder, Barbel. *The early growth of logic in the child.* Translated by E.A. Lunzer and D. Papert. New York: Harper and Row, 1964.

Polanyi, Michael. *The study of man.* Chicago: University of Chicago Press, 1963.

Sanders, Donald P. Educational inquiry as developmental research *Educational Researcher,* March 1981, pp. 8–13.

Sarason, Seymour Bernard. *The culture of the school and the problem of change.* Boston: Allyn and Bacon, 1971.

Steiner, George. *Language and silence.* New York: Atheneum, 1970.

Stockton, William. Creating computers to think like human beings. *The New York Times Magazine,* December 7, 1980, p. 40.

Theobald, Robert. *Habit and habitat.* Englewood Cliffs, N.J.: Prentice-Hall, 1972.

Wiener, Norbert. *The human use of human beings: cybernetics and society.* 2nd ed. rev. Garden City, N.Y. Doubleday, Anchor, 1954.

12

Today's Issues: Tomorrow's Possibilities

Barbara Bowman and
Elizabeth H. Brady

To know the future needs of American young children and their families is impossible. Future needs depend on a myriad of unforeseeable social and economic forces both in the United States and abroad. On the other hand, there is a continuity in individual human development and a similar continuity that shapes the development of peoples. Indeed, the interdependency between an individual or a group and the environment in which they live is a central principle in both developmental psychology and anthropology. The inner core of the individual, the central tendency of a group, are both responsive to and shape the events that affect their lives. We may guess at what may happen in the future because our past and present condition is such a powerful determiner of what we will make of tomorrow.

The research community has a unique opportunity to observe and describe the current state of both individuals and groups and, therefore, is at least as able as most to hazard some guesses about the problems and the solutions we will make for ourselves in the future. The following represents the authors' assessment of the issues for young children and their families that arose during the Needs of the Nineties Conference in Anaheim, June 1981.

Women's Roles

The most dramatic change in society in the last twenty years has been in women's roles, particularly mothers' return to, or entry into, the work force. The provision of care for millions of preschool and school-age children has raised a whole series of questions: How should child care be paid for? Who should provide it? Government? Not-for-profit agencies? Churches? Public schools? Business? What kind of training should care givers receive? How large or small should groups be? How should group size vary for children of different ages? What are the social and personal ramifications of the way we answer these questions? The question of whether or not day care is good or bad for children between the ages of three and six is no longer controversial, although the possibility that poor-quality group care may have ill effects, particularly on infants, continues to be a concern.

One of the issues especially relevant to these changes in women's roles and, therefore, in men's roles, is that of sex-role education. Clearly, what boys and girls are taught today will largely determine the ease or stress they will feel as adults in a world in which the roles that each has in the society are more similar to each other than is true for us today. Reports on nonsexist education do not suggest that this shift in roles will be easily accomplished. Research reveals that despite the best efforts of some of us, we continue to treat boys and girls differently and in ways that reinforce traditional sex-role patterns. Even in programs staffed by teachers with an explicit commitment to nonsexist education, the staff continues to encourage traditional behaviors. This kind of unconscious and uncontrolled adult behavior gives us fair notice that sex roles are buried deeply in our understanding of our own identity and that of others; conflict about roles may continue to be a problem for both men and women into the nineties and beyond.

Another of the women's issues that looks as though it will be with us into the 1990s is that of economic disparity between men and women. The pay differential between women and men continues without much change. A serious inequity in itself, the fact that on the average, women earn 59 percent of what men earn has more serious consequences: many of these women are the sole support of children. As a consequence, large numbers of children are living lives of poverty in homes headed by women. This suggests that the need for programs of intervention, remediation, foster placement, and the like, will continue to grow.

Special Needs

Programs for children with special needs as prescribed under Public Law 94–142 are based on the premise that children, handicapped or not, should learn together. Further, this learning best occurs under conditions which represent the least restrictive environment for every child.

An enormous amount of effort, time, and inventiveness have been and are being spent to implement the intent of laws protecting the handicapped; nevertheless, some hard questions need to be asked.

What, for example, has been the cost of Individual Education Plans? Could we persuade a school district to design a study which might reveal not only direct costs such as cost of conference time spent on IEPs, or auxiliary costs such as clerical time, files, and communication, but also hidden costs such as the functions of school psychologists and teachers that have been displaced to allow time for the IEP? Has staff been added—or are certain things no longer being accomplished?

Aside from fiscal and administrative matters, there are more difficult and subtle concerns: the basic premises of the educational values inherent in the interaction between handicapped and nonhandicapped children. We need to know how each child is affected and what individual differences result from interactions among children in least restrictive environments. Are there varying degrees of success at different chronological ages? Do nonhandicapped children experience changes of attitude and in what direction and form?

Implementation of PL 94-142 has brought about other interactions: parents with school personnel, teachers with resource specialists, school personnel with "experts" supporting parents and children in hearings. More well-documented information is needed to understand the impact of these encounters and their effects on interpersonal relations and self-regard; many of these human reactions are stressful.

Government support for handicapped children can best be described as an administrative mess in almost every state. Confusing and confused funding patterns, conflicts between lead agencies and delegate agencies, turf battles between state agencies, within agencies, and between public and private agencies, leave many workers weary and unproductive.

What can be done to help those who are trying to cope with the many demands on their emotional energy and especially professionals who must attempt to adjust their skills to new services and requirements? No matter what the immediate fate of PL 94-142, there is considerable work to be done into the 1990s if we are to understand the effects of this genuinely revolutionary program.

Those Who Work with Children

Uri Bronfenbrenner is credited with pointing out that it takes human beings to make human beings. This deceptively simple observation is exceptionally relevant to the quality of interactions between children and those who care for them, and to those factors which may affect the humanness of both the adults and the children.

For instance, a study of stresses experienced by the child-care worker (Hubner 1981), argues that the children in the care of a worker undergoing chronic stress will be adversely affected. There seems little doubt that an underpaid adult, worried about her own life situation, will provide less than optimal care for children, whether she be a parent or a care "deliverer." Nor can frequent changes among the adults who take care of children be beneficial.

A Sources of Stress Inventory (Hubner 1981) has been designed to identify factors affecting the quality of interaction between children and the adults who care for them. H.H. Hubner assumes that the child-care provider understands and should meet children's developmental needs, and not merely act as custodian. In the minutes of a recent advisory panel on financing elementary and secondary education (Lederberg 1980) one member warns that talented women no longer provide a readily accessible labor pool from which to draw teachers and that low salaries may reflect the fact that teachers are from the least-talented members of the labor pool. This, by extension, could be still more true of those who draw a minimum wage, if that—this includes most child-care workers. There is a clear need for more studies regarding the effects of wages and working conditions on the behavior of care givers and the effects of that behavior on children. Such studies must thread their way carefully between practices which have clear and predictable developmental impacts and those that reflect social class and cultural variation and which color or shape development, but do not compromise it. Most likely we will find that stress caused by unpleasant working conditions is a serious deterrent to quality child care and that our professional organizations will need to take a more active role in finding solutions to this problem.

There is a very real need for curriculum material that can assist in training Child Development Associate candidates, for infant care, for working with handicapped children. We must be careful, however, not to look on such materials as a substitute for direct training and supervision.

Several authors have suggested, in other chapters, that a teacher who holds a strong conviction about a sound theory of child development will be better able to provide curriculum and classroom activities that are appropriate for children and, further, will be able to resist introducing practices which are merely faddish or actually inimical to children's growth and development. With the increasing marketing of curriculum materials, learning machines, and other commercial programs, it is more important than ever for teachers and administrative personnel to have a well-developed theoretical base if they are to be open-minded without being open-headed.

A number of studies, such as chapter 2 and chapter 3 in this volume, call our attention to the stresses of parenthood, particularly those of the single parent. These studies remind us of the difficulty many parents have in meeting their own needs as well as the needs of their children. Descriptions of strategies for developing parent education, parent support and network systems, and parent involvement programs help those of us who are practitioners provide for the parental humanness that Bronfenbrenner reminds us is essential if children are to be human. The emphases on parents, their roles and functions, will certainly not decrease in the 1990s. In fact, programs in support of parents will be needed more than ever, and our need to understand how to get these programs to work effectively will be greater.

Minorities' Roles

The increasing participation of minorities in the American scene is drawing considerable attention, and as a result, we are becoming concerned with ways to deliver service programs more effectively to minority families. Model programs have been developed which aim at providing services in ways that make it more likely that minority families will participate and profit from the services offered.

Differences between minority group behaviors and those of mainstream Americans are important to recognize. Contact with Southeast Asians, our newest immigrant group, reveals much about cultural differences. The Vietnamese, for example, exhibit behaviors showing deference and respect to elders that contrast sharply with our tendencies to worship youth. Behaviors that may look quite similar on the surface, but have quite different meaning, are illustrated by the avoidance of eye contact—it symbolizes respect to the Vietnamese, guilt or passive hostility to many Americans. The importance of group and family identity as opposed to individual and personal identity is also evidenced in behavioral configurations that differ among cultural groups. Children's behaviors are judged differently at different ages, as in the tolerance, even encouragement, of dependence in Vietnamese children while early independence is highly valued among white Americans, and even more among black Americans.

The unanswered question, however, is the extent to which educational institutions should reflect and reinforce the cultural practices and identities of minorities as ends in themselves, and to what extent knowledge of cultural difference is simply to be used as a tool to Americanize the culturally different child and his parents. This is a question of values and cannot be answered by research or by professionals alone. We can be influential, however, in helping the public understand the differences.

Curriculum

Despite the emphasis on skill and drill and formal learning in preschool and kindergarten being called for by parents, legislators, and commercial publishers, those who work with young children are calling for meaningful and age-appropriate curricular experiences for them. Consistent with this is an approach to reading which emphasizes reading as a process that emerges from children's efforts to make sense of their world. Attention to the development of language as prereading communication is also currently receiving attention. An organic approach to reading instruction will in the long run yield better results than rote learning of empty skills. It looks as though the controversy over reading methods will be with us in the nineties as it has been throughout most of the century.

Stuart Reifel's study (chapter 10) of early representational play with blocks makes a strong statement about the cognitive nature of play and the importance of including play in school programs for young children. One of the authors of this chapter is reminded of the satisfaction her oldest child had in block play in a kindergarten in which there were plenty of blocks and the teacher let children keep block structures up for continuous elaboration over a period of days. Classroom observers have seen blocks disappear not only from primary grades but also from kindergartens in the last twenty years, and have heard young teachers remark sadly that they do not know how to use blocks in their educational programs.

Even highly sensitive and observant teachers, we note sadly, may not have an opportunity to see how children use blocks to convey their understanding of the world, given the constraints that operate in many schools: "Don't build high!" "Only take two blocks at a time!" In a setting with too few blocks and too many children expected to reproduce something demanded by the teacher—the airport, the supermarket—blocks soon lose their charm. Perhaps enough well-done and well-communicated research will help to restore to schools an experience in play essential to the development of young children.

Evaluation

Irving Lazar (chapter 1) suggests that the 1980s will bring more demands for formal evaluation of programs. Current attempts include videotaping as a new method of data collection, as well as continuous process evaluation. *Continuous process* acknowledges the multifaceted requirements of true program evaluation; it is designed to permit self-correction of the intervention process. It is also called *formative evaluation* which focuses on the child in the family, an approach recommended by many of our colleagues.

While evaluation has tended to be quantitative and correlational, it is apparent that some other models of evaluation are being considered. What has been referred to as "a fine grained analysis" of what goes on in programs has been recommended (Roberts and Daniels 1981), a form of evaluation that allows time for a clearly analyzed framework of values and principles that evolves from continous interaction of a small and dedicated staff. Although this type of evaluation may lack the accountability documentation required by many programs, it may also allow for more sensitive diagnostic and treatment efforts.

Those who are interested in different kinds of evaluation may also be interested in Elliot Eisner's (1979) notion of connoisseurship and criticism as a technique for evaluating. Eisner takes his ideas from the arts, a field in which the informed critic assesses the artistic product using judgment and analysis.

These two evaluative measures, judgment and analysis, lack the glamorous pseudoscientific image of statistics and taxonomies of standardized tests and rating forms. But after seventy-five years of trying to apply natural science techniques to behavioral science problems with often devastating results, it might be time to look to the arts as well as to science for evaluation instruments. If we take a recent disclosure—that one can cram for Scholastic Aptitude Tests and get a higher score, our suspicion that so-called objective methods of assessment are inadequate should be reinforced.

Eisner's position (1978) is that education is a complicated art and can best be improved by helping teachers to observe and think about what they do. He suggests that we must learn to analyze teaching and learning situations not so much for what we like but for understanding and appreciation of what is happening to the learner.

We think it significant that many of our colleagues are emphasizing the importance of underlying assumptions in data collection and that they stress the need to avoid assumptions of pathology when looking at the families of the poor, of minorities, of single parents. This is certainly a step forward in our understanding of development and human interaction. We trust that in the 1990s we will continue our search for better ways of understanding children.

Public Policy

Public policy often assumes a set of commonly held values, and it often assumes the development of a rational plan that ties programs to these values. Neither of these assumptions is warranted. In a nation as diverse as ours, not one single set of beliefs but a literal potpourri of values derive from the differing national heritages of the peoples who make up the United States and from their varying experiences here. Over the past fifteen or twenty years, we have given up the old concept of the melting pot (some of our peoples could not melt) in favor of the salad bowl—certainly a far more accurate analogy. But in our bowl we have a variety of differing opinions on how life should be lived and what programs and institutions are needed.

Nonsexist education is an example of how differences in values complicate our efforts to implement policy; different cultural groups have different expectations, different beliefs, about appropriate sex-typed behavior. Respect for cultural differences may conflict with nonsexist-role teaching. Similarly, the political-philosophical question of whether the United States should be an English-speaking or a multilingual country produces controversy. The failure to clarify these questions of values subjects programs to vacilating policies, conflicting expectations, and often mandated standards imposed from government bureaus and restricted by communities.

Just as the first assumption, that we have a commonly held set of values is not justified, neither is the assumption that public policy represents a rational plan. In many respects, the American public in general and our legislators and jurists in particular, have a love affair with experimental, quantitative research as a base for public policy. Its objectivity appeals to our democratic ideals, its predictive capability appeals to our sense of economy, and its explicitness appeals to our open, pragmatic character. Further, this kind of research has been enormously successful in the physical and natural sciences. But research—particularly research on human beings—is frequently misleading, contradictory and just plain wrong. (Kenneth Carlson has an excellent article, "Ways in Which Research Methodology Distorts Policy Issues," in *The Urban Review,* vol. 2, no. 1, 1979.) Even when research evidence is relatively clear, often public policy does not reflect the findings because public policy does not take form in a laboratory; it is not a rational process based on scientific principles. Public policy is as often determined by issues of self-interest and power politics as it is by understanding and planning.

We are frequently told not to be discouraged because the role of research and the experience of professionals often counts so little in developing and implementing public policy. We are urged to see our role as providing information to the public and to package our data in ways that have meaning to our audiences. As the Children's Defense Fund puts it, "Information is the key to effective advocacy." (1980, p. 1)

Public policy is something we all need to be concerned about. It is something that those of us who are concerned about the welfare of children and families—all children and all families—must educate ourselves about and be prepared to take a position on. However, we cannot do everything for all of the areas of human need that exist. We must identify priorities for action, some guiding principles on which to base such public policy. Prevention has emerged as one such principle. It is the principle likely to pay off best in terms of conserving both our money and our people. Additionally, it is more humane than remediation. The case for a preventive approach for the human services is clear. It is not, however, easily achieved. There are a number of issues that complicate effective implementation of such policy. Four of these will be mentioned here.

First is the issue of being penny-wise and pound-foolish. An example of this is our special education program. If we balance the cost of full implementation of PL 94–142 against the cost of public assistance, institutionalization, and against the entire social welfare system designed to combat personal and social pathology that results from untreated handicapped conditions, we find it is more expensive not to provide appropriate education than it would be to provide an effective intervention program.

We have data to demonstrate the economic advantages of preventive intervention (Sweinhart 1981). Although one might wish that talk about improving the quality of life for children and families would be enough to get needed resources, many of our advocacy experts admonish us to learn to speak more than one language when we are trying to get things for children—and the language of money is a good one to learn to speak. And the language of votes, and the language of subtle pressure, coalitions, and public education.

The second issue concerns our emphasis on individuals rather than on society. We have been focusing on treatments for individuals already damaged by preventable social conditions. Programs aimed at reducing child abuse, programs aimed at reducing the effects of poverty and prejudice, programs aimed at relieving the emotional scars of exploitation are certainly important and praiseworthy. But such programs also reflect our tendency to attend to the personal pathology in individuals rather than to the social pathology of society and its institutions.

As Americans, we have an inclination to select a person-by-person solution to problems rather than societal ones. This concern with the individual accounts for the ease with which one small child's personal tragedy can evoke in us more emotion, more willingness to act, than can the plight of hundreds of thousands. This distinctly American characteristic can also be seen in our willingness to spend millions in the attempt to save a single child from parental abuse while millions of children's lives are distorted and undermined by hunger, preventable disease, automobile carelessness, and poor education.

While we know that the causes of child abuse and neglect are multiple and hard to predict, we also know that the risk is greatest for children whose parents are poor, unemployed, and without sufficient emotional and social resources. Yet the programs that might help prevent abuse, the programs that provide employment, mental health care, day care, housekeeping services, and parent education, tend to be less attractive to us than tracking down and punishing a single parent abusing a single child. Clearly, as researchers we must be aware of the social issues that underlie the conditions we study and we must be sure that we do not condone this one-by-one route to salvation. As advocates for children we need to learn to take a more sociological perspective. We need to look at the system that is causing the problem and change it rather than trying to treat each individual case. Most families are doing as well as they can under the circumstances. It is our responsibility to try to change the circumstances and not the families.

R.H. deLone in *Small Futures* (1979) makes a similar point when he says the mechanisms used by society to eliminate poverty are based on the erroneous premise that poverty is the result of individual inadequacies rather than the distributional mechanisms of our society's economic structure.

Societal inequities, deLone goes on to say, provide jobs for large numbers of persons in the helping professions. This includes all of us who study the victims of society. As beneficiaries of oppression, inequality, and poverty, it is essential that we keep clearly in mind the need to change the system that gives us our work. We, more than others, must support far-reaching changes in our social system, the system that perpetuates poverty, oppression, and victimization.

A third issue is our willingness to permit strong interest groups to bias public policy to the advantage of their private or special interest. A case in point is the exploitation of poor women. We are currently spending large sums of tax money for research and development of intrauterine techniques for the identification of abnormal prenatal conditions in the fetus (amniocentesis). This information may give the mother reason to terminate the pregnancy; it is her constitutional right to do so. On the other hand, we refuse to provide tax money for poor women to avail themselves of this option. Without impugning the motives of those who oppose abortion, it is important that we note the vulnerability of the poor. Tax money may be spent to improve the lives of the middle class while denying the poor those benefits. This kind of special-interest oppression based on class and caste is one of the most pervasive aspects of American life and results in some of the greatest inconsistencies in our public policy.

Special-issue politics has an uncanny tendency to weigh most heavily on the poor, the meek, the defenseless, whether the issue is abortion, equal pay for women, day care, or comprehensive child care. Although some of us may buy exemption from such oppression, many of us cannot. All of us, however, must pay the price for underfinanced families, unwanted children, abused and neglected children, unsupervised and poorly socialized children.

A final point about public policy is what may be called its "boomerang effect." The Aswan Dam project is a case in point. Recognizing the need to increase the food supply if Egyptian citizens were to have a higher standard of living, policymakers saw the dam as a preventive project which would improve nutrition and decrease disease. Unfortunately, after the dam was constructed and the water began to be used for the irrigation of crops, the government became aware of the spread of a serious disease, schistosomiasis. Although food production increased, so too did this disease; thus the project increased human anguish and necessitated a host of new programs.

The boomerang effect of a public policy decision is as familiar to us as it is to the Egyptians. Screening for handicaps and genetic diseases are familiar cases in point. Many screening programs intended to benefit children have resulted in deprivation; the tendency to treat a child as if he *were* his handicap, once early identification has occurred, often means that, ergo, he is very quickly more handicapped. Early identification, labeling, special programs, all can easily result in this boomerang effect. New programs must be carefully monitored for unexpected effects if the programs are not to create larger problems than the ones they were designed to cure.

It is clear that research has an important role to play in many of the areas critical to the healthy development of children and the functioning of families. As researchers and practitioners, we have a critical role to play in monitoring the quality of this research and in disseminating the results. We have a role to play in advocating on behalf of children and families, many of whom cannot advocate for themselves. On the other hand we have an obligation to ensure that the work we do does not simply serve our own self-interest but truly serves to improve the quality of life of young children and their families.

Irving Lazar suggests we bury the eighties and just move along to the nineties when we will have learned our lessons and again be ready to expend resources on children, their care, and education. However, we must not succumb to defeatism. We can, we must, continue to work and work hard to understand, plan, evaluate, and advocate for children and families. All of us need to persevere through the Awful Eighties, so we can say in the nineties what one of Martin Luther King's workers said during the civil rights struggles in the sixties: "My feets is tired, but my soul is at rest."

References

Children's Defense Fund. *Where do you look? Whom do you ask? How do you know? Information resources for child advocates.* Washington, D.C., Children's Defense Fund, 1980.

deLone, R.H., and the Carnegie Council. *Small futures: children, inequality and the limits of liberal reform.* New York: Harcourt Brace Jovanovich, 1979.

Eisner, E.W. On the uses of educational connoisseurship and criticism for evaluating classroom life. *Teachers College Record* 78:345–358, 1978.

Eisner, E.W. *The educational imagination.* New York: Macmillan, 1979.

Hubner, H.H. Source of stress of family day care providers. Paper presented at Needs of the Nineties Conference, Anaheim, Calif., June 1981.

Lederberg, V. *Minutes of the advisory panel on financing elementary and secondary education.* Washington, D.C., November 1980.

Roberts, C.A., and P.A. Daniels. The process evaluation system: an integrated framework for future trends in early intervention. Paper presented at Needs of the Nineties Conference, Anaheim, Calif., June 1981.

Sweinhart, L. Young children grow up: effects of the Perry preschool program of youths through age 15. Paper presented at Needs of the Nineties Conference, Anaheim, Calif., June 1981.

Index

Abortion, factor of, 25
Abram, M.J., 13
Abuse: child, 50–52, 57, 61; drug, 59;
  legacy of, 62; physical, 68; sexual, 50,
  68; verbal, 53
Achievement: educational, 154–156;
  reading, 78
Action for Children's Television, 158
Administrators and administrative activities,
  9, 44, 51, 125, 149, 209
Adolescence, problems of, 30–33
Adult: authority, 58; and child ratio,
  115–116, 120; education, 44; learning,
  22; male role, 67; social role, 40;
  thinking, 25; violence, 47
Advisory Committee for Young Children
  with Special Needs, 130, 135–136, 140
Afterschool programs, 6
Age and aging, levels of, 2, 30, 80
Agencies: government, 73; medical, 50;
  state, 185, 209
Aggressiveness, trait of, 49, 155
Aid to Families with Dependent Children
  (AFDC), 4
Ainsworth, M.D.S., 90, 113, 123
Akers, R.L., 63
Alfren, S.H., 159
Amatruda, C., 93
Ambrose, J.A., 91
Ammon, P.R., 131
Anderson, B.J., 94–95, 104, 199
Anthropology, field of, 207
Anticipatory role, 32–33
Antisocial behavior, 14, 25
Anxiety, levels of, 53
Apfel, N., 11
Appalachian Regional Commission, 9
Aries, E.J., 12, 159
Aspirations: educational, 154–156;
  occupational, 151–154
Assault: on children, 50; on women, 50
Assessment paradigms, 73–75, 79–81
Astrology, fascination with, 7, 13
Audiotapes, use of, 22
Audio-visual aids, 162
Auerbach, A.B., 44
Authority and authoritarianism, 17, 21, 58,
  62
Automation, factor of, 9
Awareness, parental, 18–20, 25
Axelrod, S., 113, 123–125

Babbling, infant stages of, 91–92, 96–104
Baby-sitting cooperatives, 24
Bailey, M.W., 174
Bakeman, R., 159
Ball, T.S., 130–131
Ban, P.L., 96
Bandura, A., 63, 65
Bane, M.J., 23
Barnes, Donna, 194
Bartel, J.M., 11
Barten, S.S., 172
Bates, E., 172
Battered: children, 56; women, 53–55, 60
Behavior: antisocial, 14, 25; classroom, 186;
  insecure, 123; management, 4–5;
  maternal, 112–14, 123; nontraditional,
  162; nonviolent, 66; parental, 22, 158;
  patterns, 21, 58–59, 64, 156;
  professional, 140; sex-appropriate, 66,
  156–158; social, 1; super-macho, 65;
  techniques, 130
Bell, S.M., 11, 90, 113, 123
Belsky, J., 111
Benedek, T., 29, 31
Bennie, E., 51
Bereiter, C., 171
Bergman, A., 36
Berko, F., 134
Beuf, A., 154
Bianchi, B.P., 159
Biber, B., 173
Bijou, S., 131
Binet, Alfred, 78, 83, 131
Biology, influence of, 155–156
Birth: control, 67; rates, 148
Black ethnic group, 4, 94, 154, 211
Blair, J.A., 80
Block, J., 157
Block(s): classroom use, 171–173;
  representational-play structures,
  173–178, 182–185, 212
Bloom, L., 132, 134, 142
Blumberg, M., 48
Bolton, F.G., 58
Books, 12; child care, 14; picture, 158
Booth, A., 152
Bowlby, J., 89, 92
Bowman, Barbara, 207–217
Brady, Elizabeth H., 207–217
Brannon, R., 154, 159
Braun, S., 132

219

About the Contributors

Barbara Bowman is director of graduate studies for the Erikson Institute for Advanced Study of Child Development in Chicago. Her professional activities include work abroad as well as in the United States. Currently she is president of the National Association for the Education of Young Children, which has a membership of over 33,000.

Elizabeth H. Brady is professor and chair, Department of Educational Psychology, California State University, Northridge. Currently her professional activities are in the field of early childhood education, including teacher education, child care, and development of educational programs for children and families. She has been active in educational programs in intergroup relations, human relations, and school desegregation.

Helen F. Durio received the Ph.D. from the University of Texas at Austin. She taught educational psychology and published some twenty articles relating to education, psychology, and child development. She was coauthor, with Robert Hughes, Jr., of an annotated bibliography, *Parent Concerns: A Reading Guide for Parents of School-Age Children*. At the time of her accidental death, she was working toward the cooperative completion of the chapter published in this book.

Doris Fromberg is professor of early childhood and elementary education at Hofstra University in Hempstead, New York, and received the Ed.D. from Columbia University. She serves as director of Early Childhood Teacher Education and is the director of the Hofstra/Westbury Teacher Corps Project. Among her writings is *Early Childhood Education: A Perceptual Models Curriculum*.

Robert Hughes, Jr. received the Ph.D. from the University of Texas at Austin. He has recently completed a study of parents' information needs and is coauthor with Helen F. Durio of an annotated bibliography, *Parent Concerns: A Reading Guide for Parents of School-Age Children*. Currently, he is a senior research psychologist at the Research Development Center for Teacher Education at the University of Texas at Austin.

Irving Lazar is professor and chairman of the Department of Human Service Studies at Cornell University. He has served as chairman of the Consortium for Longitudinal Studies whose most recent findings demonstrate the positive effects of early intervention on the later achievement of low-income children. He received the Ph.D. in child development from Columbia University. Dr. Lazar has numerous publications on day care and parent programs.

Jeanne Kohl received the Ph.D. from the University of California at Los Angeles in sociology of education after having been an elementary-school teacher for several years. She has written and spoken frequently on the topic of sex-role development, and is a coauthor of *Growing Up Equal: Activities and Resources for Parents and Teachers of Young Children.* Currently she is a university administrator and is working on a Title IX project.

Mildred Daley Pagelow received the Ph.D. in sociology from the University of California at Riverside. She was one of the first sociologists to study family violence, particularly woman battering, and as a result has provided expert testimony to a number of governmental agencies. The report of her study, *Woman Battering: Victims and Their Experiences,* was published in 1981.

Rosemary F. Peterson received the Ph.D. in educational psychology from the University of California at Berkeley. She is the author of several articles and two books: *Why's and How's in Beginning Reading for ECE and the Bilingual Classroom* and *Piaget: A Handbook for Parents and Teachers of Children in the Age of Discovery, Preschool—Third Grade* (with V. Felton). Currently she is associate professor of psychology and education at Saint Mary's College, Moraga, California.

Stuart Reifel is currently assistant professor in the Department of Curriculum and Instruction at the University of Texas at Austin, where he directs the Child Study Laboratory. He received the Ed.D. from the University of California at Los Angeles. His research focuses on the significance of traditional early childhood activities for children's development. Many of his research interests developed while he taught nursery school and kindergarten.

Elizabeth C. Ringsmuth brings personal experience to a developmental perspective on adapting to multiple social roles. Simultaneously she was wife, housekeeper, mother, student, and full-time university instructor. She received the Ed.D. from the University of California at Los Angeles. She is currently associate professor in the Department of Educational Psychology, California State University, Northridge.

Barbara J. Tardif received the Ph.D. in curriculum and instruction from the University of California at Berkeley. She is a consultant for the California

Commission for Teacher Preparation and Licensing, the state teacher-credentialing agency. Previously, she taught at California State University, Sacramento. She has written numerous articles on early childhood education, particularly in the area of parenting education.

Richard R. Valencia received the Ph.D. in early childhood education from the University of California at Santa Barbara. Since 1978 he has been assistant professor of education and coordinator of the Bilingual/Multicultural Emphasis Credential Program at the University of California at Santa Cruz. His major area of research specialization is the study of sociocultural influences of family and school on intellectual development and academic achievement of Mexican American children.

Sylvia Ann White received the Ph.D. in child development from Florida State University. Since 1975 she has held various positions in San Diego, California, including: faculty member in child development, San Diego State University; director of a program for teenaged parents and their infants for the San Diego Unified School District; and project leader for the Family Day Care Provider Training Project, San Diego Community College District.

Alan L. Ziajka is currently chairman of the Child Development Department and assistant professor of education at the University of La Verne. He has also served as a researcher for various public and private organizations concerned with improving education. His most recent publication is *Prelinguistic Communication in Infancy.*

About the Editors

B.J. Barnes received the Ph.D. in education from the Claremont Graduate School. Since 1972 she has been a faculty member at California State University, Fullerton, where her work has focused primarily on the preparation of teachers for elementary-school classrooms and on concerns related to early childhood education. She is coauthor of *Schoolmaking,* which describes and examines a unique approach to the preparation of teachers.

Shirley Hill is currently a professor of education at California State University, Fullerton. She has directed the Institute of Early Childhood Education and has been editor of *ECE Update* for five years. She received the Ed.D. from the University of Arizona. Many of her professional activities have focused on parent education and the role of parents in their children's education.